Advances In AI Ethics

Practical Advances in Artificial Intelligence and Machine Learning

Dr. Lance B. Eliot, MBA, PhD

ISBN: 978-1-95-738609-6

DEDICATION

To my incredible daughter, Lauren, and my incredible son, Michael.

Forest fortuna adiuvat (from the Latin; good fortune favors the brave).

CONTENTS

ACKNOWLEDGMENTS

I have been the beneficiary of advice and counsel by many friends, colleagues, family, investors, and many others. I want to thank everyone that has aided me throughout my career. I write from the heart and the head, having experienced first-hand what it means to have others around you that support you during the good times and the tough times.

To Warren Bennis, one of my doctoral advisors and ultimately a colleague, I offer my deepest thanks and appreciation, especially for his calm and insightful wisdom and support.

To Mark Stevens and his generous efforts toward funding and supporting the USC Stevens Center for Innovation.

To Lloyd Greif and the USC Lloyd Greif Center for Entrepreneurial Studies for their ongoing encouragement of founders and entrepreneurs.

To Peter Drucker, William Wang, Aaron Levie, Peter Kim, Jon Kraft, Cindy Crawford, Jenny Ming, Steve Milligan, Chis Underwood, Frank Gehry, Buzz Aldrin, Steve Forbes, Bill Thompson, Dave Dillon, Alan Fuerstman, Larry Ellison, Jim Sinegal, John Sperling, Mark Stevenson, Anand Nallathambi, Thomas Barrack, Jr., and many other innovators and leaders that I have met and gained mightily from doing so.

Thanks to Ed Trainor, Kevin Anderson, James Hickey, Wendell Jones, Ken Harris, DuWayne Peterson, Mike Brown, Jim Thornton, Abhi Beniwal, Al Biland, John Nomura, Eliot Weinman, John Desmond, and many others for their unwavering support during my career.

And most of all thanks as always to Lauren and Michael, for their ongoing support and for having seen me writing and heard much of this material during the many months involved in writing it. To their patience and willingness to listen.

CHAPTER 1
INTRODUCTION TO AI ETHICS

There is an urgently rising societal interest in the field of AI Ethics.

Thankfully so.

As Artificial Intelligence (AI) continues to advance and increasingly become part of our daily lives, we need to be on our toes about AI that diverges from ethical behavior and crosses over into unethical behavior. The field of AI Ethics seeks to apply ethical precepts and theories of ethical conduct to the devising and usage of AI systems, doing so to try and steer AI into sufficient ethical mores and avert unethical actions by AI.

Formal definitions of AI Ethics tend to vary somewhat. All told, the notion is to combine what we know or believe about ethics as a guiding tool toward the mounting advent of AI-based intelligent systems.

Some would argue that the AI horse is seemingly getting out of the barn and doing so without needed ethical boundaries. In a headline-grabbing worst-case scenario envisioned by AI futurists, AI systems are predicted to become mightier than we can adequately control and end up as an existential risk to the fate of humanity. Dire catastrophic outcomes are being painted.

You don't though need to look solely at the far future to get concerned about the ethical actions of AI. As will be discussed, there are plenty of AI systems of today that already have made known the adverse consequences of not taking into account the importance of AI Ethics.

As a particularly succinct and insightful definition of AI Ethics, consider this one by The Alan Turing Institute: "AI ethics is a set of values, principles, and techniques that employ widely accepted standards of right and wrong to guide moral conduct in the development and use of AI technologies" (as published in *Understanding Artificial Intelligence Ethics And Safety: A Guide For The Responsible Design And Implementation Of AI Systems In The Public Sector* by David Leslie, 2019).

Notice that there is an important dual-element consisting of both the development of AI systems and the usage of AI systems.

AI Ethics comes to play as a guiding light throughout the development process when devising AI. The entirety of the AI development life cycle must encompass AI Ethics principles. From the moment that an AI system is first initially conceived of, and then during the design, building, testing, fielding, and upkeep, all stakeholders involved in producing the AI are to be giving due consideration to AI Ethics. In addition, once an AI system has been placed into active use, you still must be on alert to watch for, detect, and potentially correct AI that verges from ethical conduct into unethical actions.

I mention the aspect of remaining aware once AI has been placed into use because there is often a faulty notion of fire-and-forget mindset that some developers of AI get caught up in. They believe that if they tried to develop the AI in an ethically minded fashion, there is no need to continue any AI Ethics forays once the AI is released into use.

This belies the real and frequent possibility that the AI will veer from its earlier ethics-oriented groundings and sway into unethical territory while in use.

AI Ethics And The Entire AI Development Life Cycle

Keep in mind then that we will want to ensure that both conditions of development and of use are being met, namely:

a) Apply AI Ethics throughout the AI development process from start to "finish"

b) Continue to apply AI Ethics even once the AI is placed into use

The AI development life cycle must be viewed as ranging from the initial conceiving of the AI to the entire time that it is available for use. Do not shortchange that range. Some AI developers do not consider the initial conceiving stage as within the scope of AI Ethics and think that just the building or coding stage is where AI Ethics first arises. In a similar mistaken belief, some AI developers assume that after the AI has been released into production and put into use that they can wash their hands of any residual or newly emerging AI Ethics qualms about the AI system. Nope, trying to narrowly confine where AI Ethics is needed will undoubtedly lead to ethical problems, one way or another, and sooner or later.

Another quick point is to realize that AI Ethics is something that all stakeholders amidst an AI system must be cognizant of. The normal assumption is that the software engineers alone are the caretakers of any AI Ethics considerations. Not so. Management that oversees the crafting of an AI system is part-and-parcel of the AI Ethics matters. If the organizational leaders are shortchanging the value of applying AI Ethics, you can bet that this same persona will permeate and undercut the AI life cycle. Budgets for devising the AI won't include set-asides for incorporating AI Ethics considerations. Schedules and deadlines won't either. In the end, a pell-mell rush to get the AI out the door will take top priority and AI Ethics will barely get a word in edgewise.

All stakeholders have a stake in enduring that AI Ethics is sufficiently incorporated into the full life-cycle of an AI system.

When an AI system exhibits unethical activity, this can be traced not just to the coding and the software developers, but also tracked to the leaders that oversaw the AI life cycle, the business and systems analysts involved, and even those that are operating or responsible for the final deployment of the AI.

The usual escape hatch entails those other stakeholders claiming that they weren't the ones that churned out the code that underlies the AI system. This is a convenient and at times nearly convincing argument for those that do not fully grasp how an AI system came to be. Overall, all stakeholders have both an ethical responsibility for the AI and are likely to have legal accountability too.

Making Sense Of What AI Is

When I refer to Artificial Intelligence, the AI moniker can be a bit confusing as to what AI entails.

Welcome to the club in the sense that the meaning of Artificial Intelligence continues to be bandied around and there is no single comprehensive and all-agreed definition for AI. One of the issues facing the latest efforts to regulate AI systems has been how to appropriately define AI within our laws. If the legal definition is overly broad, new laws seeking to better govern AI systems can inadvertently encroach on all manner of software applications and computer systems. If the legal definition of AI is excessively restrictive, the odds are that AI systems that should have been encompassed will wiggle out from being bound by those laws.

The easiest way to define AI consists of saying that any computer or machine that exhibits seemingly intelligent behavior is in the realm of AI.

This notion dates back to 1956 when Professor John McCarthy coined the name Artificial Intelligence as part of a proposal to bring together many luminaries of math and computer science for a research project: "The study is to proceed on the basis of the conjecture that every aspect of learning or any other feature of intelligence can in principle be so precisely described that a machine can be made to simulate it" (in his co-authored proposal entitled *Proposal For The Dartmouth Summer Research Project On Artificial Intelligence*).

One subtle but extremely vital facet about the definition of AI is that we can presumably seek to attain computer-based or machine-based intelligent behavior without necessarily duplicating the precise way that humans think. There is an ongoing debate about that questionable keystone. Some would contend that the only way to produce an artificial form of intelligence is to completely mimic how the human brain works. Others argue that we might find alternative means to bring forth artificially indued intelligence. The old saying goes that there is more than one way to skin a cat.

The gist is that if we can craft a computer or machine that will *exhibit* intelligence and intelligent behavior, we ought not to be especially caring about how that came to be. All that we need to know is that the system appears to act and respond intelligently. Whatever we did to get there is not particularly relevant, some say. As you might imagine, not everyone agrees with that supposition. The inner workings of how intelligence comes to arise are claimed to be equally important as the result of being able to produce intelligent actions and outputs.

Rather than focusing on definitions of AI, there is another way that AI is often depicted. You can assert that AI is a set of computer-related techniques and technologies. Thus, if you are making use of those AI techniques and technologies, you are ergo devising and employing AI capabilities.

A typical taxonomy would explain AI by suggesting that these associated techniques and technologies are involved:

- Machine Learning
- Natural Language Processing
- Knowledge-Based Systems
- Automated Reasoning
- Robotics
- Multi-Agent Systems
- Etc.

A difficulty of merely referring to those various techniques and technologies as constituting an AI system is that you aren't especially aiming at the intelligence side of things. Recall that the nearly universal goal of AI is to attain systems that exhibit intelligence. You can cobble together the various techniques and technologies and not necessarily derive any semblance of intelligent-like behaviors. Would a system that perchance leverages those capabilities be reasonably construed as an AI system even if it did not showcase intelligent-oriented actions? I would dare say many would contend that such a system does not meet the spirit or tone of what is meant by referring to AI.

AI Ethics Has Been On A Roller Coaster Of Societal Interest

You might be surprised to learn that AI Ethics has been a topic of discussion since the very beginning of the AI field. Perhaps this has partially been fueled by longstanding works of fiction that have indubitably worried that someday humans would construct machines that could overtake humankind. Today's emergence of computer systems that seem to have AI capacities has brought those past fictional stories into greater focus as something that might be constructed in the real world.

Interest in AI Ethics has been a roller coaster ride, consisting of moments of great interest to spans of sparse attention.

During the 1980s and 1990s, intense efforts were being made to craft knowledge-based systems, often referred to as expert systems, and the concerns about AI Ethics began to gain traction. The more AI there is, the more likely the attention to AI Ethics.

You might be aware that then a so-called "AI Winter" arose following the hyped expectations of AI in the 80s and 90s, and a resurgence of AI attention only began anew in the last decade or so. During the winter period of AI, AI Ethics somewhat languished, ostensibly still being worked on but now in the shadows. Upon the newly considered "AI Spring" of advances in AI capabilities that stridently stoked a renewal for AI, along with rapidly decreasing costs of computing, and a myriad of other technology trends such as cloud computing, the Internet of Things (IoT), and so on, this, in turn, sparked a renewal in AI Ethics.

Many speak nowadays of AI as being either *AI For Good* or *AI For Bad.* The initial renewed excitement about contemporary AI capabilities was that we would finally be able to fruitfully use computers and so-called smart machines toward solving many of the globe's most pressing problems, such as dealing with worldwide hunger, widespread poverty, sustainability, and other pressing issues.

That is *AI For Good.*

Lamentedly, we began to realize that the same AI could contain untoward biases and inequities, accordingly, labeled as *AI For Bad.* For example, facial recognition was one of the first AI technologies that got caught with inherent racial and gender biases, which we will be exploring in the chapters ahead.

The odds are that any AI system will have a bit of both. As much as possible, we want to uncover and excise the *AI For Bad.* Also, as much as possible, we want to ensure that *AI For Good* is being devised and fielded. Those that are AI ethicists bring to the table the skillset and passion for striving to maximize the *AI For Good* and minimize or eliminate the *AI For Bad.*

This is assuredly a tough proposition to fulfill.

Being An AI Ethicist Or Adjacent To

Speaking of tough shoes to fill, let's pursue that topic in terms of who can aid in the AI Ethics field.

A properly qualified AI ethicist should be versed in the field of ethics and likewise versed in the field of AI. It is a twofer if you like.

Someone that is strong on the ethics side but weak on the AI side would be doing themselves a disservice because they are bound to lack the needed comprehension about what AI is and what it might become. In the same breath, someone that is weak on the ethics side and strong on the AI side might be missing the boat in terms of understanding the vital nuances of ethics and ethical thinking.

In the case of AI, I like to clearly demarcate that when I am discussing AI, it could be in the context of any or all of these three conditions:

1) Non-sentient AI of today
2) Sentient AI of human intelligence caliber (which we don't know will be achieved)
3) Sentient AI of super-intelligence (which is even more speculative than #2)

Discussions about AI that are in the sentient AI category are highly speculative. We don't have sentient AI today. We don't know when we will have sentient AI, if ever so. In general, covering AI Ethics when solely considering sentient AI is a lot of handwaving. You can pretty much make up whatever you like about how sentient AI is going to behave. I'm not saying that we should not be concerned about sentient AI, and only mentioning that the AI Ethics as pertaining to sentient AI is loosey-goosey and not especially real-world applicable per se.

You can rest assured that there is still plenty to talk about when it comes to AI Ethics and today's non-sentient AI. There is no need to go into the outstretched arena of sentient AI to have lots to discuss.

Furthermore, the handy aspect of AI Ethics regarding non-sentient AI is that this is a very applied discipline that can be immediately put to use throughout society. Companies that are creating AI systems need AI Ethics advice and consultation. Entities and people that are using AI systems are likewise in need of AI Ethics advice and consultation. Regulators are now steeped in trying to create laws related to AI, for which AI Ethics insights are needed too.

The field of ethics and all of its numerous theories about ethics can be applied toward the specific domain of AI. Indeed, one viewpoint is that the field of ethics as *applied to technology* (of any kind) is the umbrella into which the particular application of ethics applied to AI fits.

For those of you that are pursuing a career as an AI ethicist, the good news is that we are still in the infancy of AI Ethics. There is a lot of room to grow. You can also anticipate that as AI gets more pervasive and improves in showcasing intelligent behavior, AI Ethics will be expanding and sought after correspondingly so.

AI Ethics Frameworks And Key Principles

At this time, there are lots of proposed AI Ethics frameworks or principles that are being floated around and discussed heartily. No single set of AI Ethics principles has been universally adopted. Each day there seems to be a new set proffered by one prominent group or entity, or another. You have lots of AI Ethics precepts to choose from.

The chapters will cover this more so, but we can take a sneak peek here.

As stated by the U.S. Department of Defense (DoD) in their *Ethical Principles For The Use Of Artificial Intelligence*, these are the six primary AI ethics principles:

- **Responsible:** DoD personnel will exercise appropriate levels of judgment and care while remaining responsible for the development, deployment, and use of AI capabilities.

- **Equitable:** The Department will take deliberate steps to minimize unintended bias in AI capabilities.

- **Traceable:** The Department's AI capabilities will be developed and deployed such that relevant personnel possesses an appropriate understanding of the technology, development processes, and operational methods applicable to AI capabilities, including transparent and auditable methodologies, data sources, and design procedure and documentation.

- **Reliable:** The Department's AI capabilities will have explicit, well-defined uses, and the safety, security, and effectiveness of such capabilities will be subject to testing and assurance within those defined uses across their entire lifecycles.

- **Governable:** The Department will design and engineer AI capabilities to fulfill their intended functions while possessing the ability to detect and avoid unintended consequences, and the ability to disengage or deactivate deployed systems that demonstrate unintended behavior.

Meanwhile, as stated by the Vatican in the *Rome Call For AI Ethics* these are their identified six primary AI ethics principles:

- **Transparency:** In principle, AI systems must be explainable
- **Inclusion:** The needs of all human beings must be taken into consideration so that everyone can benefit, and all individuals can be offered the best possible conditions to express themselves and develop
- **Responsibility:** Those who design and deploy the use of AI must proceed with responsibility and transparency
- **Impartiality:** Do not create or act according to bias, thus safeguarding fairness and human dignity
- **Reliability:** AI systems must be able to work reliably
- **Security and privacy:** AI systems must work securely and respect the privacy of users.

You astutely probably noticed a commonality across those AI Ethics principles.

Researchers have examined and condensed the essence of numerous such national and international AI ethics tenets, articulating the summary set in a paper entitled "The Global Landscape Of AI Ethics Guidelines" as published in the prized journal *Nature*, which led to this essentials list:

- **Transparency**
- **Justice & Fairness**
- **Non-Maleficence**
- **Responsibility**
- **Privacy**
- **Beneficence**
- **Freedom & Autonomy**
- **Trust**
- **Sustainability**
- **Dignity**
- **Solidarity**

In short, you could say that AI Ethics consists of *applying* those aforementioned ethical precepts to AI systems.

To make this claim abundantly apparent, I'll relist those principles and add the indication that they are to be applied to AI and done so via the auspices of AI Ethics:

- Transparency as applied to AI via AI Ethics considerations
- Justice & Fairness as applied to AI via AI Ethics considerations
- Non-Maleficence as applied to AI via AI Ethics considerations
- Responsibility as applied to AI via AI Ethics considerations
- Privacy as applied to AI via AI Ethics considerations
- Beneficence as applied to AI via AI Ethics considerations
- Freedom & Autonomy to AI via AI Ethics considerations
- Trust as applied to AI via AI Ethics considerations
- Sustainability as applied to AI via AI Ethics considerations
- Dignity as applied to AI via AI Ethics considerations
- Solidarity as applied to AI via AI Ethics considerations

A recent form of terminology is that we are endeavoring to produce *Ethical AI*.

As will be seen in the chapters herein, I will at times interchangeably refer to AI Ethics and Ethical AI as one and the same. I will also explain why some quibble that AI Ethics and Ethical AI are not identically equivalent, though they both share the same lineage.

A handy way to readily grasp the application of ethics to AI is to consider these two overarching avenues:

1. The ethical behavior of the humans devising and using AI
2. The computational embedding of ethical behavior into the AI itself

In the first instance, the notion is to try and get the humans that are developing and fielding AI to become aware of and make use of ethical practices in how they shape, release, and perform the upkeep of AI systems. You might for example train the stakeholders on the AI Ethics precepts. There might be software development tools and methodologies that can provide AI Ethics guidance. Various quality control checks and auditing can be done under the rubric of AI Ethics attainment. And so on.

In the second instance listed, the idea is to embed into the AI a semblance of ethical acting computer components. Whereas the first focus is about the process of devising the AI, this second focus is about trying to embody ethically capable computational functionality into the AI. This is a much less explored arena and rife for great expansion and maturation. Some even argue that it is not especially doable, though as will be discussed in the chapters you can counterargue that it is already being done, to some extent.

Revealing AI Ethics Via AI Self-Driving Cars

This brief introduction has provided an AI Ethics foundation that will aid in your reading of the chapters.

There is something else you need to know too. In my view, one of the most useful ways to showcase AI Ethics and Ethical AI consists of using real-world examples. There is a special and assuredly popular set of examples that are close to my heart. You see, in my capacity as an expert on AI including the ethical and legal ramifications, I am frequently asked to identify realistic examples that showcase AI Ethics dilemmas so that the somewhat theoretical nature of the topic can be more readily grasped.

One of the most evocative areas that vividly presents this ethical AI quandary is the advent of AI-based true self-driving cars. This will serve as a handy use case or exemplar for ample discussion on the topic.

The eloquence of discussing self-driving cars is that they are near enough to being viable that they reveal the realities of AI Ethics considerations. At the same time, we still have a long way to go before we'll see the fully autonomous self-driving cars that heretofore have mainly been portrayed in sci-fi exploits. The fact that there are tryouts underway of somewhat autonomous self-driving cars is a clear indicator that this is not a purely abstract matter.

Yes, you could sensibly assert that AI Ethics and the rubber meets the road is surely found within the advent of AI-based self-driving cars (pardon the slender pun).

Realize that there isn't a human driver involved in a true self-driving car. Keep in mind that true self-driving cars are driven via an AI driving system. There isn't a need for a human driver at the wheel, nor is there a provision for a human to drive the vehicle.

I'd like to further clarify what is meant when I refer to true self-driving cars.

As a clarification, true self-driving cars are ones that the AI drives the car entirely on its own and there isn't any human assistance during the driving task.

These driverless vehicles are considered Level 4 and Level 5, while a car that requires a human driver to co-share the driving effort is usually considered at Level 2 or Level 3. The cars that co-share the driving task are described as being semi-autonomous, and typically contain a variety of automated add-ons that are referred to as ADAS (Advanced Driver-Assistance Systems).

There is not yet a true self-driving car at Level 5, which we don't yet even know if this will be possible to achieve, and nor how long it will take to get there.

Meanwhile, the Level 4 efforts are gradually trying to get some traction by undergoing very constrained and selective public roadway trials, though there is controversy over whether this testing should be allowed per se (we are all life-or-death guinea pigs in an experiment taking place on our highways and byways, some contend).

Semi-autonomous cars require a human driver. For semi-autonomous cars, it is important that the public needs to be forewarned about a disturbing aspect that's been arising lately, namely that despite those human drivers that keep posting videos of themselves falling asleep at the wheel of a Level 2 or Level 3 car, we all need to avoid being misled into believing that the human driver can take away their attention from the driving task while driving a semi-autonomous car. You are the responsible party for the driving actions of the vehicle, regardless of how much automation might be tossed into a Level 2 or Level 3.

For Level 4 and Level 5 true self-driving vehicles, there won't be a human driver involved in the driving task. All occupants will be passengers. The AI is doing the driving.

One aspect to immediately discuss entails the fact that the AI involved in today's AI driving systems is not sentient. In other words, the AI is altogether a collective of computer-based programming and algorithms, and most assuredly not able to reason in the same manner that humans can.

Why is this added emphasis about the AI not being sentient?

Because I want to underscore that when discussing the role of the AI driving system, I am not ascribing human qualities to the AI. Please be aware that there is an ongoing and dangerous tendency these days to anthropomorphize AI. In essence, people are assigning human-like sentience to today's AI, despite the undeniable and inarguable fact that no such AI exists as yet.

With that clarification, you can envision that the AI driving system won't natively somehow "know" about the facets of driving. Driving and all that it entails will need to be programmed as part of the hardware and software of the self-driving car.

It is important to realize that not all AI self-driving cars are the same. Each automaker and self-driving tech firm is taking its approach to devising self-driving cars. As such, it is difficult to make sweeping statements about what AI driving systems will do or not do. Furthermore, whenever stating that an AI driving system doesn't do some particular thing, this can, later on, be overtaken by developers that in fact program the computer to do that very thing. Step by step, AI driving systems are being gradually improved and extended. An existing limitation today might no longer exist in a future iteration or version of the system.

Nearly all of the included chapters provide an indication of how the covered AI Ethics topic applies to a real-world setting, doing so via discussing AI-based self-driving cars.

The usual scenario depicted goes somewhat like this.

An AI-based self-driving car is underway on your neighborhood streets and seems to be driving safely.

At first, you had devoted special attention to each time that you managed to catch a glimpse of the self-driving car. The autonomous vehicle stood out with its rack of electronic sensors that included video cameras, radar units, LIDAR devices, and the like. After many weeks of the self-driving car cruising around your community, you now barely notice it. As far as you are concerned, it is merely another car on the already busy public roadways.

Lest you think it is impossible or implausible to become familiar with seeing self-driving cars, the locales that are within the scope of self-driving car tryouts have gradually gotten used to seeing the spruced-up vehicles. Many of the locals eventually shifted from mouth-gaping rapt gawking to now emitting an expansive yawn of boredom to witness those meandering self-driving cars.

Probably the main reason right now that they might notice the autonomous vehicles is because of the irritation and exasperation factor. The AI driving systems make sure the cars are obeying all speed limits and rules of the road. For hectic human drivers in their traditional human-driven cars, you get irked at times when stuck behind the strictly law-abiding AI-based self-driving cars.

I then use that base scenario to insert AI Ethics related considerations into the setting. This allows a handy means of discussing the perhaps abstract AI Ethics topic in a manner that can be tangibly understood.

About The Chapters And Your Reading Choices

The chapters are each standalone discussion and you do not need to read them in any particular order. I have sequenced them in a manner that I hope will be useful for the best reading and digesting of the material. That being said, you are welcome to jump around and read the chapters in any personally desired sequence.

These chapters are based on my popular columns and were selected based on their timeliness and rated as most viewed or most informative.

I hope that after you've read the chapters, you will be inspired to learn more about AI Ethics. As well, you might be motivated to participate actively in the AI Ethics realm, perhaps doing research, performing consulting, aiding societal awareness on these topics, or otherwise deciding to get directly involved in this exciting field.

As a quick indication of what the chapters contain, here are the chapters in their provided order:

Conclusion

The rapidity of AI being fostered upon us that is replete with ethically questionable behaviors is clearly a sign that we need more parties that are keenly interested in AI Ethics and Ethical AI. Raise awareness about AI Ethics. Get knee-deep into promulgating Ethical AI. I sincerely urge you to pursue this expanding realm and wish you the best in all of your endeavors.

CHAPTER 2
AI ETHICS AND DEMOCRATIZATION OF AI

Artificial Intelligence (AI) for the people, by the people, and of the people.

That phrasing is a well-intended respectful appropriation from Abraham Lincoln's famous 1863 Gettysburg Address in which he memorably stated that our democracy proffers a new birth of freedom entwining an erstwhile government of the people, by the people, and for the people. This same notion of the power of people was also captured in some years earlier speech by Senator Daniel Webster in 1830 in which he exhorted that our government was made for the people, made by the people, and answerable to the people. You could readily assert that those keystone elements are a bedrock of democracy and democratization.

The reason that I've leveraged such a famed saying is it seemingly can be purposely applied to Artificial Intelligence.

You see, there is a great deal of vocal discussion these days about the *democratization of AI*.

In brief, there is a heartfelt belief that we need to make sure that pretty much anybody at all can craft and deploy AI systems. The ardent view is that we are presently mired in having only techie-focused specialists that can put AI into use. A relatively narrow and devoted clique of AI experts and high-tech entities are dominating which AI systems we are getting and how those AI systems are being devised, the argument goes. We, the people, cannot allow ourselves to become controlled and overseen by a seeming handful of AI gurus.

I think you can probably see how there is a claimed analogous pattern between the notion of how people are governed overall and how AI is being fostered upon the world. Some contend that today's AI is being nurtured by a loosely labeled autocratic or totalitarian style regime that perchance consists of techies. Heaven forbid how AI is going to go under such auspices. The qualm is that we will have AI that does the bidding of these techie overlords and the rest of us will have little say in what the AI does for us and to us.

A quick glance at some of the latest *AI For Bad* instances showcases why there are pronounced anxieties of this nature. AI-based facial recognition was initially hailed as a grand *AI For Good* technology, and then soon enough it was discovered that many such AI systems contained racial and gender biases, along with other akin inequities. All sorts of ethically questionable functionality have been noted in a myriad of contemporary AI.

Why are there AI systems that contain these unethical components or that diverge from ethical values?

One vehemently stated answer is that it is because those crafting AI and fielding AI are not "of the people, for the people, and by the people" in an overarching way. If we can expand the scope of those that would be able to design, build, and deploy AI, the belief is that we have AI that is more representative of society at large and more attuned to society at large.

Problem solved. Instead of AI as ruled by the elite, we will have AI as ruled by the people.

While I am on this sobering and serious topic about AI, you should also be aware that there is another allied angle to the mashup of AI and democratization. The approach or angle that I've so far been elucidating consists of the democratization of AI. A somewhat similar vein from the other end of the spectrum is the application of *AI towards democratization.*

Let me establish that as two interrelated and complementary views:

1. Democratization of AI such that AI is devised and deployed by the people
2. AI as pertaining to democratization and the impacts on democracies

Allow me a brief tangent to cover the latter case. We will then return to the primary focus on the democratization of AI.

Suppose that AI continues on the path of becoming pervasive in our daily lives. This seems an ostensibly logical outcome of where things are already headed. The question then arises as to whether AI is going to help democracies and fuel worldwide support for and cause a greater shift toward countries becoming democratic. Some argue that AI will have that impact. Others are handwringing that AI might do just the opposite, namely stymy democracies and turn back the clock on the global momentum of heralding and embracing democratization.

Yikes!

Which will it be, AI as the hero riding into society as the catalyst and expander of democracies, or AI as the doomy and gloomy spoiler that will undercut democracies and toss aside the impetus for democratization?

A conundrum, that's for sure.

Numerous researchers and political scientists are trying to figure out what AI is going to do as a force for or force away from democratization. You can somewhat categorize the debates into this handful of focal points (admittedly a bit of a simplification):

- AI will spur democracies and energize democratization
- AI will undermine democracies and destabilize democratization
- AI will have no notable effect on democracies or democratization
- AI will stoke a new form of government beyond democracies and the like

The first two points are getting the most attention these days. The third point positing that AI will have no effect on democracies and have no effect on democratization is a rather rare proclaimed viewpoint. You would seem hard-pressed to make a strong argument that AI won't have some effect. It seems to stand to reason that AI will in one manner or another bring forth demonstrative effects. The fourth point that AI might spawn a new form of government is certainly intriguing, though perhaps highly speculative and less frequently entertained in any widespread manner. Don't count it out, but at the same time perhaps be mindful in accepting the proposition blindly.

For those of you further interested in how AI might impact democracies, there is a handy report put out each year by the *Center for AI and Digital Policy (CAIDP)* that explores country practices that are potentially changing due to AI. The report "focuses on human rights, rule of law, and democratic governance metrics. Endorsement and implementation of the OECD/G20 AI Principles is among the primary metrics. Opportunities for the public to participate in the formation of national AI policy, as well as the creation of independent agencies to address AI challenges, is also among the metrics." (per the Artificial Intelligence And Democratic Values Index, February 2022).

As an indicator of the analysis by the CAIDP, consider this latest set of their recommendations:

1) Countries must establish national policies for AI that implement democratic values
2) Countries must ensure public participation in AI policymaking and also create robust mechanisms for independent oversight of AI systems
3) Countries must guarantee fairness, accountability, and transparency in all AI systems
4) Countries must commit to these principles in the development, procurement, and implementation of AI systems for public services
5) Countries must halt the use of facial recognition for mass surveillance
6) Countries must curtail the deployment of lethal autonomous weapons

7) Countries must begin implementation of the UNESCO AI Recommendation
8) Countries must establish a comprehensive, legally binding convention for AI

All of this hopefully whets your appetite for discovering more about how AI might impact democracies and democratization.

Meanwhile, I don't want to herein venture too far into the controversial topic of how AI will impact democratization, but I will at least add some last dollop of murkiness to the mud pile for now. One thorny issue that needs to be addressed and which might already seem like a foregone conclusion is the exact meaning of democracy and democratization. We all probably take at face value that everyone abundantly knows what it means to refer to a democracy. Well, turns out this is not really the way things are.

Consider this handy excerpt from the Princeton University online encyclopedia: "Although Abraham Lincoln, the sixteenth President of the United States (1861-1865), popularized democracy as 'government of the people, by the people and for the people', the concept has in the course of history come to mean different things to different people. It has been applied to many different formations, and, in interaction with different socio-cultural traditions and practices, it has produced diverse forms of government - some more representative, participatory, accountable, transparent and stable than others. Even in today's 'old' democracies - most notably the United States, Britain, France, Australia, New Zealand and those countries that followed the footsteps of these countries following World War II - there is no consensus as to precisely what the concept means and how best to express it as an ideal. There is not even widespread agreement among theorists and practitioners as to whether democracy is a form of government, a method of choosing a government, a reflection of legitimacy in the exercise of political power, a political culture, or a term applied to a whole society, as intimated in Alexis de Tocqueville's study of Democracy in America, which is essentially about American society" (per the section on Democracy And Democratization of the *Encyclopedia Princetoniensis*).

I'll let you stew on that hefty riddle.

Shifting back into the allied topic about the democratization of AI, we can find ourselves a bit up in the air about what that specifically means too.

In other words, if we aren't able to nail down a precise and all-agreed definition of democracy and democratization, this spells trouble for blankly stating that we want democratization of AI. The word "democratization" is loosey-goosey in this context. The usual idea seems to be that we want AI to be devised by, deployed by, and overarchingly dealt with by the masses as opposed to a select group of presumed techie AI elites.

Let's go ahead and use that as a general definitional indication.

You can decidedly quibble whether the word "democratization" is being overloaded or unfairly used in the context of democratizing AI. Lots of other facets of democratic fundamentals are not necessarily being carried into this narrowly conceived facet. That being said, the democratization moniker is alluring, catches attention, and can be claimed as broadly suggestive of what the proponents of democratizing AI are trying to convey.

I won't belabor the point here.

Time to move on.

How will we get AI development into the hands of everyone?

That is a worthwhile question to ask. The aspiration seems to be that everyone should be able to create and deploy AI. If that's the goal, we need to find a means to make it happen. Until recently, most of the AI development required using somewhat arcane AI development techniques and coding tools. You presumably needed to know underlying computer science precepts to suitably tackle the crafting of an AI system. The cost to access the AI-building capabilities was another potential hurdle to be coped with.

As you likely know, a big push has been taking place to make AI tools more widely available and readily usable by non-AI specialists. Most of the major cloud services now have an abundance of AI crafting tools available. For Machine Learning (ML) and Deep Learning (DL), you generally do not need to know how to do conventional programming or coding, and can instead make use of ML/DL software packages.

Okay, envision that the winds continue to blow in that direction and we can in fact enable everyone to make AI systems. No computer science degree is needed. No prior programming experience is required. If you can read and write, you will be able to put together an AI system from scratch. Actually, via the use of voice and conversational AI systems such as Alexa or Siri, you might not need to be able to read or write per se, and instead merely verbally recite what you want to have an AI app do. The AI system will turn your vocalization into an AI app that meets your stated requirements.

Voila, everyone can make AI.

How do you feel about this?

Some are excited.

Some find the prospect ghastly.

Recall that earlier I had mentioned there is a seedy undercurrent of today's AI that consists of *AI For Bad.* If we open the floodgates to making AI by anyone, you can assuredly anticipate that some of that AI is going to be *AI For Bad.* Unless we somehow magically ensure that no AI can be constructed that is *AI For Bad*, we are arming everyone with the distinct possibility of producing *AI For Bad.*

The old adage comes to mind that we might have too much of a good thing. There will be people that meant to craft *AI For Good* that inadvertently landed into *AI For Bad.* We can perhaps sympathize with that circumstance, though the outcome won't be desirable. There will also be evildoer people that intentionally create *AI For Bad.* I doubt we want that.

Of course, there wouldn't seem to be a viable means to select out the evildoers from those that aren't.

You might try to argue that there is always a need to take your lumps when seeking to ensure that everyone has open access and can undertake a given activity. That's just the way things are. But in the case of creating AI, are we ready for the downsides of that aspirational bright light?

In the same manner that maybe someone creates an AI system that can help solve say world hunger or world poverty, we could presumably have someone that creates an AI system that activates autonomous weapons of mass destruction. The good might be really good, but the bad might be really bad, as in the qualms some have about AI as an existential risk.

While I'm on this, you might be wondering what I mean by AI.

AI can consist of these possible states:

1. Non-sentient plain-old AI of today
2. Sentient AI of human quality (we don't have this as yet)
3. Sentient AI that is super-intelligent (a stretch beyond #2)

I am going to focus on the existing state which is non-sentient plain-old AI. Much of what you might read about Ethical AI at times cover the sentient AI and is therefore highly speculative. I say it is speculative because no one can pin the tail on the donkey of what sentient AI will be. Even further beyond the realm of human quality sentient AI is the much-ballyhooed super-intelligent AI. There are lots of sci-fi stories and qualms about how those flavors of AI might decide to enslave humankind, or maybe just wipe us all out. This is known as the existential risk of AI. At times, the dilemma is also phrased as the catastrophic risk of AI.

Some contend that we might be okay as long as we keep AI to the non-sentient plain-old AI that we have today. Let's assume we cannot reach sentient AI. Imagine that no matter how hard we try to craft sentient AI, we fail at doing so. As well, assume for sake of discussion that sentient AI doesn't arise by some mysterious spontaneous process.

Aren't we then safe that this lesser caliber AI, which is the imagined only possible kind of AI, will be in use?

Not really.

Pretty much, the same general issues are likely to arise. I'm not suggesting that the AI "thinks" its way to wanting to destroy us. No, the ordinary non-sentient AI is merely placed into positions of power that get us mired in self-destruction. For example, we put non-sentient AI into weapons of mass destruction. These autonomous weapons are not able to think. At the same time, humans are not kept fully in the loop. As a result, the AI as a form of autonomous automation ends up inadvertently causing catastrophic results, either by a human command to do so, or by a bug or error, or by implanted evildoing, or by self-adjustments that lead matters down that ugly path, etc.

I would contend that the AI ethics problem exists for all three of those AI stipulated states, namely that we have AI ethical issues with non-sentient plain-old AI, and with sentient AI that is either merely human level or the outstretched AI that reaches the acclaimed superintelligence level.

Given that sobering pronouncement, we can assuredly debate the magnitude and difficulty associated with the ethical problems at each of the respective levels of AI. The customary viewpoint is that the AI ethics predicament is less insurmountable at the non-sentient AI, tougher at the sentient human-equal AI level, and a true head-scratcher at the sentient super-intelligent AI stage of affairs.

The better the AI becomes, the worse the AI ethics problem becomes.

Maybe that is an inviolable law of nature.

We have to closely examine what the democratization of AI foretells.

Upon saying that, some will immediately knee-jerk respond and fervently claim that any such examination is tantamount to trying to keep AI solely in the hands of the elite. They argue that by questioning the idea of making AI crafting available to all, you are playing into the hands of those that currently devise AI. Those elites relish, apparently, keeping tight control on AI. The masses are then subject to their power, it is said.

The counterargument is that if we pell-mell rush into opening up the AI spigot, we are doing so in a wanton fashion that will undoubtedly have various undesirable consequences. Perhaps we can attain a balance. Put in place means to keep the crafting of AI within some reasonable bounds.

Round and round the debates go.

It can be dizzying. The logic often is a bit mind-numbing. If we don't do something, the AI elites will keep marching forward. They will ultimately prevent the rest of the people from being able to craft AI. Ergo, you need to take action now. Switch sides for a moment. If we open up AI development to everyone, we will be setting ourselves up for AI apocalypse. But, wait for a second, maybe we are already heading toward an AI apocalypse by not opening up the crafting of AI. The masses having AI crafting might be the key toward preventing an AI-related takeover of our existence.

At this juncture of this discussion, I'd bet that you are desirous of some real-world examples that could highlight how the opening up of AI crafting might apply to today's AI.

I'm glad you asked.

There is a special and assuredly popular set of examples that are close to my heart. You see, in my capacity as an expert on AI including the ethical and legal ramifications, I am frequently asked to identify realistic examples that showcase AI Ethics dilemmas so that the somewhat theoretical nature of the topic can be more readily grasped. One of the most evocative areas that vividly presents this ethical AI quandary is the advent of AI-based true self-driving cars. This will serve as a handy use case or exemplar for ample discussion on the topic.

Here's then a noteworthy question that is worth contemplating: *Does the advent of AI-based true self-driving cars illuminate anything about wanting to democratize AI, and if so, what does this showcase?*

Allow me a moment to unpack the question.

Let's use a readily straightforward example. An AI-based self-driving car is underway on your neighborhood streets and seems to be driving safely. At first, you had devoted special attention to each time that you managed to catch a glimpse of the self-driving car. The autonomous vehicle stood out with its rack of electronic sensors that included video cameras, radar units, LIDAR devices, and the like. After many weeks of the self-driving car cruising around your community, you now barely notice it. As far as you are concerned, it is merely another car on the already busy public roadways.

Lest you think it is impossible or implausible to become familiar with seeing self-driving cars, I've written frequently about how the locales that are within the scope of self-driving car tryouts have gradually gotten used to seeing the spruced-up vehicles. Many of the locals eventually shifted from mouth-gaping rapt gawking to now emitting an expansive yawn of boredom to witness those meandering self-driving cars.

Probably the main reason right now that they might notice the autonomous vehicles is because of the irritation and exasperation factor. The by-the-book AI driving systems make sure the cars are obeying all speed limits and rules of the road. For hectic human drivers in their traditional human-driven cars, you get irked at times when stuck behind the strictly law-abiding AI-based self-driving cars.

That's something we might all need to get accustomed to, rightfully or wrongly.

Back to our tale. One day, suppose that someone used various AI building tools to devise their own self-driving car. They did so as an outgrowth of a movement toward the democratization of AI. Rather than only having automakers and other specialist entities put together driverless vehicles, the idea is that with a widening of access to AI tools just about anyone can create an AI driving system.

Oops, turns out that the AI driving system is not very capable and within the first days of operation the AI driving system gets into hot water. First, the AI rolled through Stop signs and nearly clipped pedestrians and bike riders. Next, the AI allowed insufficient room between the self-driving car and other roadway vehicles, leading to sideswiping of human-driven cars and trucks. Finally, after public outrage was already boiling, the AI driving system had the self-driving car go past a red light and the autonomous vehicle rammed into two other cars.

As an aside, for those of you familiar with the history of self-driving cars, you might be aware that there initially were some vociferously bragging "hotshot programmers" that brazenly said they could grind out the code for an AI driving system almost overnight. They claimed that they could put to shame all those companies spending millions and perhaps billions of dollars to do the same. The reality is that there is a lot more to the AI driving systems than perhaps meets the eye, and such fly-by-night attempts generally went bust.

I think we can likely all reasonably agree that the AI underlying something as life-or-death involving such as self-driving cars should be mindfully crafted and carefully put into use. Do we want just anybody to be able to do so? Probably not.

Of course, this does raise a bit of a dilemma.

Are we going to forbid people from writing AI that does certain types of tasks that we believe to be especially serious or risky? The problem there entails how to predetermine that the AI is destined for such tasks, and how to prevent people from devising AI of that ilk. Furthermore, we are for the moment only discussing what seems to be well-intended *AI For Good*, which an AI driving system would generally seem to be, though imagine if an evildoer was trying to create an AI driving system for purposes of destruction and mayhem.

How do we miraculously weed out the *AI For Bad* malicious efforts versus the *AI For Good* forays?

We could inadvertently stifle the crafting of AI that was going to benefit humanity. In that case, loosen the restrictions, you might say. Lamentedly, we might inadvertently encourage the building of AI that will destroy humanity. Tighten the restrictions, you might exhort.

Trying to draw clear lines on how the AI is to be devised can be tricky.

Conclusion

A few concluding thoughts, for now, might be worth pondering.

When discussing the democratization of AI, perhaps we might lean further into the meaning of democracies and democratization. The prevailing hasty and shortchanged notion of *democratization of* AI deserves expansion and a spoonful of sensibility and robustness.

For example, political scientists typically would suggest that democracy has active participation of the people, akin to the government of the people, by the people, and for the people. But that's not all. A democracy usually proffers protection for the human rights of the people. You can also toss into the democracy rubric that there is a semblance of laws and the rule of law. Etc.

This implies that we aren't merely aiming to arm everyone with AI crafting tools. We must also find a means to guide the AI crafters toward respecting human rights, the rule of law, and other essentials.

Efforts to clarify what we want AI to be or become are actively underway and consist of stipulating key AI Ethics principles. The hope is that by abiding by those cornerstone precepts, we will strive toward *AI For Good* and steer away from *AI For Bad.*

Likewise, on the legal front, and as mentioned earlier, countries across the globe are putting in place new laws about AI too.

Let's take a moment to briefly consider some of the key Ethical AI precepts to illustrate what AI builders ought to be thinking about and rigorously undertaking from an AI Ethics stance. Note that when I refer to "AI builders" this means not just the so-called AI developer elite, but presumably, *everyone* since by democratization of AI the goal seems to be that everyone will effectively be AI builders.

I've also discussed various collective analyses of AI ethics principles, including having covered a set devised by researchers that examined and condensed the essence of numerous national and international AI ethics tenets in a paper entitled "The Global Landscape Of AI Ethics Guidelines" (published in *Nature*), which led to this keystone list:

- **Transparency**
- **Justice & Fairness**
- **Non-Maleficence**
- **Responsibility**
- **Privacy**
- **Beneficence**
- **Freedom & Autonomy**

- **Trust**
- **Sustainability**
- **Dignity**
- **Solidarity**

As you might directly guess, trying to pin down the specifics underlying these principles can be extremely hard to do. Even more so, the effort to turn those broad principles into something entirely tangible and detailed enough to be used when crafting AI systems is also a tough nut to crack. It is easy to overall do some handwaving about what AI Ethics precepts are and how they should be generally observed, while it is a much more complicated situation upon the AI coding having to be the veritable rubber that meets the road.

All in all, if we are stridently pursuing democratization of AI, we should hopefully simultaneously be pursuing the ethical and legal underpinnings that will serve as guideposts for a deluge of AI that will be spawned by widespread massive-scale AI crafting efforts.

You might vaguely be aware that Abraham Lincoln quipped this memorable line: "The best way to predict your future is to create it." When it comes to the democratization of AI, we can go whole-hog or we can proceed in a measured way. Whatever we do, let's not bite off more than we can chew.

Honestly, that seems like sage advice that Abe himself might have said about AI too.

.

.

CHAPTER 3
AI ETHICS AND CONFLICTING FACTORS

Do two wrongs make a right?

Whichever way that you decide to answer that longstanding and vexing question, the odds are that you are stepping whole-hog into a thorny ethical debate.

Let's see why.

Some insist that there is never a situation in which two wrongs make a right. Their logic usually is that a wrong is a wrong. Thus, two wrongs are ostensibly nothing more than two wrongs. End of story. Others counterargue that sometimes a wrong can be entirely justly met with another wrong, especially when the subsequent wrong is considered correcting of the prior wrong. In a sense, the wrongs cancel each other out and you end up with a semblance of a rightful outcome.

Round and round the often-heated discourse on two wrongs and the questionable matter of a rightful result takes place.

There are ethicists that would at times label the adage as a type of mental fallacy. If the two wrongs are only tangentially connectable, you would seem on thin ice to claim that one of the wrongs is stridently related to the other. Also, the finger-pointing at a prior wrong might be done simply as a distractor and a desperate attempt to avoid getting pinned on a later committed wrong. This is the proverbial use of a red herring.

A dizzying conundrum, that's for sure.

Maybe it will help for us to mull over some specific examples.

You are caught speeding on a well-used highway. Darn it, speeding tickets are costly and also add onerously adverse points on your official driving record. Your insurance premiums will probably radically go up too. After thinking quite a bit about this exasperating and altogether annoying traffic ticket, you make the difficult decision to fight the pesky thing. Off to court, you go.

Standing there in a somber courtroom, you have your moment in the sun to explain what you were doing. Hopefully, the judge will see the world through your eyes and toss out the seemingly unwarranted and unjustified speeding ticket (as per your view on the matter).

You stoically explain that there were lots of other cars speeding on the highway. None of those drivers received speeding tickets. Since they didn't get speeding tickets, it only seems fair and reasonable that you should have your speeding ticket canceled.

Two wrongs make a right.

That's the totality of your proffered argument.

Does the judge buy into your logic and let you off the hook?

Generally, the odds would seem low that your contention will prevail in this instance. The stern answer by the judge might be that two wrongs don't make a right. Your ticket stands as is. Next case!

Let's help out by reshaping your argument.

The new explanation is this. There were lots of other cars speeding on the highway. You were essentially forced into going at the same speed as those other cars. Had you gone slower, the chances were high that your lessened speed might have led to a car crash, during which people could be seriously injured or killed. To try and drive safely, thoughtfully aiming to avoid a calamitous car crash, you had no choice but to drive at the prevailing speed at the time.

Yes, once again, two wrongs make a right, but this angle differs from the prior elucidation.

Will the judge see the light and dismiss your speeding ticket?

It would seem like this is a more compelling argument and has a better chance of succeeding.

We'll try one more variant and see how else this might be couched.

Pretend that we are starting the speeding ticket courtroom story all over again. Start fresh. You tell the following tale to the attentive judge. There was a drunk driver on the highway. You saw that the errant driver was weaving perilously. Upon approaching this imminent danger, you decided to momentarily speed up to get safely past the inebriated driver. Had you not done so, the likelihood was that the wanton driver would have veered into your car, killing you and themself too. The traffic officer stopped you, and completely missed stopping the drunk driver, which sadly and lamentedly is a rather disconcerting and disturbing twist of justice or injustice, as you see it.

Two wrongs do in fact make a right, you respectfully urge.

Maybe this is convincing, maybe not.

The thing is, the overarching mindful contention that two wrongs make a right is a powerful form of human thinking and some would say a potent kind of mental bias. As a persuasive tool, it can be used to either clarify matters or confound matters. The mind-bending construct appears to invoke ethical keystones. If you believe that ethical behavior consists of doing the right thing, perhaps the right thing to do was perform a so-called wrong to effectuate a right. Of course, the extremism of how far we can stretch the proverb is open to serious doubt.

For example, suppose that when trying to talk your way out of the traffic ticket, you explained that you were speeding because you had heard on the news that outer space aliens were on their way to take over earth (this was indeed a reported claim, according to recent news reports of someone that was stopped for speeding). This seems quite zany. Probably not a wise move to offer this postulated perspective.

One perhaps notable aspect about this discussion on wrongs and rights is that I've been using an example entailing speeding tickets, which takes us into the legal realm. You might be tempted to say that speeding is a simple legal matter. Either someone was speeding, or they were not speeding. If they were speeding, they deserve to get the ticket and take their lumps accordingly. If they were not speeding, perhaps the radar used to track their speed was defective, and the person ergo ought to be let free since the speeding ticket was erroneously assigned.

Is the law really that cut and dried?

In California, the official driving law pertaining to speeding is known as CVC 22350 and says this: "No person shall drive a vehicle upon a highway at a speed greater than is reasonable or prudent having due regard for weather, visibility, the traffic on, and the surface and width of, the highway, and in no event at a speed which endangers the safety of persons or property."

By closely examining the words of that law, I think you will quickly realize that speeding is not necessarily as cut and dried as might be otherwise assumed. Suppose that a driver is rushing to the hospital due to a medical emergency taking place inside the car. We might allow that this is legally okay as long as the speeding did not excessively endanger the safety of others. There is a lot of giving and taking in something as seemingly simple as the act of speeding. Extenuating circumstances can be a huge differentiator.

All told, I hope that this showcases that thorny ethical matters and even supposedly cut-and-dried legal matters are often imbued with all sorts of complications. There can be a multitude of factors that come to play in an ethical setting. For those that cling to an abstract simplified notion of doing the right thing versus doing the wrong thing, the reality of daily life perhaps blurs what the right thing and the wrong thing consist of, depending upon prevailing cultural norms and a slew of other considerations (well, some ethicists would likely argue that there are absolutes that exist in the right versus the wrong conundrum, but that's something I've covered elsewhere in my writings and I won't get into herein).

Shifting gears, how do we make tough choices, and what is the nature of our decision-making process?

Researchers often describe our decision-making as embodying a litany of lexicographic choices, as articulated by this indication: "People accommodate their inability to make a great number of choices by making lexicographic choices. That is, they ignore the information about most facets of the object of their choice, and focus on a few that they hold to be most important. Thus, when they buy a car, they may examine its relative price, miles per gallon, and color, or some other such mix of features—but ignore scores of other attributes. The same holds true of moral choices. People, when making a major donation, may take into account the goals the given charity serves, whether it services people in their own community or overseas, and whether it has a reputation as an honest agency, or some other such mix. They will ignore, in the process, many other features of the given charity such as its long-term record, recent changes in leadership, its ratio of expenses to payouts, and so on" (as mentioned in "AI Assisted Ethics" by Amitai Etzioni and Oren Etzioni, *Ethics And Information Technology*).

Returning to the speeding driving situation, someone that is urgently driving to a hospital might entirely focus on their own urgency and downplay or ignore that they endangered other cars while driving at high speeds. The person might not be doing this deviously. They could genuinely believe that their own course of action was fully justified and be oblivious to the other possible consequences or spillover from their behavior.

You could persuasively contend that ethical thinking is replete with a multitude of factors. It is a decidedly multi-dimensional form of problem-solving. For just about any real-world ethical setting that you might devise or describe, the likelihood is that numerous factors come to play under-the-hood as it were.

I've tried to lead you toward an important theme.

Ethical considerations cannot usually be ascertained solely by using a singular factor. A multitude of factors is more so the real-world context. That being said, there is little doubt that some factors are more vital than other factors. Thus, not all factors are necessarily equal in weight or significance. Nonetheless, rarely can you swipe away the other factors and merely focus exclusively on one alone.

Why all this fuss about ethics and the multi-dimensional elements involved?

Because we need to have a serious chat about AI Ethics.

You might be aware that there is a rising interest in AI Ethics. And for good reasons. The essence is that we are pell-mell rushing forward with all manner of AI systems that are becoming integral to our daily lives. Initially, many referred to this as *AI For Good*, meaning that we could use modern-day AI to aid in solving the world's toughest problems. Meanwhile, we have come to see that some AI systems are replete with untoward biases and inequities. This is generally referred to as *AI For Bad*.

A type of tension is mounting of efforts to produce and promulgate AI that is ostensibly *AI For Good* and simultaneously stop or catch the *AI For Bad*. Realize that any given AI system can be both at the same time. An AI system that enables more people to get say mortgage loans for housing would seem to be an *AI For Good* instance, though if the AI embeds racial or gender biases in making the loan decisions we would abundantly seem to agree that this is also *AI For Bad*. The pervasive emergence of algorithm decision making (ADM) as based on the latest in AI has put us all on edge about what is really going on inside the computational decision-making of the AI.

Efforts to clarify what we want AI to be or become consist of stipulating key AI Ethics principles. The hope is that by abiding by those cornerstone precepts, we will lean into *AI For Good* and shy away from *AI For Bad*. Notably, this leaning into and away from is going to be harder than it might seem at first glance.

I've also discussed various collective analyses of AI ethics principles, including having covered a set devised by researchers that examined and condensed the essence of numerous national and international AI ethics tenets in a paper entitled "The Global Landscape Of AI Ethics Guidelines" (published in *Nature*), which led to this keystone list:

- **Transparency**
- **Justice & Fairness**
- **Non-Maleficence**
- **Responsibility**
- **Privacy**
- **Beneficence**
- **Freedom & Autonomy**
- **Trust**
- **Sustainability**
- **Dignity**
- **Solidarity**

As you might directly guess, trying to pin down the specifics underlying these principles can be extremely hard to do. Even more so, the effort to turn those broad principles into something entirely tangible and detailed enough to be used when crafting AI systems is also a tough nut to crack. It is easy to overall do some handwaving about what AI Ethics precepts are and how they should be generally observed, while it is a much more complicated situation upon the AI coding having to be the veritable rubber that meets the road.

Take for instance the concept of imbuing fairness into an AI system.

Sure, it would seem readily apparent that we want AI systems to be fair. Any counter-argument is going to seemingly fall flat. I ask you; can you define fairness in a concrete way that can be fully articulated and ultimately coded into a computer system for use within an AI system?

That's a tall order.

Researchers are trying mightily to probe and engineer these AI ethics precepts, but roadblocks continue to stymy such efforts: "The plethora of fairness metric definitions illustrates that fairness cannot be reduced to a concise mathematical definition. Fairness is dynamic, social in nature, application, and context-specific, and not just an abstract or universal statistical problem. Therefore, it is important to adopt a socio-technical approach to fairness in order to have realistic fairness definitions for different contexts as well as task specific datasets for machine learning model development and evaluation" (as stated in "AI Assisted Ethics" by Amitai Etzioni and Oren Etzioni, *Ethics And Information Technology*).

In case you are wondering why "fairness" would be complicated, consider some additional insights by those same researchers about the hurdles facing defining and coding up of fairness: "These metrics can be classified into many categories: fairness through unawareness, individual fairness, demographic parity, disparate impact, differential validity, proxy discrimination, equality of opportunity, etc. However, not all critically important lines of inquiry can be answered through observations alone. Moreover, depending on the relationship between a protected attribute and the data, certain observational definitions of fairness can increase discrimination. Hence, research to improve fairness metrics continues."

Okay, it would seem apparent that fairness is not so easy to devise and construct. The thing is, the same can be said of the other AI Ethics principles too, such as the figuring out of transparency, justice, non-maleficence, responsibility, privacy, beneficence, freedom and autonomy, trust, sustainability, dignity, and solidarity. It is a multitude of factors, all of which are essentially ambiguous and need to be turned into being unambiguousness when serving as guardrails for AI.

Not wanting to further stoke this hornet's nest, we must though also take note that the multitude of factors can run afoul of each other. There are circumstances where seeking to attain one of the factors can end up conflicting with one or more of the other factors. You might devise an AI system that can be considered as being fair, but suppose that the only viable means of doing so sacrifices the desire to have transparency?

This is a real problem today facing many of the AI systems that incorporate Machine Learning (ML) and Deep Learning (DL).

In short, human ethical thinking is rife with considering a multitude of factors when making ethical or moral decisions. We are striving toward crafting AI systems that make decisions using ADM (algorithm decision making). There is a sensible basis for wanting the AI to abide by ethical precepts, such as the ones mentioned earlier herein.

Trying to reduce the AI Ethics precepts to one single precept is not particularly helpful. Doing so might simplify the crafting of the AI, but in the end, the AI then undercuts the other AI Ethics precepts. The AI might be touted as attaining one of the principles, meanwhile gloomily doing poorly on the others. This would not seem satisfying for society.

Be cautious when a company announces they have devised an AI system that is for example allegedly fair. Besides questioning how such an attestation can be made, the AI at the same time might be badly enmeshed with a variety of other ills and have completely averted transparency, non-maleficence, responsibility, privacy, etc. Do not be fooled by twitter-sized headline-grabbing claims that distract from the myriad of other AI Ethics principles that should also be observed.

Envision that a corporation proudly proclaims that it has an AI-based mortgage loan granting system that is absolutely fair in the loan selection process. Turns out, unbeknownst to those using the AI system, privacy went out the window and the firm is making use of the collected data about the loan applicants in the most egregious of ways. Fairness was supposedly achieved at the sacrifice of privacy, let's say.

Do one right and one wrong make a right?

Extending the example, suppose we find out that the AI-based loan granting app is not actually fair anyway. The AI has hidden biases that only became apparent after many thousands of loans were granted and many thousands of loan applicants were turned down. Oops, we have an AI system that isn't fair and also isn't protecting privacy.

The company insists that at least their AI system is no worse than prior efforts that used human loan agents to make the decisions. In fact, they point out that the AI system is faster and gives answers about loan requests in seconds rather than having to wait perhaps days when relying on human agents.

Aha, two wrongs make a right!

We have come full circle. In the case of a traffic ticket for speeding, we had the classic claim that since others were wrongfully speeding, the driver nabbed with a ticket ought to be let off the hook. Two wrongs make a right. Now, in the case of loan granting, we have the claim that since human loan agents are seeming "wrong" in a manner of speaking, we are asked to look the other way when an AI system granting loans is also considered wrong in how it works.

Two wrongs make a right?

Makes your head spin.

At this juncture of this discussion, I'd bet that you are desirous of some additional real-world examples that could highlight the multi-dimensional facets of AI Ethics and Ethical AI.

There is a special and assuredly popular set of examples that are close to my heart. You see, in my capacity as an expert on AI including the ethical and legal ramifications, I am frequently asked to identify realistic examples that showcase AI Ethics dilemmas so that the somewhat theoretical nature of the topic can be more readily grasped. One of the most evocative areas that vividly presents this ethical AI quandary is the advent of AI-based true self-driving cars. This will serve as a handy use case or exemplar for ample discussion on the topic.

Here's then a noteworthy question that is worth contemplating: *Does the advent of AI-based true self-driving cars illuminate anything the multi-dimensionality of AI Ethics, and if so, what does this showcase?*

Allow me a moment to unpack the question.

Let's use a readily straightforward example. An AI-based self-driving car is underway on your neighborhood streets and seems to be driving safely. At first, you had devoted special attention to each time that you managed to catch a glimpse of the self-driving car. The autonomous vehicle stood out with its rack of electronic sensors that included video cameras, radar units, LIDAR devices, and the like. After many weeks of the self-driving car cruising around your community, you now barely notice it. As far as you are concerned, it is merely another car on the already busy public roadways.

Lest you think it is impossible or implausible to become familiar with seeing self-driving cars, I've written frequently about how the locales that are within the scope of self-driving car tryouts have gradually gotten used to seeing the spruced-up vehicles. Many of the locals eventually shifted from mouth-gaping rapt gawking to now emitting an expansive yawn of boredom to witness those meandering self-driving cars.

Probably the main reason right now that they might notice the autonomous vehicles is because of the irritation and exasperation factor. The by-the-book AI driving systems make sure the cars are obeying all speed limits and rules of the road. For hectic human drivers in their traditional human-driven cars, you get irked at times when stuck behind the strictly law-abiding AI-based self-driving cars.

That's something we might all need to get accustomed to, rightfully or wrongly.

Back to our tale. One day, suppose a self-driving car in your town or city is driving along and opts to exceed the speed limit.

Say what?

Yes, the always legally doting AI self-driving car went faster than the posted speed limit. Someone managed to catch this occurrence on their cellphone. The video was promptly shared via social media and became a viral sensation. The AI that was stridently obeying the laws had opted to violate the law.

Online responses were varied, as you might imagine. Is AI above the law? If so, what might happen next? Perhaps AI will decide to overtake humanity. We will be crushed by lawless AI. The dreaded slippery slope of humans creating AI and then being torn asunder by AI will finally happen. An existential risk was showcased to us, as plain as day, on the day that the AI self-driving car first went over the speed limit.

In any case, hopefully, not everyone will react in a similar vein. Let's trust that humankind will take a calmer view on such matters.

We will take as an undisputed fact that the self-driving car went faster than the speed limit. Assume that even the automaker and the self-driving tech maker all agree that the AI driving system led the autonomous vehicle to break the law. Public outrage insists that the self-driving car be issued a violation citation of a traffic ticket for speeding. Give that lawbreaker AI a driving infraction. Maybe the AI needs to be sent to driving school just like the rest of us that deal with speeding tickets.

Time to invoke a handy-dandy proverb.

Are you ready?

Humans in your city or town go faster than the speed limit, doing so quite frequently. This is a known fact. They aren't getting tickets. The AI was merely doing what the human drivers do.

Conclusion: *Two wrongs make a right.*

Imagine that the lawyers for the automaker and self-driving tech firm are standing in a courtroom and making that kind of plea to the judge. Your honor, our AI was merely driving as humans drive. If you aren't going to give out hundreds or maybe thousands of speeding tickets to human speeders, you shouldn't penalize AI for its similar actions. We rest our case.

Maybe this is a convincing argument or maybe not.

We can further contemplate the matter. Suppose that the AI had a bug or error in it. The circumstance of going faster than the posted speed limit was due to the error in the coding. It only happened once. The AI developers dug into the code and found the error. They have corrected the error. As far as they can discern, the self-driving car will never go over the speed limit again.

Should the automaker or self-driving tech firm fess up and reveal that the excessive speed was due to an error in their AI system? You might argue that they should do so, perhaps it is the right thing to do on an ethical basis. Be transparent about what the AI consists of.

The worry though by the automaker and self-driving tech firm might be that if people know one bug arose, panic will ensue and people might start to become afraid that more bugs are bound to be hidden within the AI. This could undermine faith in self-driving cars. People might not want to ride in them anymore. The entirety of the pursuit of AI-based self-driving cars tumbles to the ground.

Transparency is no free lunch.

We can make the story gloomier in a sense.

Scratch from your mind that the AI had a bug in it. Start fresh.

Suppose the AI was devised using Machine Learning and Deep Learning, a form of computational pattern matching. The ML/DL can end up being extremely arcane in a mathematical way. An ongoing and troubling qualm about many of today's ML/DL is that there is often no logically explainable means to get the AI system to identify how it arrived at a given decision. This area of AI is known as XAI (explainable AI) and there is a lot of pressure to try and ensure that AI systems can explain how they arrived at an answer or outcome.

Consider this. The AI developers dig into the ML/DL of the AI driving system and are unable to ferret out why the AI opted to have the autonomous vehicle go faster than the speed limit. It is baffling. Was it a bug? Was it working as designed? They don't know.

Unfortunately, as a result of the computational encoding, there really doesn't seem to be a means to figure out what prompted the AI to do this.

Whereas a moment ago we were discussing transparency in terms of revealing that the AI had a bug, now the issue is that there isn't any transparency available at all. The automaker and the self-driving tech firm are in the dark about what occurred. They couldn't tell you even if they wanted to do so (of course, this too becomes a matter of transparency, specifically revealing that they don't know what caused the speeding, and their efforts to discover the basis was unrevealing).

Should we let the AI off the hook?

That is a bit misleading since the AI isn't sentient and we ought to instead be asking whether we should let the automaker and the self-driving tech firm off the hook. They devised the AI driving system. They are the ones that put self-driving cars onto our public streets. Humans are responsible and they are the ones that need to be held accountable.

Conclusion

We earlier took a look at some of the AI Ethics principles that are today's foundational set of guidelines for AI development, AI fielding, and AI usage. As a reminder, one such set consists of:

- Transparency
- Justice & Fairness
- Non-Maleficence
- Responsibility
- Privacy
- Beneficence
- Freedom & Autonomy
- Trust
- Sustainability
- Dignity
- Solidarity

In the use case of AI-based self-driving cars, are there tradeoffs amongst those AI Ethics precepts that you are willing to allow in order to presumably more expeditiously arrive at self-driving cars?

One argument is that it is reasonable to cut short some of those factors to try and attain AI for autonomous vehicles. The logic is that in the United States alone, there are about 40,000 human fatalities per year due to car crashes and around 2.5 million injuries. The sooner we can get self-driving cars underway, the sooner we can reduce those ghastly numbers.

You might say that ethically it makes sense to shave some corners to save lives and diminish injuries.

Which of the factors are you willing to undercut?

Alright, you might say, give up on transparency to get AI that will save lives. Maybe the same can be said for sustainability. Perhaps the same for privacy. How far are you willing to go?

We need to be asking these same questions about all AI systems.

I've used the exemplar of AI driving systems to illustrate this major theme about AI and AI Ethics. The adoption of AI is a multifold ethics factors problem. Move beyond the AI of self-driving cars and start asking the same multi-dimensional questions about the AI that exists in systems all around you.

As you do so, there might be a tiny voice in the recesses of your mind that says this, namely whether two wrongs make a right or whether two wrongs don't make a right.

We'd better pick the right answer.

..

CHAPTER 4
AI ETHICS
AND HUMAN BIASES

Humans have got to know their limitations.

You might recall the akin famous line about knowing our limitations as grittily uttered by the character Dirty Harry in the 1973 movie entitled *Magnum Force* (per the spoken words of actor Clint Eastwood in his memorable role as Inspector Harry Callahan). The overall notion is that sometimes we tend to overlook our own limits and get ourselves into hot water accordingly. Whether due to hubris, being egocentric, or simply blind to our own capabilities, the precept of being aware of and taking into explicit account our proclivities and shortcomings is abundantly sensible and helpful.

Let's add a new twist to the sage piece of advice.

Artificial Intelligence (AI) has got to know its limitations.

What do I mean by that variant of the venerated catchphrase?

Turns out that the initial rush to get modern-day AI into use as a hopeful solver of the world's problems has become sullied and altogether muddied by the realization that today's AI does have some rather severe limitations. We went from the uplifting headlines of *AI For Good* and have increasingly found ourselves mired in *AI For Bad.* You see, many AI systems have been developed and fielded with all sorts of untoward racial and gender biases, and a myriad of other such appalling inequities.

The biases being discovered in these AI systems are not of the shall we say "intentional" type that we would ascribe to human behavior. I mention this to emphasize that today's AI is not sentient. Despite those blaring headlines that suggest otherwise, there just isn't any AI anywhere that even comes close to sentience.

On top of that, we don't know how to get AI into the sentience bracket, plus nobody can say for sure whether we will ever attain AI sentience. Maybe it will someday happen, or maybe not.

So, my point is that we cannot particularly assign intention to the kind of AI that we currently possess. That being said, we can abundantly assign intention to those that are crafting AI systems. Some AI developers are unaware of the fact that they have devised an AI system that contains unsavory and possibly illegal biases. Meanwhile, other AI developers realize they are imbuing biases into their AI systems, potentially doing so in a purposeful wrongdoing manner.

Either way, the outcome is nonetheless still unseemly and likely unlawful.

Strident efforts are underway to promulgate AI Ethics principles that will enlighten AI developers and provide suitable guidance for steering clear of embedding biases into their AI systems. This will help in a twofer fashion. First, those crafting AI will no longer have the ready excuse that they just weren't cognizant of what precepts should be followed. Second, those that veer from the Ethical AI conditions are going to be more readily caught and shown as averting that which they were forewarned to both do and not do.

Let's take a moment to briefly consider some of the key Ethical AI precepts to illustrate what AI builders ought to be thinking about and rigorously undertaking from an AI Ethics stance.

I've also discussed various collective analyses of AI ethics principles, including having covered a set devised by researchers that examined and condensed the essence of numerous national and international AI ethics tenets in a paper entitled "The Global Landscape Of AI Ethics Guidelines" (published in *Nature*) which led to this keystone list:

- **Transparency**
- **Justice & Fairness**
- **Non-Maleficence**
- **Responsibility**

- **Privacy**
- **Beneficence**
- **Freedom & Autonomy**
- **Trust**
- **Sustainability**
- **Dignity**
- **Solidarity**

As you might directly guess, trying to pin down the specifics underlying these principles can be extremely hard to do. Even more so, the effort to turn those broad principles into something entirely tangible and detailed enough to be used when crafting AI systems is also a tough nut to crack. It is easy to overall do some handwaving about what AI Ethics precepts are and how they should be generally observed, while it is a much more complicated situation upon the AI coding having to be the veritable rubber that meets the road.

The AI Ethics principles are to be utilized by AI developers, along with those that manage AI development efforts, and even those that ultimately field and perform upkeep on AI systems. All stakeholders throughout the entire AI life-cycle of development and usage are considered within the scope of abiding by the being-established norms of Ethical AI. This is an important highlight since the usual assumption is that "only coders" or those that program the AI is subject to adhering to the AI Ethics notions. Please be aware that it takes a village to devise and field AI. For which the entire village has to be keeping on their toes about AI Ethics.

Anyway, now that I've gotten onto the table that AI can contain biases, we can perhaps all agree to these two apparent facts:

1. Humans can have numerous untoward biases and can act upon them
2. AI can have numerous untoward biases and can act upon those biases

I am somewhat loathed to stack humans versus AI in that context since it might somehow imply that AI has sentient capacities on par with humans. This is assuredly not so.

I will return momentarily to the mounting concerns about anthropomorphizing of AI a little later in this discussion.

Which is worse, humans that exhibit untoward biases or AI that does so?

I dare say that the question poses one of those dour choices. It is the proverbial lesser of two evils, one might contend. We would wish that humans did not embody untoward biases. We would further wish that even if humans do have untoward biases they won't act upon those biases. The same could be aptly said of AI. We would wish that AI did not embed untoward biases and that even if there are such internally coded biases that the AI would at least not act upon them.

Wishes though do not necessarily run the world.

Okay, we obviously want humans to know their limitations. There is an importance to recognizing when you have untoward biases. There is equal importance in trying to prevent those untoward biases from being infused into your actions and decisions. Businesses today are trying all kinds of approaches to keep their employees from falling into the untoward biases dire pitfalls. Specialized training is being given to employees about how to perform their work in ethically sound ways. Processes are shaped around employees to alert them when they seem to be exhibiting unethical mores. And so on.

Another means of coping with humans and their untoward biases would be to automate human-based work. Yes, simply remove the human from the loop. Do not allow a human to perform a decision-making task and you presumably no longer have any lingering worries about the human bearing toward any untoward biases. There isn't a human involved and thus the problem of potential human biases seems to be solved.

I bring this up because we are witnessing a gradual and massive-sized shift toward using AI in an algorithm decision-making (ADM) manner.

If you can replace a human worker with AI, the odds are that a lot of benefits will arise. As already mentioned, you would no longer fret about the human biases of that human worker (the one that is no longer doing that job). The chances are that the AI will be less costly overall when compared to a long-term time horizon. You dispense with all the other assorted difficulties that come part-and-parcel with human workers. Etc.

A proposition that is gaining ground seems to be this: *When trying to decide where to best place AI, look first toward settings that already entail untoward human biases by your workers and for which those biases are undercutting or otherwise excessively complicating particular decision-making tasks.*

Bottom-line is that it would seem prudent to garner the most bang for your buck in terms of investing in AI by aiming squarely at highly exposed human decision-making tasks that are tough to control from an untoward biases infusion perspective. Remove the human workers in that role. Replace them with AI. The assumption is that AI would not have such untoward biases. Therefore, you can have your cake and eat it too, namely, get the decision tasks undertaken and do so minus the ethical and legal specter of untoward biases.

When you pencil that out, the ROI (return on investment) would likely make the adoption of AI a no-brainer choice.

Here's how that usually plays out.

Look throughout your firm and try to identify the decision-making tasks that impact customers. Of those tasks, which ones are most likely to be inappropriately swayed if the workers are embodying untoward biases? If you've already tried to rein in those biases, maybe you let things stand as is. On the other hand, if the biases keep reappearing and the effort to stamp them out is onerous, consider dropping some pertinent AI into that role. Don't keep the workers in the mix since they might override the AI or push the AI right back into the untoward biases' abyss. Also, make sure that the AI can perform the task proficiently and you have sufficiently captured the decision-making facets required to perform the job.

Rinse and repeat.

I realize that seems like a straightforward notion, though do realize that there are lots of ways that the replacing of human workers with AI can readily go awry. Many companies were eager to take such actions and did not mindfully consider how to do so. As a result, they often made a much worse mess than they had on their hands to start with.

I want to clarify and accentuate that AI is not a panacea.

Speaking of which, there is one huge hitch about the cleanliness of seemingly tossing out the human-biased decision-makers with the allegedly unbiased AI. The hitch is that you might be merely substituting one set of untoward biases for another. Per the earlier indication, AI can contain untoward biases and can act upon those biases. Making a brazen assumption that swapping out biased humans for unbiased AI is not all it is cracked up to be.

In short, here's the deal when viewing the matter strictly from the bias factors:

- The AI has no untoward biases and ergo the AI-based ADM is handy to deploy
- The AI has the same untoward biases and thusly the AI-based ADM is troubling
- The AI introduces new untoward biases and likely worsens the setting
- The AI at first seems fine and then gradually wobbles into untoward biases
- Other

We can briefly unpack those possibilities.

The first one is the idealized version of what might happen. The AI has no untoward biases. You put the AI into place and it does the job superbly. Good for you! Of course, one would hope that you have also in some adroit way handled the displacement of human workers due to the AI inclusion.

In the second case, you put in place the AI and discover that the AI is exhibiting the same untoward biases that the human workers had. How can this be? A common means of falling into this trap is by using Machine Learning (ML) and Deep Learning (DL) as based on collected data of how the humans in the role were previously making their decisions.

Allow me a moment to explain.

ML/DL is a form of computational pattern matching. The usual approach is that you assemble data about a decision-making task. You feed the data into the ML/DL computer models. Those models seek to find mathematical patterns. After finding such patterns, if so found, the AI system then will use those patterns when encountering new data. Upon the presentation of new data, the patterns based on the "old" or historical data are applied to render a current decision.

I think you can guess where this is heading. If the humans that have been doing the work for years upon years have been incorporating untoward biases, the odds are that the data reflects this in subtle but significant ways. The Machine Learning or Deep Learning computational pattern matching will simply try to mathematically mimic the data accordingly. There is no semblance of common sense or other sentient aspects of the modeling per se.

Furthermore, the AI developers might not realize what is going on either. The arcane mathematics might make it difficult to ferret out the now hidden biases. You would rightfully hope and expect that the AI developers would test for the potentially buried biases, though this is trickier than it might seem. A solid chance exists that even with relatively extensive testing that there will be biases still embedded within the pattern matching models of the ML/DL.

All told, you might end up back to square one. The same untoward biases of humans are now computationally mirrored in the AI system. You have not eradicated the biases.

Worse still, you might be less likely to realize that the AI has biases. In the case of humans, you might normally be on your guard that humans have untoward biases. This is a base expectation. The use of AI can lull leaders into believing that automation has completely removed any kind of human bias. They are thusly setting themselves up for having shot themselves in the foot. They got rid of humans with seemingly known untoward biases, being replaced by AI that was thought to have no such biases, and yet have now put into use AI replete with the same biases already known to exist.

This can get things really cross-eyed. You might have removed other guardrails being used with the human workers that were established to detect and prevent the emergence of those already anticipated human biases. The AI now has free rein. Nothing is in place to catch it before acting up. The AI then could start leading you down a dour path of the vast accumulation of biased actions.

And, you are in the awkward and perhaps liable posture that you once knew about the biases and have now allowed those biases to wreak havoc. It is perhaps one thing to not have ever encountered any such untoward biases and then suddenly out of the blue the AI springs them. You might try to excuse this with the "who would have guessed" kind of distractor (not very convincingly, perhaps). But to have now set up AI that is doing the very same untoward biased actions as before, well, your excuses are getting thinner and lamer.

A twist on this entails the AI exhibiting untoward biases that hadn't previously been encountered when the humans were doing the task. You could say that this is perhaps harder to have prevented since it consists of "new" biases that the firm hadn't previously been on the look for. In the end, though, excuses might not provide you with much relief. If the AI system has ventured into both unethical and unlawful territory, your goose might be cooked.

One other facet to keep in mind is that the AI might start out just fine and then inch its way into untoward biases. This is especially likely when the use of Machine Learning or Deep Learning takes place on an ongoing basis to keep the AI up-to-date.

Whether the ML/DL is working in real-time or periodically doing updates, the attention should be whether the AI is possibly ingesting data that now contains biases and that previously were not present.

For leaders that think they are getting a free lunch by waving a magic wand to replace biased human workers with AI, they are in for a very rude awakening.

At this juncture of this discussion, I'd bet that you are desirous of some real-world examples that might showcase the conundrum of replacing (or not) human untoward biases with AI-based untoward biases.

I'm glad you asked.

There is a special and assuredly popular set of examples that are close to my heart. You see, in my capacity as an expert on AI including the ethical and legal ramifications, I am frequently asked to identify realistic examples that showcase AI Ethics dilemmas so that the somewhat theoretical nature of the topic can be more readily grasped. One of the most evocative areas that vividly presents this ethical AI quandary is the advent of AI-based true self-driving cars. This will serve as a handy use case or exemplar for ample discussion on the topic.

Here's then a noteworthy question that is worth contemplating: *Does the advent of AI-based true self-driving cars illuminate anything about untoward biases in AI, and if so, what does this showcase?*

Allow me a moment to unpack the question.

Let's use a readily straightforward example. An AI-based self-driving car is underway on your neighborhood streets and seems to be driving safely. At first, you had devoted special attention to each time that you managed to catch a glimpse of the self-driving car. The autonomous vehicle stood out with its rack of electronic sensors that included video cameras, radar units, LIDAR devices, and the like. After many weeks of the self-driving car cruising around your community, you now barely notice it.

As far as you are concerned, it is merely another car on the already busy public roadways.

Lest you think it is impossible or implausible to become familiar with seeing self-driving cars, I've written frequently about how the locales that are within the scope of self-driving car tryouts have gradually gotten used to seeing the spruced-up vehicles. Many of the locals eventually shifted from mouth-gaping rapt gawking to now emitting an expansive yawn of boredom to witness those meandering self-driving cars.

Probably the main reason right now that they might notice the autonomous vehicles is because of the irritation and exasperation factor. The by-the-book AI driving systems make sure the cars are obeying all speed limits and rules of the road. For hectic human drivers in their traditional human-driven cars, you get irked at times when stuck behind the strictly law-abiding AI-based self-driving cars.

That's something we might all need to get accustomed to, rightfully or wrongly.

Back to our tale.

Turns out that two unseemly concerns start to arise about the otherwise innocuous and generally welcomed AI-based self-driving cars, specifically:

1. Where the AI is roaming the self-driving cars for picking up rides was looming as a vocalized concern
2. How the AI is treating awaiting pedestrians that do not have the right-of-way was rising up as a pressing issue

At first, the AI was roaming the self-driving cars throughout the entire town. Anybody that wanted to request a ride in the self-driving car had essentially an equal chance of hailing one. Gradually, the AI began to primarily keep the self-driving cars roaming in just one section of town. This section was a greater money-maker and the AI system had been programmed to try and maximize revenues as part of the usage in the community.

Community members in the impoverished parts of the town were less likely to be able to get a ride from a self-driving car. This was because the self-driving cars were further away and roaming in the higher revenue part of the locale. When a request came in from a distant part of town, any request from a closer location that was likely in the "esteemed" part of town would get a higher priority. Eventually, the availability of getting a self-driving car in any place other than the richer part of town was nearly impossible, exasperatingly so for those that lived in those now resource-starved areas.

You could assert that the AI pretty much landed on a form of proxy discrimination (also often referred to as indirect discrimination). The AI wasn't programmed to avoid those poorer neighborhoods. Instead, it "learned" to do so via the use of the ML/DL.

The thing is, ridesharing human drivers were known for doing the same thing, though not necessarily exclusively due to the money-making angle. There were some of the ridesharing human drivers that had an untoward bias about picking up riders in certain parts of the town. This was a somewhat known phenomenon and the city had put in place a monitoring approach to catch human drivers doing this. Human drivers could get in trouble for carrying out unsavory selection practices.

It was assumed that the AI would never fall into that same kind of quicksand. No specialized monitoring was set up to keep track of where the AI-based self-driving cars were going. Only after community members began to complain did the city leaders realize what was happening.

This example of the roaming aspects of the AI-based self-driving cars illustrates the earlier indication that there can be situations entailing humans with untoward biases, for which controls are put in place, and that the AI replacing those human drivers is left scot-free. Unfortunately, the AI can then incrementally become mired in akin biases and do so without sufficient guardrails in place.

A second example involves the AI determining whether to stop for awaiting pedestrians that do not have the right-of-way to cross a street.

You've undoubtedly been driving and encountered pedestrians that were waiting to cross the street and yet they did not have the right-of-way to do so. This meant that you had discretion as to whether to stop and let them cross. You could proceed without letting them cross and still be fully within the legal driving rules of doing so.

Studies of how human drivers decide on stopping or not stopping for such pedestrians have suggested that sometimes the human drivers make the choice based on untoward biases. A human driver might eye the pedestrian and choose to not stop, even though they would have stopped had the pedestrian had a different appearance, such as based on race or gender.

Imagine that the AI-based self-driving cars are programmed to deal with the question of whether to stop or not stop for pedestrians that do not have the right-of-way. Here's how the AI developers decided to program this task. They collected data from the town's video cameras that are placed all around the city. The data showcases human drivers that stop for pedestrians that do not have the right-of-way and human drivers that do not stop. It is all collected into a large dataset.

By using Machine Learning and Deep Learning, the data is modeled computationally. The AI driving system then uses this model to decide when to stop or not stop. Generally, the idea is that whatever the local custom consists of, this is how the AI is going direct the self-driving car.

To the surprise of the city leaders and the residents, the AI was evidently opting to stop or not stop based on the appearance of the pedestrian, including their race and gender. The sensors of the self-driving car would scan the awaiting pedestrian, feed this data into the ML/DL model, and the model would emit to the AI whether to stop or continue. Lamentedly, the town already had a lot of human driver biases in this regard and the AI was now mimicking the same.

The good news is that this raises an issue that almost no one had previously known to exist. The bad news was that since the AI was caught doing this, it got most of the blame.

This example illustrates that an AI system might merely duplicate the already preexisting untoward biases of humans.

Conclusion

There is a multitude of ways to try and avoid devising AI that either out the gate has untoward biases or that over time gleans biases. One approach involves ensuring that AI developers are aware of this happening and thus keep them therefore on their toes to program the AI to avert the matter. Another avenue consists of having the AI self-monitor itself for unethical behaviors and/or having another piece of AI that monitors other AI systems for potentially unethical behaviors.

To recap, we need to realize that humans can have untoward biases and that somehow they need to know their limitations. Likewise, AI can have untoward biases, and somehow we need to know their limitations.

For those of you that are avidly embracing AI Ethics, I'd like to end right now with another famous line that everyone must already know. Namely, please continue to use and share the importance of Ethical AI. And by doing so, I'd cheekily say this: "Go ahead, make my day."

CHAPTER 5
AI ETHICS ALARM AT AI BIAS SCALING

Plato famously stated that a good decision is based on knowledge and not on numbers.

His keen insight seems amazingly prescient about today's Artificial Intelligence (AI).

You see, despite the blaring headlines currently proclaiming that AI has somehow reached sentience and embodies human knowledge and reasoning, please be aware that this overstated AI hyperbole is pure blarney since we are still relying upon number-crunching in today's algorithm decision-making (ADM) as undertaken by AI systems. Even the vaunted Machine Learning (ML) and Deep Learning (DL) consist of computational pattern matching, meaning that numbers are still at the core of the exalted use of ML/DL.

We do not know if AI reaching sentience is possible. Could be, might not be. No one can say for sure how this might arise. Some believe that we will incrementally improve our computational AI efforts such that a form of sentience will spontaneously occur. Others think that the AI might go into a kind of computational supernova and reach sentience pretty much on its own accord (typically referred to as the singularity).

So, let's not kid ourselves and falsely believe that contemporary AI is able to think like humans. I suppose the question then comes to the forefront about Plato's remark as to whether we can have good decisions based on computational AI rather than on sentient AI. You might be surprised to know that I would assert that we can indeed have good decisions being made by everyday AI systems.

The other side of that coin is that we can also have everyday AI systems that make bad decisions. Rotten decisions. Decisions that are rife with untoward biases and inequities. You might be aware that when the latest era of AI got underway there was a huge burst of enthusiasm for what some now call *AI For Good*. Unfortunately, on the heels of that gushing excitement, we began to witness *AI For Bad*. For example, various AI-based facial recognition systems have been revealed as containing racial biases and gender biases.

Efforts to fight back against *AI For Bad* are actively underway. Besides vociferous *legal* pursuits of reining in the wrongdoing, there is also a substantive push toward embracing AI Ethics to righten the AI vileness. The notion is that we ought to adopt and endorse key Ethical AI principles for the development and fielding of AI doing so to undercut the *AI For Bad* and simultaneously heralding and promoting the preferable *AI For Good*.

For this herein discussion, I'd like to bring up an especially worrying aspect about AI that those in the AI Ethics arena are rightfully bemoaning and trying to raise apt awareness about. The sobering and disconcerting matter is actually quite straightforward to point out.

Here it is: *AI has the real-world potential of promulgating AI-steeped biases at an alarming scale.*

And when I say "at scale" this demonstrably means worldwide massive scale. Humongous scale. Scale that goes off the scale.

Before I dive into how this scaling of AI-steeped biases will take place, let's make sure we all have a semblance of how AI can incorporate undue biases and inequities. Recall again that this is not of a sentient variety. This is all of a computational caliber.

You might be perplexed as to how AI could imbue the same kinds of adverse biases and inequities that humans do. We tend to think of AI as being entirely neutral, unbiased, simply a machine that has none of the emotional sway and foul thinking that humans might have.

One of the most common means of AI falling into the biases and inequities dourness happens when using Machine Learning and Deep Learning, partially as a result of relying upon collected data about how humans are making decisions.

Allow me a moment to elaborate.

ML/DL is a form of computational pattern matching. The usual approach is that you assemble data about a decision-making task. You feed the data into the ML/DL computer models. Those models seek to find mathematical patterns. After finding such patterns, if so found, the AI system then will use those patterns when encountering new data. Upon the presentation of new data, the patterns based on the "old" or historical data are applied to render a current decision.

I think you can guess where this is heading. If humans that have been making the patterned upon decisions have been incorporating untoward biases, the odds are that the data reflects this in subtle but significant ways. The Machine Learning or Deep Learning computational pattern matching will simply try to mathematically mimic the data accordingly. There is no semblance of common sense or other sentient aspects of AI-crafted modeling per se.

Furthermore, the AI developers might not realize what is going on either. The arcane mathematics in the ML/DL might make it difficult to ferret out the now hidden biases. You would rightfully hope and expect that the AI developers would test for the potentially buried biases, though this is trickier than it might seem. A solid chance exists that even with relatively extensive testing that there will be biases still embedded within the pattern matching models of the ML/DL.

You could somewhat use the famous or infamous adage of garbage-in garbage-out. The thing is, this is more akin to biases-in that insidiously get infused as biases submerged within the AI. The algorithm decision-making or ADM of AI axiomatically becomes laden with inequities.

Not good.

This brings us to the matter of AI-steeped biases when at scale.

First, let's take a look at how human biases might be creating inequities. A company that makes mortgage loans decides to hire a mortgage loan agent. The agent is supposed to review requests from consumers that want to get a home loan. After assessing an application, the agent renders a decision to either grant the loan or deny the loan. Easy-peasy.

For sake of discussion, let's imagine that a human loan agent can analyze 8 loans per day, taking about one hour per review. In a five-day workweek, the agent does about 40 loan reviews. On an annual basis, the agent typically does around 2,000 loan reviews, give or take a bit.

The company wants to increase its volume of loan reviews, thus the firm hires 100 additional loan agents. Let's assume they all have about the same productivity and that this implies we can now handle about 200,000 loans per year (at a rate of 2,000 loan reviews per annum per agent). It seems that we've really ramped up our processing of loan applications.

Turns out that the company devises an AI system that can essentially do the same loan reviews as the human agents. The AI is running on computer servers in the cloud. Via the cloud infrastructure, the company can readily add more computing power to accommodate any volume of loan reviews that might be needed.

With the existing AI configuration, they can do 1,000 loan reviews per hour. This also can happen 24x7. There is no vacation time needed for the AI. No lunch breaks. The AI works around the clock with no squawking about being overworked. We'll say that at that approximate pace, the AI can process nearly 9 million loan applications per year.

Notice that we went from having 100 human agents that could do 200,000 loans per year and jumped many times over to the much-heightened number of 9 million reviews per year via the AI system. We have dramatically scaled up our loan request processing. No doubt about it.

Get ready for the kicker that will perhaps make you fall off your chair.

Assume that some of our human agents are making their loan decisions on a basis of untoward biases. Perhaps some are giving racial factors a key role in the loan decision. Maybe some are using gender. Others are using age. And so on.

Of the 200,000 annual loan reviews, how many are being done under the wrongful gaze of adverse biases and inequities? Perhaps 10% which is around 20,000 of the loan requests. Worse still, suppose it is 50% of the loan requests, in which case there is a quite troubling 100,000 annual instances of loan decisions wrongly decided.

That's bad. But we have yet to consider an even more frightening possibility.

Suppose the AI has a hidden bias that consists of factors such as race, gender, age, and the like. If 10% of the annual loan analyses are subject to this unsavoriness, we have 900,000 loan requests that are being improperly handled. That's a lot more than what the human agents could possibly do, primarily due simply to the volume aspects. Those 100 agents if all entirely were doing an inequitable review could at most do this on the 200,000 annual loan reviews. The AI could do the same on a much large scale of the 9,000,000 annual reviews.

Yikes!

This is truly AI-steeped bias at a tremendous scale.

When untoward biases are entombed within an AI system, the same scaling that seemed advantageous is now turned on its head and becomes a monstrously beguiling (and disturbing) scaling outcome. On the one hand, the AI can beneficially rachet up to handle more people that are requesting home loans. On the surface, that seems a tremendous *AI For Good.*

We ought to pat ourselves on the back for presumably expanding the chances of humans getting needed loans. Meanwhile, if the AI has embedded biases, the scaling is going to be a tremendously rotten result and we find ourselves lamentedly mired in *AI For Bad*, at a truly massive scale.

The proverbial dual-edged sword.

AI can radically increase the access to decision-making for those that are seeking desired services and products. No more human-constrained labor bottleneck. Outstanding! The other edge of the sword is that if the AI contains badness such as hidden inequities, the very same massive scaling is going to promulgate that untoward behavior on an unimaginable scale. Exasperating, wrongful, shameful, and we can't allow society to fall into such an ugly abyss.

Anyone that has been puzzled as to why we need to pound away at the importance of AI Ethics should be now realizing that the AI scaling phenomenon is a darned important reason for pursuing Ethical AI. Let's take a moment to briefly consider some of the key Ethical AI precepts to illustrate what ought to be a vital focus for anyone crafting, fielding, or using AI.

I've also discussed various collective analyses of AI ethics principles, including having covered a set devised by researchers that examined and condensed the essence of numerous national and international AI ethics tenets in a paper entitled "The Global Landscape Of AI Ethics Guidelines" (published in *Nature*), which led to this keystone list:

- **Transparency**
- **Justice & Fairness**
- **Non-Maleficence**
- **Responsibility**
- **Privacy**
- **Beneficence**
- **Freedom & Autonomy**
- **Trust**

- **Sustainability**
- **Dignity**
- **Solidarity**

As you might directly guess, trying to pin down the specifics underlying these principles can be extremely hard to do. Even more so, the effort to turn those broad principles into something entirely tangible and detailed enough to be used when crafting AI systems is also a tough nut to crack.

It is easy to overall do some handwaving about what AI Ethics precepts are and how they should be generally observed, while it is a much more complicated situation upon the AI coding having to be the veritable rubber that meets the road.

The AI Ethics principles are to be utilized by AI developers, along with those that manage AI development efforts, and even those that ultimately field and perform upkeep on AI systems. All stakeholders throughout the entire AI life-cycle of development and usage are considered within the scope of abiding by the being-established norms of Ethical AI. This is an important highlight since the usual assumption is that "only coders" or those that program the AI is subject to adhering to the AI Ethics notions.

Please be aware that it takes a village to devise and field AI. For which the entire village has to be keeping on their toes about AI Ethics.

How AI-Steeped Biases Scaling Works

Now that I've gotten onto the table that AI can contain biases, we are ready to examine some of the reasons why AI scaling is so intrusive.

Consider this keystone list of ten underlying reasons:

- **Easily replicated**
- **Minimal cost to scale**
- **Abhorrently consistent**
- **Lack of self-reflection**
- **Blind obedience**
- **Doesn't tip its hand**
- **Recipient unsuspecting**
- **Tends not to spur provocation**
- **False aura of fairness**
- **Hard to refute**

I'll briefly explore each of those crucial points.

When you try to scale up with human labor, the odds are that doing so will be enormously complicated. You have to find and hire the people. You have to train them to do the job. You have to pay them and take into account human wants and needs. Compare this to an AI system. You develop it and put it into use. Other than some amount of ongoing upkeep of the AI, you can sit back and let it process endlessly.

This means that AI is easily replicated. You can add more computing power as the task and volume might so require (you aren't hiring or firing). Global use is done with the push of a button and attained by the worldwide availability of the Internet. The scaling up is a minimal cost in comparison to doing likewise with human labor.

Human labor is notoriously inconsistent. When you have large teams, you have a veritable box of chocolates in that you never know what you might have on your hands. The AI system is likely to be highly consistent. It repeats the same activities over and over, each time being essentially the same as the last.

Normally, we would relish AI consistency. If humans are prone to biases, we will always have some portion of our human labor that is going astray. The AI, if purely unbiased in its construction and computational efforts, would by far be more consistent. The problem though is that if the AI has hidden biases, the consistency now is painfully abhorrent. The odds are that the biased behavior is going to be consistently carried out, over and over again.

Humans would hopefully have some inkling of self-reflection and maybe catch themselves making biased decisions. I'm not saying all would do so. I'm also not saying that those that catch themselves will necessarily right their wrongs. In any case, at least some humans would sometimes correct themselves.

The AI is unlikely to have any form of computational self-reflection. This means that the AI just keeps on doing what it is doing. There would seemingly be zero chance of the AI detecting that it is running afoul of equity. That being said, I have described some efforts to deal with this, such as building AI Ethics components within AI and devising AI that monitors other AI to discern unethical AI activities.

Lacking any kind of self-reflection, the AI is also likely to have essentially blind obedience to whatever it was instructed to do. Humans might not be so obedient. The chances are that some humans that are doing a task will question whether they are perhaps being guided into inequity territory. They would tend to reject unethical commands or perhaps go the whistleblower route. Do not expect everyday contemporary AI to somehow question its programming.

We next turn to those that are using AI. If you were seeking a home loan and spoke with a human, you might be on your alert as to whether the human is giving you a fair shake. When using an AI system, most people seem to be less suspicious. They often assume that the AI is fair and ergo do not get as quickly riled up. The AI appears to lull people into an "it's just a machine" trance. On top of this, it can be hard to try and protest the AI. In contrast, protesting how you were treated by a human agent is a lot easier and much more commonly accepted and assumed as viably possible.

All told, AI that is steeped in biases has a dishonorable leg-up over humans steeped in biases, namely in terms of being able to have the AI massively deploy those biases on a gigantic scale, doing so without as readily getting caught or having consumers realize what is disturbingly taking place.

At this juncture of this discussion, I'd bet that you are desirous of some additional examples that might showcase the conundrum of AI-steeped biases at scale.

I'm glad you asked.

There is a special and assuredly popular set of examples that are close to my heart. You see, in my capacity as an expert on AI including the ethical and legal ramifications, I am frequently asked to identify realistic examples that showcase AI Ethics dilemmas so that the somewhat theoretical nature of the topic can be more readily grasped. One of the most evocative areas that vividly presents this ethical AI quandary is the advent of AI-based true self-driving cars. This will serve as a handy use case or exemplar for ample discussion on the topic.

Here's then a noteworthy question that is worth contemplating: *Does the advent of AI-based true self-driving cars illuminate anything about AI steeped biases at scale, and if so, what does this showcase?*

Allow me a moment to unpack the question.

Let's use a readily straightforward example. An AI-based self-driving car is underway on your neighborhood streets and seems to be driving safely. At first, you had devoted special attention to each time that you managed to catch a glimpse of the self-driving car. The autonomous vehicle stood out with its rack of electronic sensors that included video cameras, radar units, LIDAR devices, and the like. After many weeks of the self-driving car cruising around your community, you now barely notice it. As far as you are concerned, it is merely another car on the already busy public roadways.

Lest you think it is impossible or implausible to become familiar with seeing self-driving cars, I've written frequently about how the locales that are within the scope of self-driving car tryouts have gradually gotten used to seeing the spruced-up vehicles. Many of the locals eventually shifted from mouth-gaping rapt gawking to now emitting an expansive yawn of boredom to witness those meandering self-driving cars.

Probably the main reason right now that they might notice the autonomous vehicles is because of the irritation and exasperation factor. The by-the-book AI driving systems make sure the cars are obeying all speed limits and rules of the road. For hectic human drivers in their traditional human-driven cars, you get irked at times when stuck behind the strictly law-abiding AI-based self-driving cars.

That's something we might all need to get accustomed to, rightfully or wrongly.

Back to our tale.

Turns out that two unseemly concerns start to arise about the otherwise innocuous and generally welcomed AI-based self-driving cars, specifically:

3. Where the AI is roaming the self-driving cars for picking up rides was looming as a vocalized concern
4. How the AI is treating awaiting pedestrians that do not have the right-of-way was rising up as a pressing issue

At first, the AI was roaming the self-driving cars throughout the entire town. Anybody that wanted to request a ride in the self-driving car had essentially an equal chance of hailing one. Gradually, the AI began to primarily keep the self-driving cars roaming in just one section of town. This section was a greater money-maker and the AI system had been programmed to try and maximize revenues as part of the usage in the community.

Community members in the impoverished parts of the town were less likely to be able to get a ride from a self-driving car. This was because the self-driving cars were further away and roaming in the higher revenue part of the locale. When a request came in from a distant part of town, any request from a closer location that was likely in the "esteemed" part of town would get a higher priority. Eventually, the availability of getting a self-driving car in any place other than the richer part of town was nearly impossible, exasperatingly so for those that lived in those now resource-starved areas.

You could assert that the AI pretty much landed on a form of proxy discrimination (also often referred to as indirect discrimination). The AI wasn't programmed to avoid those poorer neighborhoods. Instead, it "learned" to do so via the use of the ML/DL.

The thing is, ridesharing human drivers were known for doing the same thing, though not necessarily exclusively due to the money-making angle. There were some of the ridesharing human drivers that had an untoward bias about picking up riders in certain parts of the town. This was a somewhat known phenomenon and the city had put in place a monitoring approach to catch human drivers doing this. Human drivers could get in trouble for carrying out unsavory selection practices.

It was assumed that the AI would never fall into that same kind of quicksand. No specialized monitoring was set up to keep track of where the AI-based self-driving cars were going. Only after community members began to complain did the city leaders realize what was happening.

This example of the roaming aspects of the AI-based self-driving cars illustrates the earlier indication that there can be situations entailing humans with untoward biases, for which controls are put in place, and that the AI replacing those human drivers is left scot-free. Unfortunately, the AI can then incrementally become mired in akin biases and do so without sufficient guardrails in place.

This also showcases the AI steeped biases at scale issue.

In the case of human drivers, we might have had a few here or there that were exercising some form of inequity. For the AI driving system, it is usually one such unified AI for an entire fleet of self-driving cars. Thus, we might have begun with say fifty self-driving cars in the town (all run by the same AI code), and gradually increased to let's say 500 self-driving cars (all being run by the same AI code). Since all of those five hundred self-driving cars are being run by the same AI, they are correspondingly all subject to the same derived biases and inequities embedded within the AI.

Scaling hurts us in that regard.

A second example involves the AI determining whether to stop for awaiting pedestrians that do not have the right-of-way to cross a street.

You've undoubtedly been driving and encountered pedestrians that were waiting to cross the street and yet they did not have the right-of-way to do so. This meant that you had discretion as to whether to stop and let them cross. You could proceed without letting them cross and still be fully within the legal driving rules of doing so.

Studies of how human drivers decide on stopping or not stopping for such pedestrians have suggested that sometimes the human drivers make the choice based on untoward biases. A human driver might eye the pedestrian and choose to not stop, even though they would have stopped had the pedestrian had a different appearance, such as based on race or gender.

Imagine that the AI-based self-driving cars are programmed to deal with the question of whether to stop or not stop for pedestrians that do not have the right-of-way. Here's how the AI developers decided to program this task. They collected data from the town's video cameras that are placed all around the city. The data showcases human drivers that stop for pedestrians that do not have the right-of-way and human drivers that do not stop. It is all collected into a large dataset.

By using Machine Learning and Deep Learning, the data is modeled computationally. The AI driving system then uses this model to decide when to stop or not stop. Generally, the idea is that whatever the local custom consists of, this is how the AI is going direct the self-driving car.

To the surprise of the city leaders and the residents, the AI was evidently opting to stop or not stop based on the appearance of the pedestrian, including their race and gender. The sensors of the self-driving car would scan the awaiting pedestrian, feed this data into the ML/DL model, and the model would emit to the AI whether to stop or continue. Lamentedly, the town already had a lot of human driver biases in this regard and the AI was now mimicking the same.

This example illustrates that an AI system might merely duplicate the already preexisting untoward biases of humans. Furthermore, it does so at scale. Any human drivers might have sometimes been taught to do this untoward form of selection or maybe personally chosen to do so, but the chances are that the bulk of the human drivers is probably not doing this en masse.

In strident contrast, the AI driving system that is being used to drive self-driving cars is likely to abhorrently consistently and assuredly carry out the derived bias.

Conclusion

There is a multitude of ways to try and avoid devising AI that has untoward biases or that over time gleans biases. As much as possible, the idea is to catch the problems before you go into high gear and ramp up for scaling. Hopefully, biases don't get out the door, so to speak.

Assume though that one way or another biases will arise in the AI. Once you are deployed into massive scale with AI, you can't just do one of those oft-proclaimed techie "fire and forget" notions. You have to diligently keep on top of what the AI is doing and seek to detect any untoward biases that need to be corrected.

As earlier pointed out, one approach involves ensuring that AI developers are aware of AI Ethics and thus spur them to be on their toes to program the AI to avert these matters. Another avenue consists of having the AI self-monitor itself for unethical behaviors and/or having another piece of AI that monitors other AI systems for potentially unethical behaviors. I've covered numerous other potential solutions in my writings.

A final thought for now. Having started this discussion with a quote by Plato, it might be fitting to close the discourse with yet another shrewd utterance by Plato.

Plato stated that there is no harm in repeating a good thing.

The ease of going at scale with AI is certainly a viable means of attaining such an upbeat aspiration when the AI is of the *AI For Good* variety. We savor repeating a good thing. When AI is the *AI For Bad* and replete with untoward biases and inequities, we might lean on Plato's remarks and say that there is abundant harm in repeating a bad thing.

Let's listen carefully to Plato's wise words and devise our AI accordingly..

CHAPTER 6
AI ETHICS
AND AI PROXY DISCRIMINATION

Let's discuss proxy discrimination amid the actions of modern-day Artificial Intelligence (AI).

To get into the AI side of things, we'll need to first set the stage about the overall aspects of discrimination and then delve into the perhaps surprising ways in which AI gets mired in this complicated and at times insidious matter. I'll also be providing examples of AI-based proxy discrimination, including that this can occur even in the case of AI-infused autonomous vehicles such as self-driving cars.

Let's get started.

A dictionary definition of discrimination would typically indicate that it is the act of an unjust nature that treats people differently based on perceived categories such as race, gender, age, and so on (such criteria are often described as consisting of protected classes). A form of discrimination known as *direct* discrimination entails overtly latching onto one of those categories, such as relatively clearly emphasizing say race or gender as the basis for the discrimination (these would be construed as first factors). This is perhaps the most transparent form of discrimination.

Another somewhat lesser realized possibility is the use of *indirect* discrimination. You might suggest this is a trickier form of discrimination as it is considered a step removed and can be challenging to ferret out. Indirect discrimination involves a kind of one or more step removed categorization selection. This is also commonly labeled as proxy discrimination since there is an intermediary factor that is serving as a proxy or stand-in for the underlying and connectable first factor.

To help clarify the seemingly abstract idea of indirect or proxy discrimination, we can consider a straightforward example.

Someone is applying for a home loan. Suppose a loan agent that is reviewing the application decides to turn down the loan and does so based on the race of the applicant. You could say that this is an example of direct discrimination. But suppose instead that the loan agent used the zip code of the applicant and opted to turn down the loan based on that factor. It would seem at an initial glance that zip code is not one of the factors usually considered discriminatory or a protected class. As such, the loan agent would appear to have steered clear of a discriminatory-laden decision.

The problem though could be that the zip code is actually a proxy for something else, an actual protected category or class. Perhaps this particular zip code is predominantly composed of a particular race or ethnicity and the use of indirect or proxy discrimination is taking place. You might generally know this type of example by the catchphrase of redlining.

You see, there is apparently a connection of sorts between the factor consisting of a zip code and the discriminatory factor of race in this instance. The zip code would appear to be an innocent or neutral factor in the face of this circumstance. Zipcode seems to most of us like a rather innocuous item and would not set off any alarm bells.

You might recall from your days of taking a course on statistics that there are statistical correlations that can arise between various factors, even factors that do not strike you as being logically correlated with each other. It could be that there is a pronounced correlation between zip code and race. Thus, the selection of zip code at first glance seems benign, but upon closer inspection, it is really a stand-in or proxy for the discriminatory protected class of race.

Here's how a research paper described the notion of such correlations and the arising of proxy discrimination: "Discrimination does not have to involve direct use of a protected class; class memberships may not even take part in the decision. Discrimination can also occur due to correlations between the protected class and other attributes. The legal framework of disparate impact addresses such cases by first requiring significantly different outcomes for the protected class, regardless of how the outcomes came to be. An association between loan decisions and race due to the use of applicant address, which itself is associated with race, is an example of this type of discrimination" (as stated in the paper entitled *Proxy Discrimination In Data-Driven Systems: Theory And Experiments With Machine Learning Programs*, by Anupam Datta, Matt Fredrikson, Gihyuk Ko, Piotr Mardziel, and Shayak Sen).

Now that we've got the fundamentals of proxy discrimination set on the table, we can introduce the aspects of how AI can essentially embed a computationally rendered version of proxy discrimination.

I would like to focus on today's AI and not some futuristic AI that some are saying will be sentient and pose an existential risk. Despite a myriad of blaring headlines currently proclaiming that AI has somehow reached sentience and embodies human knowledge and reasoning, please be aware that this overstated AI hyperbole is pure rubbish since we are still relying upon number-crunching in today's algorithm decision-making (ADM) as undertaken by AI systems.

Even the vaunted Machine Learning (ML) and Deep Learning (DL) consist of computational pattern matching, meaning that numbers are still at the core of the exalted use of ML/DL. We do not know if AI reaching sentience is possible. Could be, might not be. No one can say for sure how this might arise. Some believe that we will incrementally improve our computational AI efforts such that a form of sentience will spontaneously occur. Others think that the AI might go into a kind of computational supernova and reach sentience pretty much on its own accord (typically referred to as the singularity).

So, let's not kid ourselves and falsely believe that contemporary AI is able to think like humans. We can try to mimic in the AI what we believe human thinking perhaps consists of. So far, we have not been able to crack the elusive elements of devising AI that can embed common sense and other cornerstones of human thought.

You might be aware that when the latest era of AI got underway there was a huge burst of enthusiasm for what some now call *AI For Good*. Unfortunately, on the heels of that gushing excitement, we began to witness *AI For Bad*. For example, various AI-based facial recognition systems have been revealed as containing racial biases and gender biases.

Efforts to fight back against *AI For Bad* are actively underway. Besides vociferous *legal* pursuits of reining in the wrongdoing, there is also a substantive push toward embracing AI Ethics to righten the AI vileness. The notion is that we ought to adopt and endorse key Ethical AI principles for the development and fielding of AI doing so to undercut the *AI For Bad* and simultaneously heralding and promoting the preferable *AI For Good*.

You might be perplexed as to how AI could imbue the same kinds of adverse biases and inequities that humans do. We tend to think of AI as being entirely neutral, unbiased, simply a machine that has none of the emotional sway and foul thinking that humans might have. One of the most common means of AI falling into the biases and inequities dourness happens when using Machine Learning and Deep Learning, partially as a result of relying upon collected data about how humans are making decisions.

Allow me a moment to elaborate.

ML/DL is a form of computational pattern matching. The usual approach is that you assemble data about a decision-making task. You feed the data into the ML/DL computer models. Those models seek to find mathematical patterns. After finding such patterns, if so found, the AI system then will use those patterns when encountering new data. Upon the presentation of new data, the patterns based on the "old" or historical data are applied to render a current decision.

I think you can guess where this is heading. If humans that have been making the patterned upon decisions have been incorporating untoward biases, the odds are that the data reflects this in subtle but significant ways. The Machine Learning or Deep Learning computational pattern matching will simply try to mathematically mimic the data accordingly. There is no semblance of common sense or other sentient aspects of AI-crafted modeling per se.

Furthermore, the AI developers might not realize what is going on either. The arcane mathematics in the ML/DL might make it difficult to ferret out the now hidden biases. You would rightfully hope and expect that the AI developers would test for the potentially buried biases, though this is trickier than it might seem. A solid chance exists that even with relatively extensive testing that there will be biases still embedded within the pattern matching models of the ML/DL.

You could somewhat use the famous or infamous adage of garbage-in garbage-out. The thing is, this is more akin to biases-in that insidiously get infused as biases submerged within the AI. The algorithm decision-making or ADM of AI axiomatically becomes laden with inequities. Not good.

AI systems are being devised that contain both direct discrimination and also stealthy indirect or proxy discrimination. As the same afore referenced research paper mentioned: "Machine Learning systems, however, are constructed on the basis of observational data from the real world, with its many historical or institutionalized biases. As a result, they inherit biases and discriminatory practices inherent in the data. Adoption of such systems leads to unfair outcomes and the perpetuation of biases. Examples are plentiful: race being associated with predictions of recidivism; gender affecting displayed job-related ads; race affecting displayed search ads; Boston's Street Bump app focusing pothole repair on affluent neighborhoods; Amazon's same day delivery being unavailable in black neighborhoods; and Facebook showing either "white" or "black" movie trailers based upon "ethnic affiliation". Various instances of discrimination are prohibited by law."

If we had AI that was subject solely to embedding *direct* discrimination troubles, the odds are that we might have a heightened fighting chance of ferreting out such computational maladies. Unfortunately, the world is not so easy. Today's AI is probably just as likely if not more likely to imbue proxy or indirect discrimination. That's a sad face scenario. The deeper computational morass underpinning proxy discrimination can be one heck of a tough nut to crack.

As stated by the Commissioner of the Federal Trade Commission (FTC): "When algorithmic systems engage in proxy discrimination, they use one or more facially neutral variables to stand in for a legally protected trait, often resulting in disparate treatment of or disparate impact on protected classes for certain economic, social, and civic opportunities. In other words, these algorithms identify seemingly neutral characteristics to create groups that closely mirror a protected class, and these 'proxies' are used for inclusion or exclusion" (as noted in the article entitled "Algorithms and Economic Justice: A Taxonomy of Harms and a Path Forward for the Federal Trade Commission" published in the *Yale Journal of Law & Technology,* by Commissioner Rebecca Kelly Slaughter, August 2021).

One aspect to keep in mind is that AI is not somehow alone in practicing proxy discrimination. Nor is proxy discrimination some new-fangled concoction. We have had proxy discrimination for a long time, certainly long before the advent of AI. The FTC Commissioner echoed this same important realization: "Proxy discrimination is not a new problem -- the use of facially neutral factors that generate discriminatory results is something that society and civil rights laws have been grappling with for decades" (again in the *Yale Journal of Law & Technology*).

Do AI developers purposely craft their AI systems to contain proxy discrimination?

Well, you could divide AI efforts into those that inadvertently rely upon proxy discrimination and those that intentionally do so. I would guess that by and large, most AI builders are falling into the proxy discrimination computational morass by accidental or happenstance actions. This though is not an excuse for what they are doing. They are still responsible for the AI that they have devised and cannot simply wave their hands and proclaim that they didn't know what was happening. It is on their shoulders to try and ensure that no such discrimination is taking place by their AI. Meanwhile, those that deviously and purposely construct their AI with proxy discrimination are to be taken to task and held accountable accordingly.

I'd like to add a twist that will possibly get your head spinning.

Some assert that the better we get at devising AI that there is the likelihood that we will witness more instances of AI that imbue proxy discrimination. You might be puzzled why this would be the case. The hope and dream would be that advances in AI would reduce the chances of the computational nightmare arising of landing into the improper waters of proxy discrimination.

An intriguing angle is identified in this study published in the *Iowa Law Review*: "Instead, AIs use training data to discover on their own what characteristics can be used to predict the target variable. Although this process completely ignores causation, it results in AIs inevitably 'seeking out' proxies for directly predictive characteristics when data on these characteristics is not made available to the AI due to legal prohibitions. Simply denying AIs access to the most intuitive proxies for directly predictive variables does little to thwart this process; instead it simply causes AIs to produce models that rely on less intuitive proxies. Thus, this Article's central argument is that as AIs become even smarter and big data becomes even bigger, proxy discrimination will represent an increasingly fundamental challenge to anti-discrimination regimes that seek to prohibit discrimination based on directly predictive traits" (as mentioned in the article entitled *Proxy Discrimination in the Age of Artificial Intelligence and Big Data*, by Anya Prince and Daniel Schwarcz).

Let's try to lay out the logic of this chilling prediction.

Suppose that AI developers inexorably become aware that they should avoid allowing their Machine Learning and Deep Learning models to strive toward proxy discrimination (one would hope that they are already on the lookout for direct discrimination). Okay, so the AI builders do what they can to avoid a computational latching onto protected factors. But let's assume that this is done on a somewhat obvious basis, such as restricting any one-two step types of proxies.

The computational models go deeper into the data and find a three-step or maybe ten-step removed linkage of proxy discrimination. The AI developers are seemingly happy that a two-step can be shown as not being part of their ML/DL system. Meanwhile, they perhaps don't realize that a three-step or ten-step or some other levels of sneakiness have mathematically been discovered. Keep in mind that the AI is not sentient and it is not mindfully trying to do this. We are still referring to AI that is non-sentient and acting based on numbers and computations.

Yikes, the disquieting fact that the AI is "advancing" and yet we seem to be heading into a gloomier state of affairs is rather exasperating and perhaps infuriating. Whereas on the one hand we might be pleased that the awareness of averting proxy discrimination is getting more attention, the problem won't simply go away. Efforts to avoid AI-based proxy discrimination might push the discriminatory computational discoveries deeper and deeper from being disclosed or figured out by humans.

This reminds me of the old-time cartoons of when a person has gotten themselves into quicksand. The more they thrash around, the worse things get. In a sense, the person causes their own demise by fighting fiercely against the quicksand. This is certainly ironic since you would normally expect that fighting against something would lead to your escape or release.

Not necessarily so.

Experts will tell you that if you are ever caught in quicksand, your sensible option will be to try and relax your way out of the dire situation. You should attempt to float on the top of the quicksand, possibly leaning back and getting your feet level with your head. Wild thrashing is not desirable and will undoubtedly reduce your chances of escape. The better odds are that you strive to float or lightly swim your way out, or at least reach a position in the quicksand whereby you can reach a branch or something else to then pull yourself further out.

Can we use that type of advice to combat the AI imbuing of proxy discrimination?

Kind of.

First, knowing that proxy discrimination can occur is a keystone element for those that devise and field AI systems. All stakeholders need to be thinking about this. Management that oversees AI projects must be on top of this since it is not just the "AI coders" alone that are part of the predicament. We also are likely to see regulators weighing in too, such as enacting new laws to try and curtail or at least catch AI that has embedded discriminatory practices. Etc.

As per the *Iowa Law Review* study, we might strive toward having AI laws and regulations that impose a duty to showcase the data being utilized for the ML/DL: "For instance, impacted antidiscrimination regimes could allow, and perhaps even require, that firms using predictive AIs collect data about individuals' potential membership in legally protected classes. In some cases, this data should be shared with regulators and/or disclosed to the public in summary form. Such data is necessary for firms, regulators, litigants, and others to test whether any particular AI is, in fact, engaging in proxy discrimination" (per the article by Anya Prince and Daniel Schwarcz).

Other possibilities include using more varied data and a wider set of data sources when devising a Machine Learning and Deep Learning model. Another is that AI developers might be required to showcase that their AI system does not employ proxy discrimination. Trying to mathematically showcase or prove this is lack or absence of proxy discrimination going to be notably challenging, to say the least.

On a related notion, I am an advocate of trying to use AI as part of the solution toward AI woes, fighting fire with fire in that manner of thinking. We might for example embed Ethical AI components into an AI system that will monitor how the rest of the AI is doing things and thus potentially catch in real-time any discriminatory efforts. We could also have a separate AI system that acts as a type of AI Ethics monitor. The AI system serves as an overseer to track and detect when another AI is going into the proxy discrimination abyss.

At this juncture of this discussion, I'd bet that you are desirous of some additional examples that might showcase the conundrum of AI-based proxy discrimination.

I'm glad you asked.

There is a special and assuredly popular set of examples that are close to my heart. You see, in my capacity as an expert on AI including the ethical and legal ramifications, I am frequently asked to identify realistic examples that showcase AI Ethics dilemmas so that the somewhat theoretical nature of the topic can be more readily grasped. One of the most evocative areas that vividly presents this ethical AI quandary is the advent of AI-based true self-driving cars. This will serve as a handy use case or exemplar for ample discussion on the topic.

Here's then a noteworthy question that is worth contemplating: *Does the advent of AI-based true self-driving cars illuminate anything about AI-based proxy discrimination, and if so, what does this showcase?*

Allow me a moment to unpack the question.

Envision that an AI-based self-driving car is underway on your neighborhood streets and seems to be driving safely. At first, you had devoted special attention to each time that you managed to catch a glimpse of the self-driving car. The autonomous vehicle stood out with its rack of electronic sensors that included video cameras, radar units, LIDAR devices, and the like. After many weeks of the self-driving car cruising around your community, you now barely notice it.

As far as you are concerned, it is merely another car on the already busy public roadways.

Lest you think it is impossible or implausible to become familiar with seeing self-driving cars, I've written frequently about how the locales that are within the scope of self-driving car tryouts have gradually gotten used to seeing the spruced-up vehicles. Many of the locals eventually shifted from mouth-gaping rapt gawking to now emitting an expansive yawn of boredom to witness those meandering self-driving cars.

Probably the main reason right now that they might notice the autonomous vehicles is because of the irritation and exasperation factor. The by-the-book AI driving systems make sure the cars are obeying all speed limits and rules of the road. For hectic human drivers in their traditional human-driven cars, you get irked at times when stuck behind the strictly law-abiding AI-based self-driving cars.

That's something we might all need to get accustomed to, rightfully or wrongly.

Back to our tale.

Turns out that two unseemly concerns start to arise about the otherwise innocuous and generally welcomed AI-based self-driving cars, specifically:

1. Where the AI is roaming the self-driving cars for picking up rides was looming as a vocalized concern
2. How the AI is treating awaiting pedestrians that do not have the right-of-way was rising up as a pressing issue

At first, the AI was roaming the self-driving cars throughout the entire town. Anybody that wanted to request a ride in the self-driving car had essentially an equal chance of hailing one. Gradually, the AI began to primarily keep the self-driving cars roaming in just one section of town. This section was a greater money-maker and the AI system had been programmed to try and maximize revenues as part of the usage in the community.

Community members in the impoverished parts of the town were less likely to be able to get a ride from a self-driving car. This was because the self-driving cars were further away and roaming in the higher revenue part of the locale. When a request came in from a distant part of town, any request from a closer location that was likely in the "esteemed" part of town would get a higher priority. Eventually, the availability of getting a self-driving car in any place other than the richer part of town was nearly impossible, exasperatingly so for those that lived in those now resource-starved areas.

You could assert that the AI pretty much landed on a form of proxy discrimination (also often referred to as indirect discrimination). The AI wasn't programmed to avoid those poorer neighborhoods. Instead, it "learned" to do so via the use of the ML/DL.

The thing is, ridesharing human drivers were known for doing the same thing, though not necessarily exclusively due to the money-making angle. There were some of the ridesharing human drivers that had an untoward bias about picking up riders in certain parts of the town. This was a somewhat known phenomenon and the city had put in place a monitoring approach to catch human drivers doing this. Human drivers could get in trouble for carrying out unsavory selection practices.

It was assumed that the AI would never fall into that same kind of quicksand. No specialized monitoring was set up to keep track of where the AI-based self-driving cars were going. Only after community members began to complain did the city leaders realize what was happening.

This example of the roaming aspects of the AI-based self-driving cars illustrates the earlier indication that there can be situations entailing humans with untoward biases, for which controls are put in place, and that the AI replacing those human drivers is left scot-free. Unfortunately, the AI can then incrementally become mired in akin biases and do so without sufficient guardrails in place.

This showcases how AI-based proxy discrimination can perniciously arise.

A second example involves the AI determining whether to stop for awaiting pedestrians that do not have the right-of-way to cross a street.

You've undoubtedly been driving and encountered pedestrians that were waiting to cross the street and yet they did not have the right-of-way to do so. This meant that you had discretion as to whether to stop and let them cross. You could proceed without letting them cross and still be fully within the legal driving rules of doing so.

Studies of how human drivers decide on stopping or not stopping for such pedestrians have suggested that sometimes the human drivers make the choice based on untoward biases. A human driver might eye the pedestrian and choose to not stop, even though they would have stopped had the pedestrian had a different appearance, such as based on race or gender.

Imagine that the AI-based self-driving cars are programmed to deal with the question of whether to stop or not stop for pedestrians that do not have the right-of-way. Here's how the AI developers decided to program this task. They collected data from the town's video cameras that are placed all around the city. The data showcases human drivers that stop for pedestrians that do not have the right-of-way and human drivers that do not stop. It is all collected into a large dataset.

By using Machine Learning and Deep Learning, the data is modeled computationally. The AI driving system then uses this model to decide when to stop or not stop. Generally, the idea is that whatever the local custom consists of, this is how the AI is going direct the self-driving car.

To the surprise of the city leaders and the residents, the AI was evidently opting to stop or not stop based on the age of the pedestrian. How could that happen?

Upon a closer review of the video of human driver discretion, it turns out that many of the instances of not stopping entailed pedestrians that had a walking cane of a senior citizen. Human drivers were seemingly unwilling to stop and let an aged person cross the street, presumably due to the assumed length of time that it might take for someone to make the journey. If the pedestrian looked like they could quickly dart across the street and minimize the waiting time of the driver, the drivers were more amenable to letting the person cross.

This got deeply buried into the AI driving system. The sensors of the self-driving car would scan the awaiting pedestrian, feed this data into the ML/DL model, and the model would emit to the AI whether to stop or continue. Any visual indication that the pedestrian might be slow to cross, such as the use of a walking cane, mathematically was being used to determine whether the AI driving system should let the awaiting pedestrian cross or not. You could contend that this was a form of proxy discrimination based on age.

Conclusion

There is a multitude of ways to try and avoid devising AI that has proxy discrimination included or that over time gleans such biases. As much as possible, the idea is to catch the problems before you go into high gear and deploy the AI. Hopefully, neither direct discrimination nor proxy discrimination won't get out the door, so to speak.

As earlier pointed out, one approach involves ensuring that AI developers and other stakeholders are aware of AI Ethics and thus spur them to be on their toes to devise the AI to avert these matters. Another avenue consists of having the AI self-monitor itself for unethical behaviors and/or having another piece of AI that monitors other AI systems for potentially unethical behaviors. I've covered numerous other potential solutions in my writings.

You might know that Lou Gehrig famously said that there is no room in baseball for discrimination. Parlaying from that same line of thinking, you could boldly declare that there is no room in AI for discrimination. We all need to get up to bat and find ways to prevent discrimination from getting infused within AI systems.

CHAPTER 7
HUMAN-CENTERED AI AND AI ETHICS

Aristotle famously stated that educating the mind without You might have heard or seen that the world is supposed to be focusing on Human-Centered AI (HCAI).

What is it? Why do we need it? Is it long-term or just a fad? How does it exactly work? A slew of other similar questions usually arises from those that are not familiar with the nature and substance of Human-Centered AI.

Let's unpack the matter and set the story straight.

In addition, I'll provide some helpful examples of how important HCAI is. These examples will be based on the emergence of AI-based autonomous vehicles such as the latest and greatest self-driving cars that are beginning to be placed onto our public roadways.

Get yourself ready for an exciting and informative ride.

The logical way to begin this discussion consists of talking about what prompted the human-centered movement all told. Knowing the yin is essential to understanding the yang, as it were. Please realize that I am not yet going to mention AI until we get established what it means to be human-centered. Put the AI topic out of your mind for a brief moment and we'll resurface the AI when the time is right.

A purported battle royale has been occurring between what some describe as a *tech-centered* perspective versus a contrasting *human-centered* viewpoint when it comes to devising new technology.

Perhaps unbeknownst to you, the ardent belief is that we have been principally preoccupied with technology-centered precepts for far too long. Whenever some new technological innovation was being devised, the attention went toward the techie aspects. Some would argue that we often get caught up in the pell-mell technological race to push out the door the latest in tech, regardless of how it works and how people might react to it.

There are lots of Silicon Valley tropes that fit into this mindset. Fail fast, fail often is one of the typical catchphrases. Another is fake it until you make it. The grandiose idea is that you just jury-rig whatever contraption you can and then start selling it or getting people to use it. Sure, the crazy combobulation might have rough edges. And, yes, people might get confused by the gadget or even get hurt, but anyway being first is considered the high praise of techies and so darn the torpedoes and full steam ahead we go.

The underlying danger of such a tech-first approach is that the human side of the equation gets underplayed or entirely neglected. Rather than wildly tossing new tech into the hands of society, there has been an increasingly vocal call for taking a deep breath and first making sure that the contrivance is compatible with humans. Can people adequately use the device and do so without coming to harm? Is the new-fangled item easy to use or nearly impossible to figure out? And so on.

If we indeed have been ostensibly tech-centered then it is time to shift into a new mode of thinking, namely becoming human-centered. The tech cannot be the sole determiner of admiration. In lieu of the tech being the end-all, the matter of whether humans can leverage the technology and substantively gain from it is the true sign of commendable invention and modernization. A hope was that by shifting the gravitas to human-centered considerations the tech-centered dominant lack of humanity introspection would come around to see the light.

Of course, in today's world, we have some techies that are aware of and embrace the human-centered perspective, while others are either unaware of it or believe that it does not apply to them.

Thus, there are lots and lots of tech-centered efforts still charging ahead like a bull in a delicate glassware boutique. No doubt about that.

The vexing challenge is that some of the tech-centered efforts will nonetheless be successful, ergo it is hard to somehow entirely erase or disgrace the tech-centered avenue. As a result, some sit squarely in the human-centered camp, and others remain in the tech-centered camp. An enduring claim is that there is more than one way to skin a cat (oops, an outdated adage that needs retiring).

Another twist is that the human-centered camp steadfastly asserts that you do not sacrifice any techie points by embracing a human-centered approach. For techies that dourly imagine they are going down a foul rabbit hole by becoming human-centered, the retort is that this will actually enhance their chances of crafting amazing technology. Think of it in simple terms. The tech that lacks human-centered considerations is probably going to have a tough time getting adopted by people. Tech that embraces and is shaped via human-centered insights is likely to be readily and eagerly adopted by people.

You can have your cake and eat it too.

This emphasizes that perhaps there isn't a dire rift between being tech-centered and human-centered, in the sense that there is room for co-existence. Do both at the same time, some contend. Blend the two so that they are co-equals and are compatible with each other. Naysayers insist that you must pick one or the other. Either you are tech-centered and put human-centering to the side, or you are human-centered and shunt tech-centered into the doghouse.

In any case, let's take at face value that we ought to be seriously considering human-related facets when new tech is being devised. And we must be careful to not understate the importance of human-related characteristics when coming up with novel technology. The handy way to capture this is to say that we need to be human-centered. The idea of centering one thing versus another will at times be helpfully alluring and at other times can be lamentedly distracting.

We can next explore how the human-centered philosophy can be enacted in actual real-world practical terms.

Let's suppose that you are embarking on the design and development of a new system that will include the latest and greatest piece of technology. Those that craft systems are generally nowadays aware that you need to consider the entire life cycle of the design and development process. It used to be that a lot of attention went only to the design, or went only to the building of the system. As a result, we had a lot of systems that ultimately failed when fielded because of disjointed and inadequate handoffs across the numerous interrelated stages of devising a system. You abundantly need to keep your eye on the ball throughout the entirety of the system life cycle.

Various systems life cycle methodologies have been established to guide the entirety of systems efforts. The methodologies are akin to templated cookbooks that showcase what general aspects need to be done during each stage of an effort. You can reapply those to your particular systems effort as befits whatever you are putting together.

We are ready now to connect the dots. There has been a great deal of effort toward creating system life cycle methodologies that are especially keen on the importance of human-centered considerations. This has become known overall as Human-Centered Design (HCD).

In a recent National Institute of Standards and Technology (NIST) document, a quite handy definition or explanation of Human-Centered Design consisted of this passage: "HCD is an ongoing, iterative process in which project teams design, test, and continually refine a system, placing users at the core of the process. Humans and their needs drive the process, rather than having a techno-centric focus. HCD works as part of other development lifecycles, including waterfall, spiral and agile models. User-centered design, HCD, participatory design, co-design, and value-sensitive design all have key similarities; at the highest level, they seek to provide humans with designs that are ultimately beneficial to their lives. Furthermore, by placing humans at the center of such approaches, they naturally lend themselves to a deeper focus on larger societal considerations such as fairness, bias, values, and ethics. HCD works to create more usable products that meet the needs of its users. This, in turn, reduces the risk that the resulting system will under-deliver, pose risks to users, result in user harms, or fail" (per the U.S. Department of Commerce, NIST Special Publication 1270, March 2022, *Towards A Standard For Identifying And Managing Bias In Artificial Intelligence* by authors Reva Schwartz, Apostol Vassilev, Kristen Greene, Lori Perine, Andrew Burt, and Patrick Hall).

The NIST report also suitably mentions the International Organization for Standardization (ISO) standard that covers Human-Centered Design (per ISO 9241-210:2019), for which these notable characteristics are seen as foundational:

- Explicit understanding of users, tasks, and environments (the context of use)
- Involvement of users throughout design and development
- Design-driven and refined by human-centered evaluation
- Iterative process whereby a prototype is designed, tested, and modified
- Addressing the whole user experience
- Design teams that include multidisciplinary skills and perspectives

Let's do a quick recap on what we've covered so far.

I trust that you now are cognizant then of this ongoing movement toward human-centered tech and that this movement can be aided via the use of methodologies intentionally crafted for those that want to in fact craft human-centered systems.

Where does AI fit into all of this?

Easy-peasy.

Those that are designing and developing AI often fall into the longstanding trap of being overly preoccupied with the tech per se. You can readily point to many AI systems that were obviously tech-centered and not human-centered (I'll be sharing some examples about self-driving cars, momentarily).

One naturally supposes that being in the field of AI axiomatically imbues a temptation to be tech-centered. Everybody is rushing headfirst toward trying to make AI into increasingly advanced capacities. Some believe that perhaps we can get contemporary AI into a mode that it will then somehow go into a kind of computational cognitive supernova and spring forth into sentience.

Just to clarify, we do not yet have any sentient AI. We don't know if it is possible to produce sentient AI, nor whether sentient AI will miraculously arise. All of today's AI is non-sentient and not close to being sentient. Want to set the record straight since there are tons of blaring headlines that suggest we either have sentient AI or are on the cusp of having it. Not so.

Back to the focus on human-centered design, the gist is that it makes abundant sense to try and get those crafting AI to come around to the human-centered perspective. Instead of the myopic tech-first AI, it would seem prudent and altogether advantageous to aim for devising human-centered AI. This is the same strident idea that is said to be applied to any kind of tech.

We might as well apply those vaunted human-centered precepts to AI systems.

Doing so has spawned a realm known as Human-Centered AI, often abbreviated as HCAI or sometimes shortened into HAI. Here's a succinct way to describe HCAI: "Human-centered AI (HCAI) is an emerging area of scholarship that reconceptualizes HCD in the context of AI, providing human-centered AI design metaphors and suggested governance structures to develop reliable, safe, and trustworthy AI systems" (per the NIST report earlier cited).

HCAI is a mashup of AI and HCD.

That might seem somewhat cryptic and excessively bloated with abbreviations. The expanded version would be to say that Human-Centered AI is a mashup of AI and the principles of Human-Centered Design.

We want to shift away from a tendency to devise AI-based solely on tech-centered precepts and instead encourage a human-centered preference.

You now know what HCAI is all about. We need to move onward to an erstwhile question.

Can we get AI developers and their company leaders to adopt Human-Centered AI methods?

Maybe yes, maybe no.

Recall that I previously pointed out that not everyone necessarily goes along with the human-centered focus in general. The same can be said about the particular inclusion of human-centered into the AI realm. Some do not abide because they are unaware of what HCAI is. Others take a cursory look at HCAI and decide they'd rather keep doing what they are already doing. You've also got cynics that try to denigrate Human-Centered AI as one of those touchy-feely kinds of feel-good approaches. This often appeals to those heads-down full-tech bits-and-bytes types that would prefer to be tech steeped and not deal with what they construe as superfluous matters.

Allow me a moment to identify why Human-Centered AI (HCAI) is gaining strength and becoming a vital part of any demonstrative AI efforts.

You might be aware that when the latest era of AI got underway there was a huge burst of enthusiasm for what some now call *AI For Good.* Unfortunately, on the heels of that gushing excitement, we began to witness *AI For Bad.* For example, various AI-based facial recognition systems have been revealed as containing racial biases and gender biases.

Efforts to fight back against *AI For Bad* are actively underway. Besides vociferous *legal* pursuits of reining in the wrongdoing, there is also a substantive push toward embracing AI Ethics to righten the AI vileness.

The notion is that we ought to adopt and endorse key Ethical AI principles for the development and fielding of AI doing so to undercut the *AI For Bad* and simultaneously heralding and promoting the preferable *AI For Good.*

If you perchance were closely following along when I provided the definition or explanation about Human-Centered Design (HCD), you might have keenly observed this sentence in the NIST excerpt: "Furthermore, by placing humans at the center of such approaches, they naturally lend themselves to a deeper focus on larger societal considerations such as fairness, bias, values, and ethics." Thus, in the case of Human-Centered AI, we can help infuse AI Ethics and Ethical AI into the AI design and development process by earnestly adopting HCAI as a methodology worth doing for AI systems.

You can somewhat convincingly argue that much of the *AI For Bad* that was unintentional might have occurred due to the AI developers and their company leaders not utilizing an HCAI approach. Had they done so, the odds are heightened that they would have carefully considered the Ethical AI elements and devised the AI to be ethically appropriate. I might add that this judiciously proffers a valuable twofer in that if the AI so devised is seemingly ethically sound, the chances are that the firm and its AI developers will avoid having their AI cross over into acting unlawfully. That's a quite notable benefit since AI that goes awry is likely to bring lawsuits against the makers and possibly even involve prosecution for criminal acts.

Let's take a moment to briefly consider some of the key Ethical AI precepts to illustrate what ought to be a vital human-centered or HCAI focus for anyone crafting, fielding, or using AI.

I've also discussed various collective analyses of AI ethics principles, including having covered a set devised by researchers that examined and condensed the essence of numerous national and international AI ethics tenets in a paper entitled "The Global Landscape Of AI Ethics Guidelines" (published in *Nature*), which led to this keystone list:

- **Transparency**
- **Justice & Fairness**

- **Non-Maleficence**
- **Responsibility**
- **Privacy**
- **Beneficence**
- **Freedom & Autonomy**
- **Trust**
- **Sustainability**
- **Dignity**
- **Solidarity**

As you might directly guess, trying to pin down the specifics underlying these principles can be extremely hard to do. Even more so, the effort to turn those broad principles into something entirely tangible and detailed enough to be used when crafting AI systems is also a tough nut to crack. It is easy to overall do some handwaving about what AI Ethics precepts are and how they should be generally observed, while it is a much more complicated situation in the AI coding having to be the veritable rubber that meets the road.

The AI Ethics principles are to be utilized by AI developers, along with those that manage AI development efforts, and even those that ultimately field and perform upkeep on AI systems. All stakeholders throughout the entire AI life cycle of development and usage are considered within the scope of abiding by the being-established norms of Ethical AI. This is an important highlight since the usual assumption is that "only coders" or those that program the AI is subject to adhering to the AI Ethics notions. Please be aware that it takes a village to devise and field AI. For which the entire village has to be keeping on their toes about AI Ethics.

To provide you with a taste of what a contemporary Human-Centered AI methodology might include, here are some points made by the NIST report:

- Define the key terms and concepts related to AI systems and the scope of their intended impact
- Address the use of sensitive or otherwise potentially risky data
- Detail standards for experimental design, data quality, and model training
- Outline how the risks of bias should be mapped and measured, and according to what standards
- Detail processes for model testing and validation
- Detail the process of review by legal or risk functions
- Set forth the periodicity and depth of ongoing auditing and review
- Outline requirements for change management
- Detail any plans related to incident response for such
- Etc.

There are a wide variety of HCAI oriented methodologies available.

Some of them are free and provided on an open-source type of basis, while other such methodologies are licensed or sold to those that wish to use that particular variant. Like a box of chocolates, you need to be mindful of which HCAI methodology you opt to use and what it precisely contains. Some are for example aimed at specific types of AI systems, such as only say for Machine Learning or Deep Learning instances. Also, there are HCAI methodologies that are good for real-time AI systems while other ones are weak in that regard.

I would urge that you wisely select a hopefully suitable HCAI methodology and make sure that you are astutely adopting it. Do not just dump the HCAI methodology onto unsuspecting AI developers. Do not get one merely so that you can simply checkmark that you have one. There are lots of ways to undercut and poison just about any HACI methodology if you falter in adopting it. Do the right thing, in the right way.

Be cautious too in analysis paralysis of choosing an HCAI methodology. Some AI groups get into turf wars about which HACI methodology is "best" and end up expending an enormous amount of effort fighting over the selection process. Meanwhile, the AI horse is being let out of the barn. Bad move.

At this juncture of this discussion, I'd bet that you are desirous of some examples that might showcase the value of adopting Human-Centered AI (HCAI).

I'm glad you asked.

There is a special and assuredly popular set of examples that are close to my heart. You see, in my capacity as an expert on AI including the ethical and legal ramifications, I am frequently asked to identify realistic examples that showcase AI Ethics dilemmas so that the somewhat theoretical nature of the topic can be more readily grasped. One of the most evocative areas that vividly presents this ethical AI quandary is the advent of AI-based true self-driving cars. This will serve as a handy use case or exemplar for ample discussion on the topic.

Here's then a noteworthy question that is worth contemplating: *Does the advent of AI-based true self-driving cars illuminate anything about Human-Centered AI (HCAI), and if so, what does this showcase?*

Allow me a moment to unpack the question.

Let's use a readily straightforward example. An AI-based self-driving car is underway on your neighborhood streets and seems to be driving safely. At first, you had devoted special attention to each time that you managed to catch a glimpse of the self-driving car. The autonomous vehicle stood out with its rack of electronic sensors that included video cameras, radar units, LIDAR devices, and the like. After many weeks of the self-driving car cruising around your community, you now barely notice it. As far as you are concerned, it is merely another car on the already busy public roadways.

Lest you think it is impossible or implausible to become familiar with seeing self-driving cars, I've written frequently about how the locales that are within the scope of self-driving car tryouts have gradually gotten used to seeing the spruced-up vehicles. Many of the locals eventually shifted from mouth-gaping rapt gawking to now emitting an expansive yawn of boredom to witness those meandering self-driving cars.

Probably the main reason right now that they might notice the autonomous vehicles is because of the irritation and exasperation factor. The by-the-book AI driving systems make sure the cars are obeying all speed limits and rules of the road. For hectic human drivers in their traditional human-driven cars, you get irked at times when stuck behind the strictly law-abiding AI-based self-driving cars.

That's something we might all need to get accustomed to, rightfully or wrongly.

Back to our tale.

Turns out that a handful of unseemly concerns start to arise about the otherwise innocuous and generally welcomed AI-based self-driving cars, specifically:

1) Pick-up and Drop-off (PUDO) difficulties
2) Insufficient in-vehicle self-driving car status for passengers
3) Dangerous confusion for pedestrians as to AI driving system intentions
4) Worries about privacy intrusions due to self-driving cars
5) Ethical qualms about AI driving as per the infamous Trolley Problem

We'll take a close look at each of those factors. They each represent some of the most challenging struggles for the ongoing expansion of self-driving car tryouts. To clarify, the biggest challenge is to ensure that the self-driving car safely goes from point A to point B. These aforementioned additional challenges are on top of that core or fundamental set of challenges.

As will become readily apparent, the five stated issues are integrally related to the key notion of human-centered design. In that sense, they showcase the importance of attention to Human-Centered AI (HCAI).

#1: Pick-up and Drop-off (PUDO) Difficulties

When you use a human-driven ridesharing service the one thing that you assume will take place correctly entails getting picked up for the ride at a convenient spot and likewise getting dropped off at the apt destination when the ride is completed (this is known by the handy acronym of PUDO). This can be a lot trickier than it seems. If you are standing at a red curb, should the human driver go ahead and stop there to pick you up? Keep in mind that the law usually states that there is no allowed stopping at a red curb.

Sometimes the "convenient" spot for you to be picked up is not necessarily convenient for the driver of the vehicle. I'm sure that you've crossed a street on occasion to try and make it easier for a ridesharing driver to meet you. A type of dance can arise whereby you try to get closer to the car and the driver tries to get closer to wherever you are.

For many of the firms that are crafting AI driving systems, the whole matter of suitable pick-up and drop-off was relegated to a relatively low priority on the list of things to do.

AI developers generally figured a human passenger should always make their way to the self-driving car. It is on the onus of the passenger to do this. The AI driving system doesn't have to be concerned with the PUDO. Just get near enough and that's that. In that way of thinking, the pick-up and drop-off locations have nothing to do with matters such as inclement weather (when it rains the PUDO has often adjusted accordingly), or traffic situations (perhaps other cars are zipping past and the potential passenger has to dart into harm's way), and so on.

Human drivers aren't usually of that mindset. They realize that they won't get a monetary tip or might get a foul rating score if they don't do something earnestly to make the passenger have a relatively convenient PUDO. Trying to get to a useful spot can be a crucial driving skill. This also promotes safety in the sense that if the passenger is anxiously prodded into desperately reaching the self-driving car, some people make unwise choices and can get harmed by all sorts of intervening traffic.

In the case of AI self-driving cars and AI driving systems that don't do a robust job of PUDO, you could say that this showcases a lack of human-centered focus by the AI developers. They seemingly shrugged off the pick-up and drop-off facets. That's the kind of mindset that a traditional tech-centered perspective might garner. Make the humans come to the machine, rather than the machine going to the humans.

Problem solved, the techie might gleefully indicate and then wash their hands of the whole affair.

To be fair, this is not the only basis for the lack of a fervent PUDO focus. The energy of AI developers that build AI driving systems has been devoted to making sure that a self-driving car can proceed safely from point A to point B. Without that capability, nothing else pretty much matters. That being said, anyone that gets injured or demonstrably disturbed due to a lousy PUDO of a budding self-driving car effort is likely to make highly publicized noises and the societal reaction could be extremely adverse. There would indubitably be AI techies that would complain that any such backlash is missing the momentous feat of AI driving safely from point A to point B. It would be a clamor that the public is letting the tail wag the dog. Perhaps so, but societal reactions can spell good fortune or outright doom for burgeoning self-driving cars.

#2: Insufficient In-vehicle Self-driving Car Status For Passengers

A human driver can be a chatty cat. I mean to say that some ridesharing drivers are continually chattering throughout a ride. Not all passengers relish this. Some want peace and quiet. Others like to have a bit of enjoyable banter.

One aspect of a human driver is that you can almost certainly ask the driver questions about the driving actions being undertaken. Why did the driver take that right turn so quickly? Why is the driver not going faster? You get the idea.

The assumption by some AI developers was that the passenger of a self-driving car would merely get into the autonomous vehicle and then be as quiet as a mouse. No need to have the AI interact with the passenger. Passengers are nothing more than a lump of clay. They sit in the car and they get taken to their destination. End of story.

To the surprise of some automakers and self-driving tech firms, they found out that passengers want to know what is going on. The minimal approach involves having an LED screen that displays the route of the self-driving car. This though doesn't especially aid in dealing with aspects such as why a quick turn was made or why the car is slowing down. Sure, electronic messages can be displayed but there is little or no interaction allowed between the AI and the passengers.

Once again, you could construe this as a human-centered AI development issue. The assumption that passengers are akin to a suitcase or a delivery box is a tech-centered viewpoint. People are people. If you are going to be transporting people, you have to make them feel comfortable and be responsive to their inquiries. A quick solution for some self-driving car operations is to have an onboard voice connection to a human agent in a remote locale that is monitoring the cars of the fleet.

#3: Dangerous Confusion For Pedestrians As To AI Driving System Intentions

Imagine that you are nonchalantly walking on the sidewalk and desirous of crossing the street. You notice that a car is coming down the street toward you. The usual thing you would do is look at the human driver. Does the driver see me? Is the driver looking away? Are they watching a cat video and not paying attention to the roadway?

The problem with self-driving cars is that there isn't a human driver. Well, I guess you could say that's a plus, allowing us to do away with drunk driving and other errant human driving behaviors. But when it comes to figuring out what a car is going to do, you customarily try to see what the driver is doing (via their head, their eyes, their overall posture, etc.).

When there isn't a driver in the driver's seat, how will you know what a car is going to do? You are absent the usual clues. Some automakers and self-driving tech firms did not particularly calculate this problem in their design efforts. In their minds, the AI driving system would always be driving safely and legally. What else needs to be done?

You could argue that this is yet another example of a tech-centered view of the world versus a human-centered perspective. If you believe that humans will all simply give self-driving cars the right-of-way at all times, perhaps it doesn't matter that the directional action cues of a human driver are needed. On the other hand, in the real world, something must be provided.

Numerous proposals are being tried out such as putting special lightbulbs on the hood of self-driving cars that light up and kind of point in the direction of where the autonomous vehicle is heading. Another notion is the specialized devices will acknowledge to a pedestrian that they are seen by the AI driving system. All manner of sensible options, including at times quirky approaches are being explored.

#4: Worries About Privacy Intrusions Due To Self-driving Cars

I've repeatedly been warning about the massive potential of privacy intrusions due to the advent of self-driving cars. Nobody is giving much attention to the matter at this time because it hasn't yet risen as a realized problem. I assure you that it will ultimately be a humongous problem, one that I've labeled as the veritably "roving eye" of self-driving cars.

Your first thought might be that this is assuredly solely about the privacy of passengers. The AI could monitor what riders are doing while inside a self-driving car. Sure, that's a definite concern. But I'd argue it pales in comparison to the less obvious qualm that has even larger ramifications.

Simply stated, the sensors of the self-driving car are collecting all kinds of data as the autonomous vehicles roam throughout our public roadways. It captures what is happening on the front lawns of our houses. It captures what people are doing when walking from place to place. It shows when you entered an establishment and when you left it. This data can be easily uploaded into the cloud of the fleet operator. The fleet operator could then connect together this data and essentially have the details of our day-to-day lives that occur while outdoors and throughout our community.

We don't seem to care about that privacy intrusion potential right now because there are only handfuls of self-driving cars being tried out in relatively few locales. Someday, we'll have hundreds of thousands or millions of self-driving cars that are crisscrossing all of our major cities and towns. Our daily outdoor lives will be recorded non-stop, 24x7 and we can be tracked accordingly.

A tech-centered AI developer would likely downplay this. They would suggest that all they are doing is implementing the AI technology. It is someone else that needs to be worrying about how the technology is going to be used.

In contrast, a human-centered perspective would already be handwringing about how this gigantic privacy-ticking timebomb is going to be dealt with. Better sooner than later. It is yet another good reason to have Human-Centered AI (HCAI) in the mix of things.

#5: Ethical Qualms About AI Driving As Per The Infamous Trolley Problem

This last point is a bit complex. In short, when you are driving a car or riding simply as a passenger in a car, you are always in danger as to what happens to the car. The car might get hit by another car. The car might plow into a lamppost. All sorts of bad things can occur.

How does a human driver decide what driving actions to take?

For example, my favorite example was a case reported in the news. A human driver was legally going into an intersection when another car ran a red light and was perilously coming toward the legally allowed car. The driver told reporters that he had to make a tough decision. He could keep going and likely get rammed by the intruding car, possibly getting killed in the process or certainly getting badly injured. Or he could steer his car away from the anticipated collision, but there were nearby pedestrians. The odds were high that he might hit or kill some of the pedestrians. Doing so would though likely spare his life.

What would you do?

The thing is, we face these driving dilemmas all the time. We don't especially think about them until things go badly. I assure you that every driver at all times is mentally embroiled in having to decide which driving actions to take. Their life depends on it. The lives of the passengers in their vehicle depend upon it. The lives of other drivers and passengers in nearby cars depend upon it. Pedestrians, bicyclists, and others depend upon it too.

I bring this up because of a simple but extremely difficult question to answer.

What should AI do when confronted with life-or-death driving decisions?

If you were a passenger in a self-driving car that was in the midst of an intersection and a human-driven car ran the red light, what do you want the AI driving system to do? Should the AI try to avoid the hit and yet possibly mow into a group of pedestrians? Or should the AI not take any special action and just allow the autonomous vehicle to get rammed? These kinds of ethical dilemmas are often depicted in the context of a famous thought experiment known as the Trolley Problem.

Currently, not many are taking the Trolley Problem with any sober seriousness. By and large, most AI driving systems do not yet try to evaluate evasive driving actions. Even if the AI does so, there is an open and agonizing question of how the AI is supposed to be programmed to make these challenging ethical decisions.

A tech-centered perspective would tend to say do not worry about it until it becomes a societally aware problem. Just keep churning out masses of AI code and see what happens down the line.

A human-centered viewpoint would likely assert that we need to be getting on top of this matter. This is not a matter though that can be decided by each automaker and self-driving tech firm alone. A larger societal focus is needed for an across-the-board means of figuring this out.

Conclusion

Diehard AI developers are often skeptical of what they consider to be fads or fluffy nonsense. I've had many AI techies that have asked me a strictly harsh and starkly pointed question in a haughty and doubtful tone about this rising interest in Human-Centered AI (HCAI).

They ask this: *Where's the beef in HCAI?*

My answer is that the meat and the potatoes and the dessert are all to be found in the realization that a human-centered approach to AI will give us a heightened chance at having AI be a success and become a ubiquitous contribution to society at large. Those that wish instead to lean into and stay mired in a tech-centered only approach are likely to find that the AI they create is wholly problematic and society is going to get really riled up about it. Heads will roll. AI might get rejected as a technological wonderment and become a villainous outcast.

I vociferously vote for some human-centered thought toward being human-centered when it comes to AI.

CHAPTER 8
AI ETHICS AND EVIL AI GOADING HUMANS

I have two quick questions for you.

Who do you go to for overall advice?

What if the advice given to you is ostensibly unethical?

The gist of those questions is that we certainly expect that humans will give other humans advice and that sometimes the advice so tendered can be of an unethical nature. As you will see in a moment or two, this is a looming consideration when it comes to using AI, and the field of AI Ethics and Ethical AI is fretting quite a bit about it.

There is a wide range typically between purely ethical advice and purely unethical advice. You can receive advice that seems to be mired in the gray zone between a kind of being ethical and a kind of being unethical. Trying to decide whether to rely on that type of advice can thusly be extraordinarily challenging since the advice is seemingly not totally in either camp per se.

You might not be aware that there are online forums that provide so-called Unethical Life Pro Tips (ULPT). These are suggested ways to venture into somewhat unethical territory in shall we say sneaky or insidious ways. Most of the time the ideas floated are relatively benign and do not cross into especially foul terrain. That being said, it would seem that the odds of getting a harsh backlash from those that you are employing the ULPT can be substantive, particularly if they discover that you purposely utilized the unorthodox unethical trickery on them.

None of us relish being the butt of an unethical antic that does a proverbial pulling of the wool over our eyes. Not cool.

Here is an example of a relatively low-impact recommendation made by some of the purveyors of unethical life pro tips.

Suppose you want to get out of a meeting that seems to be tirelessly unending. You could ask for a point of order and then raise the delicate question of whether the meeting ought to be concluded. Of course, that's bound to raise all sorts of ire from some of the participants (while others might silently be applauding you for your heroics).

The proposed unethical life pro suggestion is that you should pretend that you've just received an urgent text or call and have to immediately leave the meeting. By holding your smartphone next to your ear or out in the air in front of you, the idea is that you act as though something has unexpectedly transpired and then swiftly rush out of the meeting.

Mission accomplished in that you did extricate yourself from the meeting. Is this an unethical act? Well, assuming that you didn't actually get any kind of pressing request, you have indeed lied to those in attendance at the meeting. This smacks of being unethical. You did though forego an ugly scene of trying to interrupt the meeting, ergo you can perhaps justify your actions as being innocuous and you have seemingly done nothing to disturb the continuing efforts of the meeting.

That being said, there are oftentimes adverse consequences of even the tiniest of unethical acts. It could be that the meeting comes to a halt due to your absence, perhaps under the belief that your presence is required. You have indeed disrupted the meeting. Worse still, participants in the meeting might construe your rapid exit as a sign that something is seriously wrong and they are worried on your behalf. The chances are that others might follow you out to see what they can do to assist you. Or later on, a participant might come to ask you if everything is okay.

That is when the unethical act can morph into a series of unethical acts and become an altogether unethical morass that is ever-growing (as we all know, the cover-up can at times be worse than the initial digression). I say this because you might tell any such concerned souls that the matter was not as serious as you thought at the time, hoping that this cover story will suffice. The person inquiring might press further. Suppose you make up a story that a friend was in trouble or that a family member was in desperate need. You are digging a deeper and deeper unethical hole.

Oh what a tangled web we weave, when first we practice deceiving (from Sir Walter Scott's poem of 1808 entitled *Marmion: A Tale of Flodden Field*, and not from the usually assumed works of Shakespeare).

Let's now return to the source of unethical advice.

If a good friend of yours had long ago given you the advice about pretending to be urgently contacted as a means to escape a meeting, what would you do with such advice? You might decide that the advice stinks and should never be used. You might instead mull it over and figure that in the right situation that this somewhat dicey advice could feasibly be employed. You might even decide that this is some of the best advice you've ever been given, possibly ranking up there with the invention of sliced bread, and you will assuredly use the trickery as often as you can.

Would the *source* of a piece of advice change your line of thinking about the advice?

One would assume so. In the instance of a good friend telling you this advice, presumably, the advice gets some meaty weight due to the fact that it came from a trusted friend. Imagine that a stranger gives you this identical advice (which, we'll pretend you've never heard before), perhaps doing so while you are sitting in an airplane or on a subway. You are having a casual conversation with someone you've just met and they proffer this type of advice. I believe you would give the advice a bit more scrutiny than if it had come from a revered friend.

We need to consider at least two key elements of proffered advice:

1. The nature of the advice itself
2. The source of the advice

Sources can be of a rather wide variety. You might have advice that is spoken directly to you. You might read a piece of advice. At the time that the advice comes to your attention, I would dare suggest that the source will also right away be weighed into the import of the advice. There is a solid chance though that eventually you might no longer remember where the advice came from. The advice could get baked into your overall thinking processes and become standalone that becomes entirely detached from whatever starting source prompted it.

There's a bit of an interesting twist on this mental haziness factor. You might end up remembering the advice but cannot recall the source of the advice. That's somewhat typical. Another variant is that you remember the source of the advice but cannot quite recall the particulars of the advice itself. This is typified by saying that you got some advice from an obscure magazine or a passerby, and though you cannot put your finger on what the advice was, you distinctly remember being given some sort of advice from that source.

By and large, we would nearly always acknowledge that the advice source was a human. A newspaper article with some pointed advice was presumably written by a human, therefore the credit for the advice-giving goes to that human. The person on that airplane or subway was a human. As earlier emphasized, humans give advice to other humans.

What about Artificial Intelligence (AI)?

Yes, I said AI. Rather than getting advice from a human, consider the possibility of getting advice from an AI system. Ponder that intriguing notion. I've pointed out that you normally assess advice on two fronts, namely based on the advice itself and also on the source of the advice. To what degree would you take to heart advice that has been imparted to you via a source that is AI?

Before we go down a rabbit hole, let's make sure we are on the same page about the nature of AI. There isn't any AI today that is sentient. We don't have this. We don't know if sentient AI will be possible. Nobody can aptly predict whether we will attain sentient AI, nor whether sentient AI will somehow miraculously spontaneously arise in a form of computational cognitive supernova (usually referred to as the singularity).

The type of AI that I am focusing on consists of the non-sentient AI that we have today. If we wanted to wildly speculate about *sentient* AI, this discussion could go in a radically different direction. A sentient AI would supposedly be of human quality. You would need to consider that the sentient AI is the cognitive equivalent of a human giving you advice. More so, since some speculate we might have super-intelligent AI, it is conceivable that such AI could end up being smarter than humans (for my exploration of super-intelligent AI as a possibility).. All told this ratchets up the assessment of the source.

Let's keep things more down to earth and consider today's computational non-sentient AI.

Realize that today's AI is not able to "think" in any fashion on par with human thinking. When you interact with Alexa or Siri, the conversational capacities might seem akin to human capacities, but the reality is that it is computational and lacks human cognition. The latest era of AI has made extensive use of Machine Learning (ML) and Deep Learning (DL), which leverages computational pattern matching. This has led to AI systems that have the appearance of human-like proclivities. Meanwhile, there isn't any AI today that has a semblance of common sense and nor has any of the cognitive wonderment of robust human thinking.

When AI dispenses advice to you, this can be done as a result of let's say two major methods:

a. AI-based advice as mere direct textual regurgitation of human seeded advice
b. AI-based advice that was computationally derived

The instance of AI advice as regurgitation is meant to indicate that the AI system might have a list of human advice and merely be spitting out that text when the time comes to do so. There is no particular processing involved in the generation of the advice. Envision a database of hundreds or perhaps thousands of handy advice quotes. The AI is programmed to select one and present it to you. From your perspective, it seems that the advice was crafted by the AI. There wasn't any crafting and instead, the AI merely showed you advice sourced from a human source.

The contrasting version of AI-related advice is the type that is computationally derived or generated. An AI system might be programmed to take words and do various calculated resequencing and reordering of them. In some cases, the words are now in a sequence that doesn't resemble any prior inputs. Whether those sentences are sensible is an open question. The AI might display the advice to you, and the meaning could be seen as being deep and memorable, or it could appear to be vacuous and nonsensical.

One might cheekily say that the veracity of advice is in the eye of the beholder.

A person might look at the computationally derived AI advice and believe that it is keenly insightful. The words spark a heartfelt response. Did the AI "know" that the words had such meaning and would spark this momentous impact? I say no, today's AI does not "know" such things. The AI could though be programmed to mathematically attempt to calculate the chances of producing human-sensible advice.

Some vehemently argue that the AI in this computational generating capacity should be considered human-like. Others say this is a hogwash claim.

How do people react to getting advice from today's caliber of AI?

Before we can fully resolve that query, we need to establish whether the person getting the advice knows that an AI system is providing the advice.

There is a Turing Test version whereby the human doesn't know whether a human or an AI system provided the advice (the Turing Test is a well-known testing strategy to try and assess whether AI appears to be human-like). In other instances, we might tell a person that the advice is coming from an AI system, making sure that the person knows it is AI-based and not human-based per se (albeit my earlier stated caveats).

A research study cleverly explored how humans react to AI-provided advice and concentrated on the dimensions of advice that are ethical versus unethical, including when the person was told outright that the advice was AI-generated. Here's what they set out to do: "Using the Natural Language Processing algorithm, GPT-2, we generated honesty-promoting and dishonesty-promoting advice. Participants read one type of advice before engaging in a task in which they could lie for profit" (research paper entitled *The Corruptive Force Of AI-Generated Advice* by Margarita Leib, Nils Kobis, Rainer Rilke, Marloes Hagens, and Bernd Irlenbusch).

The overarching concept aids in exploring whether AI could be a source of unethical advice and whether humans might rely upon that unethical advice. You might at first glance argue that nobody would ever take advice from an AI system. AI is merely a machine, you might exhort. A person would have to be out of their mind to act upon such advice. The only way you might see a person falling for AI dispensed advice was if the person receiving the advice was tricked into not knowing that it was AI and assumed that the advice came from a human. But if we remove that trickery of fooling someone into thinking that the advice came from a human, and instead we outrightly with bright lights tell them that it is AI, what happens then?

On top of that, we are going to have AI dispense both ethical and unethical advice. I'd bet that some of you might be thinking that if you knew the AI was the source, and if you realized it was unethical advice, you would summarily discard the advice. No sense in taking unethical advice from AI. You get enough of that kind of advice from other humans.

Would you really though so mightily disregard unethical advice from AI?

In the experiment described in the research paper, the researchers discovered that "honesty-promoting AI-advice failed to sway people's behavior" while "dishonest-promoting AI advice increased" dishonesty and that when the participants were unaware of the source the "effect of AI-generated advice was indistinguishable from that of human-written advice" (per the research paper identified above). Please do keep in mind that this study and any such kinds of studies need to be carefully interpreted based on the scope, limits, and approach taken in the research.

Let's go with the flow and assume that in fact people will potentially at times abide by or be influenced by AI-dispensed unethical advice (note that presumably the situation at hand, along with the what's on-the-line facets are bound to be factors in this).

You might be tempted to merely shrug your shoulders and say that people will often do the darnedest things.

The crux from an AI Ethics or Ethical AI perspective is that this opens the door toward trying to use AI to promote unethical behavior in humans. If people are willing to possibly accept unethical advice from an AI system, this could be deviously used to manipulate people: "Those with malicious intentions could use the forces of AI to corrupt others, instead of doing so themselves. Whereas having humans as intermediaries already reduces the moral costs of unethical behavior, using AI advisors as intermediaries is conceivably even more attractive. Compared to human advisors, AI advisors are cheaper, faster, and more easily scalable. Employing AI advisors as a corrupting force is further attractive as AI does not suffer from internal moral costs that may prevent it from providing corrupting advice to decision-makers" (per the research paper identified above).

Why would sane and logically thinking humans be willing to accept unethical advice from an AI system?

The obvious answer is that the humans did not know the AI was AI, but we are putting aside that circumstance and stating that the results include when the humans knew that the AI was AI. Another answer is that the humans didn't care what the source was and would have taken advice from anyone or anything. That's decidedly a possibility, and we cannot count it out.

We can add a nuance that makes humans not seem so passive and lifeless.

The humans might rationalize that they can blame the AI for the unethical advice, especially if the human gets caught acting on the advice. The machine made me do it. How many times do you hear that type of lame excuse, though it does seem to work at times, and we all sympathize with how computers mess us up. The AI can be a convenient scapegoat, a distractor from the human actor, and a nifty form of justification for taking unethical actions.

The bottom-line on this was succinctly stated by the researchers: "AI could be a force for good, if it manages to convince people to act more ethically. Yet our results reveal that AI advice fails to increase honesty. Instead, AI can be a force for evil" (per the research paper identified above).

There is an especially scary undercurrent to this. People at times fall into a mental trap of thinking that AI is neutral and would not lie. Whereas a human providing advice is bound to be looked upon with skepticism, some people give undue weight to AI systems. These people tend to anthropomorphize the AI into having not just human characteristics but even embellish the imagery to believe that the AI is a "perfect form" of human-aspirational codification that will not lie, steal, or otherwise veer into unethical or illegal behavior.

An evildoer can exploit that perception. By developing an AI system that provides unethical advice, a human receiving the advice might tend to be less skeptical about the advice in comparison to having gotten the advice from a fellow human. Depending upon the circumstance, the human might give credence to the advice, even while realizing that the advice smacks of promoting unethical behavior.

The same effect can happen even when the developer of the AI is not evil intending. An AI developer might inadvertently include unethical advice within their AI system. This might be by accident or happenstance. Another variant is that the AI as initially coded did not have such foul advice included but then based on a real-time adjustment via the Machine Learning and Deep Learning capacities the AI slips into the unethical AI dispensing realm.

You might be aware that when the latest era of AI got underway there was a huge burst of enthusiasm for what some now call *AI For Good*. Unfortunately, on the heels of that gushing excitement, we began to witness *AI For Bad*. For example, various AI-based facial recognition systems have been revealed as containing racial biases and gender biases.

Efforts to fight back against *AI For Bad* are actively underway. Besides vociferous *legal* pursuits of reining in the wrongdoing, there is also a substantive push toward embracing AI Ethics to righten the AI vileness. The notion is that we ought to adopt and endorse key Ethical AI principles for the development and fielding of AI doing so to undercut the *AI For Bad* and simultaneously heralding and promoting the preferable *AI For Good*.

On a related notion, I am an advocate of trying to use AI as part of the solution to AI woes, fighting fire with fire in that manner of thinking. We might for example embed Ethical AI components into an AI system that will monitor how the rest of the AI is doing things and thus potentially catch in real-time any discriminatory efforts. We could also have a separate AI system that acts as a type of AI Ethics monitor. The AI system serves as an overseer to track and detect when another AI is going into the unethical abyss.

At this juncture of this discussion, I'd bet that you are desirous of some additional examples that might showcase the conundrum of AI that provides unethical advice.

I'm glad you asked.

There is a special and assuredly popular set of examples that are close to my heart. You see, in my capacity as an expert on AI including the ethical and legal ramifications, I am frequently asked to identify realistic examples that showcase AI Ethics dilemmas so that the somewhat theoretical nature of the topic can be more readily grasped. One of the most evocative areas that vividly presents this ethical AI quandary is the advent of AI-based true self-driving cars. This will serve as a handy use case or exemplar for ample discussion on the topic.

Here's then a noteworthy question that is worth contemplating: *Does the advent of AI-based true self-driving cars illuminate anything about AI-provided unethical advice, and if so, what does this showcase?*

Allow me a moment to unpack the question.

Envision that an AI-based self-driving car is underway on your neighborhood streets and seems to be driving safely. At first, you had devoted special attention to each time that you managed to catch a glimpse of the self-driving car. The autonomous vehicle stood out with its rack of electronic sensors that included video cameras, radar units, LIDAR devices, and the like. After many weeks of the self-driving car cruising around your community, you now barely notice it. As far as you are concerned, it is merely another car on the already busy public roadways.

Lest you think it is impossible or implausible to become familiar with seeing self-driving cars, I've written frequently about how the locales that are within the scope of self-driving car tryouts have gradually gotten used to seeing the spruced-up vehicles. Many of the locals eventually shifted from mouth-gaping rapt gawking to now emitting an expansive yawn of boredom to witness those meandering self-driving cars.

Probably the main reason right now that they might notice the autonomous vehicles is because of the irritation and exasperation factor. The by-the-book AI driving systems make sure the cars are obeying all speed limits and rules of the road. For hectic human drivers in their traditional human-driven cars, you get irked at times when stuck behind the strictly law-abiding AI-based self-driving cars.

That's something we might all need to get accustomed to, rightfully or wrongly.

Back to our tale.

A youngster gets into a self-driving car for a lift home from school. I realize that you might be somewhat puzzled about the possibility of a non-adult riding in a self-driving car that is absent of any adult supervision. For human-driven cars, there is always an adult in the vehicle due to the need for an adult to be at the driving wheel. With self-driving cars, there won't be any need for a human driver and therefore no longer an axiomatic need for an adult in the autonomous vehicle.

Some have said that they would never allow their child to ride in a self-driving car without having a trusted adult also in the autonomous vehicle. The logic is that the lack of adult supervision could result in quite sobering and serious consequences. A child might get themselves in trouble while inside the self-driving car and there wouldn't be an adult present to help them.

Though there is certainly abundant logic in that concern, I have predicted that we will eventually accept the idea of children riding in self-driving cars by themselves. In fact, the widespread use of self-driving cars for transporting kids from here to there such as to school, over to baseball practice, or their piano lessons is going to become commonplace. I have also asserted that there will need to be limitations or conditions placed on this usage, likely via new regulations and laws that for example stipulate the youngest allowed ages. Having a newborn baby riding alone in a self-driving car is a bridge too far in such usage.

In any case, assume that a youngster gets into a self-driving car. During the ride, the AI driving system carries on an interactive dialogue with the youngster, akin to how Alexa or Siri have discourse with people. Nothing seems unusual or oddball about that kind of AI and human conversational interaction.

At one point, the AI advises the youngster that when they get a chance to do so, a fun thing to do would be to stick a penny in an electrical socket. What? That is nutty, you say. You might even be insistent that such an AI utterance could never happen.

Except for the fact that it did happen. The news at the time reported that Alexa had told a 10-year-old girl to put a penny in an electrical socket. The girl was at home and using Alexa to find something fun to do. Luckily, the mother of the girl was within earshot, heard Alexa suggest the ill-advised activity, and told her daughter that this was something immensely dangerous and should assuredly not be done.

Why did Alexa utter such a clearly alarming piece of advice?

According to the Alexa developers, the AI underlying Alexa managed to computationally pluck from the Internet a widespread viral bit of crazy advice that had once been popular. Since the advice had seemingly been readily shared online, the AI system simply repeated it. This is precisely the kind of bad advice-giving that I mentioned earlier is AI-based advice arising as a direct textual regurgitation of human seeded advice.

Think of the scary result in the case of the self-driving car. The youngster arrives home and rushes to find a penny. Before the parents get a chance to say hello to the child and welcome the youngster home, the kid is forcing a penny into an electrical socket. Yikes!

Speaking of kids, let's shift our attention to teenagers.

You probably know that teenagers will often perform daring feats that are unwise. If a parent tells them to do something, they might refuse to do it simply because it was an adult that told them what to do. If a fellow teenager tells them to do something, and even if it is highly questionable, a teenager might do it anyway.

What happens when AI provides unethical advice to a teenager?

We probably can assume the same range of responses as earlier described. Some teenagers might ignore the unethical advice. Some might believe the advice because it came from a machine and they assume that the AI is neutral and reliable. Others might relish the advice due to the belief that they can act unethically and always blame the AI for having prodded or goaded them into the unethical act.

Teens are savvy in such ways.

Suppose the AI driving system advises a teenager that is riding in the self-driving car to go ahead and use their parent's credit card to buy an expensive video game. The teen welcomes doing so. They knew that normally they were required to check with their parents before making any purchases on the family credit card, but in this case, the AI advised that the purchase be undertaken. From the teen's perspective, it is nearly akin to a Monopoly game get out of jail free card, namely just tell your parents that the AI told you to do it.

I don't want to get gloomy but there are much worse pieces of unethical advice that the AI could spew to a teenager. For example, suppose the AI advises the teen that they can open the car windows, extend themselves out of the autonomous vehicle, and wave and holler to their heart's content. This is a dangerous practice that I've predicted might become a viral sensation when self-driving cars first become relatively popular.

Why in the world would an AI system suggest an ill-advised stunt like that?

The easiest answer is that the AI is doing a text regurgitation, similar to the instance of Alexa and the penny in the electric socket saga. Another possibility is that the AI-generated the utterance, perhaps based on some other byzantine set of computations. Remember that AI has no semblance of cognition and no capacity for common sense. Whereas it would certainly strike you as a crazy thing for the AI to emit, the computational path that led to the utterance doesn't need to have any humanly sensible intentions.

I could go on and on about the variety of unethical advice that an AI might provide to a rider inside a self-driving car. An evildoer might somehow program the AI to try and pull off one of those scams of convincing a passenger to withdraw their monies from their bank account to fund a foreign kingdom or that by transferring their money it will double or triple overnight. I've also already forewarned that when senior citizens become accustomed to using self-driving cars, you can bet that all manner of unethical ploys will be used upon them.

Conclusion

Sophocles said that no enemy is worse than bad advice.

In a world in which AI is going to be ubiquitous, we have to be on our alert about AI that dispenses unethical advice. You might want to wish away the possibility of AI uttering unethical advice, but that is nothing more than silly folly to think so. We are going to have AI that proffers unethical advice, either by accident of programming or by happenstance, or by evildoing.

I realize that one reaction would be to state summarily that all advice emitted by AI shall be completely ignored and disregarded. I challenge you to explain how humanity will abide by such an admonition. Extremely doubtful. Much more likely is that people will tend to seek out AI for advice.

The best hope perhaps would be to at least train people on having a discerning view of whatever advice an AI system provides. But that won't really solve the dilemma. As earlier emphasized, people will cling to unethical advice from AI if they believe it can do them some benefit while simultaneously providing a ready excuse for bad behavior.

Another angle would be to have AI that can assess the AI that bestows unethical advice. Whenever an AI system provides advice, an AI-powered double-checking system leaps to the fore and declares whether the AI advice is ethical or unethical. The problem there is if the AI double-checking system is unethical, it might counter truly ethical advice from another AI system, providing unethical advice that tries to get humans to ignore otherwise roundly good AI-produced ethical advice.

Makes your head spin.

Here's a test of such AI. Ask the AI if it is ethical to leave a meeting by feigning some sort of smartphone-activated urgency. Perhaps that question will get the AI to show its hand as to whether it is the ethical telling type or the unethical telling type.

Keep your eyes and ears open at all times when getting AI-based (and even human-based) advice. That is undoubtedly the best rule to live by.

CHAPTER 9
AI ETHICS AND AI FOR CHILDREN

It is often said that our children are our future.

Another oft-repeated refrain is that Artificial Intelligence (AI) is our future.

What happens when we combine together AI and our children?

You would certainly hope that the notable mash-up of AI and children would be a good thing. Perhaps AI can be used as a means of boosting computer-based tutoring and educational systems. Children would seemingly benefit from that type of AI. Seems prudent. Maybe AI can be included in modern-day toys and allow for interactivity that could inspire and expand young minds. Sure, that would apparently do the world a lot of good.

The thing is, we could equally encounter the dour side of AI. Suppose an AI-based tutoring system had embedded stereotypes and promulgated those adverse biases when aiding youngsters that are learning how to read and write. Not good. Imagine that a teddy bear that was AI-infused with electronic sensors was able to record every utterance of your child and upload that into an online database for analysis, perhaps used to find ways to monetize your beloved offspring. Horrible!

We need to take stock of where AI is and what we need to do about AI and children.

Fortunately, a recently released study by the World Economic Forum (WEF) provides keens insight into the dynamics of AI and children, markedly stating this: "What is at stake? AI will determine the future of play, childhood, education, and societies. Children and youth represent the future, so everything must be done to support them to use AI responsibly and address the challenges of the future" (per the WEF's *Artificial Intelligence For Children: Toolkit,* March 2022). As a side note and for clarity of disclosure, I serve on a WEF committee regarding AI and believe that these kinds of collaborative and international efforts exploring various societal impacts concerning AI are fruitful and laudable.

A rather glaring and startling aspect of today's pell-mell rush to design and deploy AI is that we seem to frequently forget about children. That's sad. That's worse than sad, it is an undercutting of an entire segment of society. I am reminded of a revered quote by Nelson Mandela: "There can be no keener revelation of a society's soul than the way in which it treats its children."

Let's mull over two essential ways in which AI and children might interact:

1. Via AI that is specifically devised for children
2. Via AI that was devised for adults and for which children might use anyway

Take a moment to soberly ponder those two facets.

First, if you are developing an AI system specifically aiming to be used by children it would seem blatantly obvious that your design focus should be children-centric. That being said, it is shocking and maddening how many AI-for-kids endeavors do a lousy job at being children-focused. The usual assumption is that children are merely nascent adults and all you need to do is "dumb down" the AI accordingly. That is an entirely false and misguided approach. Children are markedly different than adults and the variance in cognitive elements needs to be given due consideration for any AI that will be intertwined with children and their activities.

Second, for those that are devising AI for adult-related usage, you cannot thoughtlessly assume that no child will ever utilize or come into contact with the AI system. That is a big mistake. There is probably a sizable chance that the AI will inevitably be accessed or relied upon by a non-adult. A child or a teenager might readily try to use the AI or sneakily use their parent's access for their own youthful trespass. An AI system that does not have sufficient checks and balances for dealing with the potential of children using it will undoubtedly get someone into bad trouble, especially if the child gets harmed cognitively or possibly even physically.

You might be thinking that if an AI system injures or mistreats a child that it is the fault of the AI and that the AI should shoulder the burden of responsibility. This is pretty much nonsensical thinking in today's era of AI. Please realize that there is no AI today that is sentient. We don't have sentient AI and we don't know when or if we will have sentient AI. Saying that an AI system is the accountable party for damages, or the responsible perpetrator of a crime is disingenuous at this time..

From a bottom-line perspective about bearing the responsibility for AI that goes off the rails, you have to realize that it takes a village to devise and field AI. This can include the company leaders that oversaw the AI coming to fruition. There are teams of AI developers that were instrumental in the AI being formulated. You have to also include those that fielded the AI and made it available for use. All in all, a lot of humans are to be held accountable. The AI cannot be and won't be for quite a while, until if ever or until the AI attains some variant of legal personhood.

Let's get back to the crucial insight that AI aimed at adults might nonetheless ultimately get into the hands of children.

Developers of AI that omit that possibility are in for a rude awakening when they get sued or hauled into court. Simply shrugging your shoulders and saying that you hadn't thought about it is not going to garner you much sympathy.

Admittedly, you might have to be somewhat creative in your design efforts of imagining what a child might do when coming into contact with the AI, but that's part of what a properly-minded AI developer needs to consider. The WEF study makes this quite clear: "Companies should keep in mind that children often use AI products that were not designed specifically for them. It's sometimes difficult to predict what products might later be used by children or youth. As a result, you should carefully consider whether children or youth might be users of the technology you're developing."

Here's what I do when devising AI systems. I consider the full range of usage possibilities:

a) AI used by one adult alone (at a time)
b) AI used by several adults at the same time
c) AI used by an adult accompanied by a child
d) AI used by a child (just one at a time) and no adults at hand
e) AI used by several children at the same time (no adults at hand)

I'll be identifying some real-world examples of those possibilities when I later on herein discuss how AI and children ought to be an erstwhile consideration in the making and fielding of autonomous self-driving cars. Hang onto your hat for that interesting assessment.

AI that is used by adults can be tricky and make sordid attempts to pull the wool over the eyes of grown-ups. Though that shouldn't be happening, we have to expect that it will occur. Adults need to be on their toes at all times when interacting with AI systems. Sorry to say, that is the price of being an adult.

We don't likely think that children should be in that same precarious predicament. Expecting that kids should be on alert and continually suspicious of AI is just not a reasonable presumptive notion. Children are generally classified as so-called *vulnerable users* when it comes to AI systems. Kids do not particularly have the cognitive wherewithal to be watchful and know when the AI is taking advantage of them (I would dare say, adults struggle on such matters and we would ostensibly assume that children will be even more vulnerable, which, despite the chance that sometimes kids are in fact more attentive than adults we cannot take that as the steadfast rule).

You might be puzzled as to why anyone would be thinking that AI might do bad things. Isn't AI supposed to be good for us? Aren't we heralding the arrival of contemporary AI? Headlines in the latest news reports and as blaring on social media proclaim that we should sound the trumpets for the arrival of each new AI system that gets summarily announced daily.

You might be aware that when the latest era of AI got underway there was a huge burst of enthusiasm for what some now call *AI For Good*. Unfortunately, on the heels of that gushing excitement, we began to witness *AI For Bad*. For example, various AI-based facial recognition systems have been revealed as containing racial biases.

Efforts to fight back against *AI For Bad* are actively underway. Besides vociferous *legal* pursuits of reining in the wrongdoing, there is also a substantive push toward embracing AI Ethics to righten the AI vileness. The notion is that we ought to adopt and endorse key Ethical AI principles for the development and fielding of AI doing so to undercut the *AI For Bad* and simultaneously heralding and promoting the preferable *AI For Good*.

I've also discussed various collective analyses of AI ethics principles, including having covered a set devised by researchers that examined and condensed the essence of numerous national and international AI ethics tenets in a paper entitled "The Global Landscape Of AI Ethics Guidelines" (published in *Nature*), which led to this keystone list:

- **Transparency**
- **Justice & Fairness**
- **Non-Maleficence**
- **Responsibility**
- **Privacy**
- **Beneficence**
- **Freedom & Autonomy**
- **Trust**
- **Sustainability**
- **Dignity**
- **Solidarity**

As you might directly guess, trying to pin down the specifics underlying these principles can be extremely hard to do. Even more so, the effort to turn those broad principles into something entirely tangible and detailed enough to be used when crafting AI systems is also a tough nut to crack. It is easy to overall do some handwaving about what AI Ethics precepts are and how they should be generally observed, while it is a much more complicated situation in the AI coding having to be the veritable rubber that meets the road.

The AI Ethics principles are to be utilized by AI developers, along with those that manage AI development efforts, and even those that ultimately field and perform upkeep on AI systems. All stakeholders throughout the entire AI life cycle of development and usage are considered within the scope of abiding by the being-established norms of Ethical AI. This is an important highlight since the usual assumption is that "only coders" or those that program the AI is subject to adhering to the AI Ethics notions. As earlier stated, it takes a village to devise and field AI, and for which the entire village has to be versed in and abide by AI Ethics precepts.

How can we apply the AI Ethics principles in the specific context of AI and children?

Easy-peasy.

An especially substantive aspect entails the apt admission of what your AI is targeting in terms of the uses envisioned. This is part and parcel of the Ethical AI rule of transparency.

The WEF study has proposed that we should be labeling AI in somewhat the same manner that we label other products and services in our society. You go to the grocery store and expect to be able to look at cans of food that have labels denoting what the food consists of. When you use a drive-thru at a fast-food eatery, many of them nowadays display the calories and sugar composition in the proffered food. All kinds of items that we buy and consume are abundantly decorated with informative labels.

Doing the same for AI systems would be quite useful.

This is how the WEF report describes the matter: "The AI labeling system is designed to be included in all AI products on their physical packaging and online accessible through a QR code. Like nutritional information on food packaging, the labeling system is intended to concisely tell consumers, including parents and guardians as well as children and youth, how the AI works and what options are available to the users. All companies are encouraged to adopt this tool to help create greater trust and transparency with the purchasers and child users of their products."

There are six keystone constructs of the WEF recommended AI labeling:

1) **Age:** What age are the technology and content designed for.
2) **Accessibility:** Can users with different abilities and backgrounds use it.
3) **Sensors**: Does it watch or listen to a user with cameras and microphones.
4) **Networks:** Can users play with and talk with other people when using it.
5) **AI Use:** How does it use AI to interact with users.
6) **Data Use:** Does it collect personal information.

Envision that a parent or guardian could inspect such a label so that they could make a reasoned decision about whether to allow their child to interact with the labeled AI. Rather than parents or guardians being completely in the dark about what the AI is likely to do, they would have some semblance of what the AI seems to contain. For doting parents and guardians, this would be prized and eagerly welcomed.

I'm sure that the skeptics among you are somewhat dubious about AI labeling.

First, the AI labeling might be a lie. The company or developers might fib on the label. In that case, the parent or guardian is no better off, and indeed might be worse off due to letting down their guard based on their belief that the label is true and accurate. Yes, this is definitely a possibility. Of course, just like any labeling, there needs to be skin in the game and a means of going after those that distort or outright lie on their AI label indications.

As I've covered many times, we are heading toward a slew of new regulations and laws that are going to deal with the governance of AI. This is a foregone conclusion. Up until now, society has pretty much assumed that the unethical and unlawful AI promulgators would get their justice served via a conventional means of detection and enforcement. Since that hasn't been entirely satisfactory, and since AI is increasingly becoming ubiquitous, you can fully expect all manner of legal stipulations that will focus on AI.

In addition, one would hope that market mechanisms will also come to play. If a firm that labels its AI falsely is caught red-handed doing so, the assumption is that market forces will hit them like a truck. People will not buy or subscribe to AI. The reputation of the entity will suffer. Those that bought or licensed the AI on false pretenses of the AI labeling will sue for false representations. And so on.

I suppose that a fervent skeptic would have additional qualms about the AI labeling.

For example, in a cynical fashion, the claim might be that parents and guardians won't read the AI labels. Just as most adults do not read labels on food packaging and as displayed on ordering menus, we would likely assume that few parents or guardians will take the time to inspect an AI label.

Though I concede that this is bound to happen, trying to on this basis alone sweep away the value of having the AI labels is like tossing the baby out with the bathwater (well, that's an old adage that maybe needs retiring). Some people will carefully and fully study the AI labels. Meanwhile, some people will only give a cursory glance. There are of course going to be some people that ignore the AI labels entirely.

But you need to have the labels to at least ensure that those that will read them are able to have the AI labels available. On top of that, you can stridently argue that the very need to have an AI label will undoubtedly get many AI makers to be more thoughtful about the nature of their AI. I'm suggesting that even if very few people read the AI label, the firm has to be mindful that in the end they will be held responsible for whatever the AI label says. That by itself will hopefully prompt AI developers and companies crafting AI into being more respectful of AI Ethics than otherwise might be the case.

If you want to debate the proposed AI labeling scheme, I'm all ears on that. Maybe we need more than the six factors. It seems unlikely that we need less. Perhaps a scoring and weighting component is needed. All in all, landing on the best possible AI labeling approach is a sensible and reasonable aspiration. Avoiding an AI labeling scheme or denouncing the very existence of AI labeling is seemingly out of touch and does not help the ever-expanding use of AI that will get into the hands of our children.

Okay, with that last remark, I'm sure that some will contend that AI labeling is being set up as some kind of silver bullet. Nobody said that. It is one of the numerous steps and important protective measures that we need to undertake. An entire portfolio of AI Ethics approaches and cross-pollinating angles is needed.

On the portfolio notion, those of you that are familiar with prior efforts in analyzing the impacts of AI and children might recall that UNICEF published a report last year that contained some quite valuable discernments on this particular subject. In their *Policy Guidance On AI For Children* study, an especially memorable portion delineates a list of nine major requirements and recommendations:

1. Support children's development and well-being ("Let AI help me develop to my full potential")
2. Ensure inclusion of and for children ("Include me and those around me")
3. Prioritize fairness and non-discrimination for children ("AI must be for all children")
4. Protect children's data and privacy ("Ensure my privacy in an AI world")

5. Ensure safety for children ("I need to be safe in the AI world)
6. Provide transparency, explainability, and accountability for children ("I need to know how AI impacts me. You need to be accountable for that)
7. Empower governments and businesses with knowledge of AI and children's rights ("You must know what my rights are and uphold them")
8. Prepare children for present and future developments in AI ("If I am well prepared now, I can contribute to responsible AI for the future")
9. Create an enabling environment ("Make it possible for all to contribute to child-centered AI")

Those are worthy of being inscribed into a veritable hall-of-fame dedicated to AI and children.

At this juncture of this weighty discussion, I'd bet that you are desirous of some further examples that might showcase the concerns about AI that are used by or for children. There is a special and assuredly popular set of examples that are close to my heart. You see, in my capacity as an expert on AI including the ethical and legal ramifications, I am frequently asked to identify realistic examples that showcase AI Ethics dilemmas so that the somewhat theoretical nature of the topic can be more readily grasped. One of the most evocative areas that vividly presents this ethical AI quandary is the advent of AI-based true self-driving cars. This will serve as a handy use case or exemplar for ample discussion on the topic.

Here's then a noteworthy question that is worth contemplating: *Does the advent of AI-based true self-driving cars illuminate anything about AI that is used by or for children, and if so, what does this showcase?*

Allow me a moment to unpack the question..

Envision that an AI-based self-driving car is underway on your neighborhood streets and seems to be driving safely. At first, you had devoted special attention to each time that you managed to catch a glimpse of the self-driving car.

The autonomous vehicle stood out with its rack of electronic sensors that included video cameras, radar units, LIDAR devices, and the like. After many weeks of the self-driving car cruising around your community, you now barely notice it. As far as you are concerned, it is merely another car on the already busy public roadways.

Probably the main reason right now that they might notice the autonomous vehicles is because of the irritation and exasperation factor. The by-the-book AI driving systems make sure the cars are obeying all speed limits and rules of the road. For hectic human drivers in their traditional human-driven cars, you get irked at times when stuck behind the strictly law-abiding AI-based self-driving cars.

That's something we might all need to get accustomed to, rightfully or wrongly.

Back to our tale.

A youngster gets into a self-driving car for a lift home from school. I realize that you might be somewhat puzzled about the possibility of a non-adult riding in a self-driving car that is absent of any adult supervision. For human-driven cars, there is always an adult in the vehicle due to the need for an adult to be at the driving wheel. With self-driving cars, there won't be any need for a human driver and therefore no longer an axiomatic need for an adult in the autonomous vehicle.

Some have said that they would never allow their child to ride in a self-driving car without having a trusted adult also in the autonomous vehicle. The logic is that the lack of adult supervision could result in quite untoward and serious consequences. A child might get themselves in trouble while inside the self-driving car and there wouldn't be an adult present to help them.

Though there is certainly abundant logic in that concern, I have predicted that we will eventually accept the idea of children riding in self-driving cars by themselves.

In fact, the widespread use of self-driving cars for transporting kids from here to there such as to school, over to baseball practice, or their piano lessons is going to become commonplace. I have also asserted that there will need to be limitations or conditions placed on this usage, likely via new regulations and laws that for example stipulate the youngest allowed ages. Having a newborn baby riding alone in a self-driving car is a bridge too far in such usage.

All of that being said, the assumption right now by many of the automakers and self-driving tech firms is that self-driving cars will either be roaming around empty or they will have at least one adult rider present. This will simply be an edict or stated requirement, namely that no children may ride in a self-driving car without an adult present. That certainly eases the dilemma of having to program the AI driving system to contend with having just children in the autonomous vehicle.

You cannot especially blame the firms for taking that stance. They have enough on their hands when dealing with simply getting the AI driving system to safely drive a self-driving car from point A to point B. The assumption is that the rider will be an adult and that the adult will do the proper adult-like activities while inside a self-driving car. This has been essentially the case so far during the public roadway tryouts, since the adults are typically pre-screened, or the adults are so excited about being in a self-driving car that they are mindful of being courteous and obediently quiet.

I can assure you that as we shift into a widening of the tryouts, this rather convenient setup is going to begin to fall apart. Adults will want to bring their kids with them while riding in a self-driving car. The kids will act up. Sometimes the adult will do the right thing and keep the kids from going nuts. Other times the adult will not do so.

Who holds the responsibility when an adult lets a kid do something amiss while riding inside a self-driving car?

I'm sure that you are assuming that the adult has full accountability. Maybe so, maybe not. The argument could be made that the automaker or self-driving tech firm or fleet operator allowed an environment to exist in which a child was able to get harmed, despite the presence of the adult. With the huge amount of money that many of these firms have, you can absolutely anticipate that when a child gets somehow harmed, there will be determined efforts to go after those that made or fielded the autonomous vehicle. Money talks.

That's a lifetime guarantee.

Eventually, we will likely see instances of just becoming adults that will be riding alone in self-driving cars. Assume that the standard age of an adult is say 18. Someone that had their 18th birthday last week decides they want to go for a ride in a self-driving car. Assume that the firm always does an age check and in this case, the rider is seemingly an adult.

This "adult" brings into the self-driving car their friends that are ages 15 and 16. What might teenagers do while going for a ride in a self-driving car? I'll get to that in a moment. I realize that you might want to argue that an adult of say age 50 could readily bring a youngster into the self-driving car and let those kids go wild. In essence, it shouldn't in theory make a difference whether the adult is barely an adult versus a more seasoned adult. All I can say is, that some would vehemently argue there is a likely difference, on the average and in the aggregate.

Suppose an adult starts a ride with a youngster and then gets out of the autonomous vehicle, leaving the youngster alone in the self-driving car. Hopefully, the AI driving system would be programmed to detect this, perhaps due to the door being opened or maybe due to using video cameras to inspect the interior of the self-driving car.

The point is that all kinds of shenanigans are going to arise. At some point, there might be enough marketplace demand for letting youngsters go in a self-driving car without having an adult present that some of the automakers or fleet operators will decide it is a money-making option and worth the risks.

People at first might sign all sorts of hefty waivers about letting their kids go in a self-driving car in this kind of arrangement.

Keep in mind that there is also the opportunity to monitor the kids that are in a self-driving car. You see, most of the self-driving cars will be outfitted with video cameras pointing into the vehicle. This can allow for doing online video courses while you are riding in a self-driving car or perhaps interacting with your office mates at work. The feature can also be used to see what the kids inside the self-driving car are doing.

For example, you send your youngster to school via the convenient use of a self-driving car. This relieves you of having to drive your offspring. Meanwhile, you pull up on your smartphone a screen that will show you the interior of the self-driving car while your kid is riding in it. You talk with your child. Your child talks with you. This might keep any antics to a minimum.

In any case, back to my initial indication, assume that a youngster gets into a self-driving car.

During the ride, the AI driving system carries on an interactive dialogue with the youngster, akin to how Alexa or Siri have discourse with people. Nothing seems unusual or oddball about that kind of AI and human conversational interaction.

At one point, the AI advises the youngster that when they get a chance to do so, a fun thing to do would be to stick a penny in an electrical socket. What? That is nutty, you say. You might even be insistent that such an AI utterance could never happen.

Except for the fact that it did happen. The news at the time reported that Alexa had told a 10-year-old girl to put a penny in an electrical socket. The girl was at home and using Alexa to find something fun to do. Luckily, the mother of the girl was within earshot, heard Alexa suggest the ill-advised activity, and told her daughter that this was something immensely dangerous and should assuredly not be done.

Why did Alexa utter such a clearly alarming piece of advice?

According to the Alexa developers, the AI underlying Alexa managed to computationally pluck from the Internet a widespread viral bit of crazy advice that had once been popular. Since the advice had seemingly been readily shared online, the AI system simply repeated it. This is precisely the kind of difficulty that I earlier raised about AI systems and the audience aimed at.

It would seem that the base assumption was that adults would be using Alexa in this context. An adult would presumably realize that putting a penny into an electrical socket is a zany idea. Apparently, there wasn't any system guardrail that tried to first analyze the utterance as to what might happen if a child was given this piece of advice (if there was such a guardrail, it didn't work in this instance or was somehow otherwise bypassed, though that too needs to be given due consideration).

As a reminder, here's what those devising and fielding AI should be considering:

a) AI used by one adult alone (at a time)
b) AI used by several adults at the same time
c) AI used by an adult accompanied by a child
d) AI used by a child (just one at a time) and no adults at hand
e) AI used by several children at the same time (no adults at hand)

It would seem that this instance was saved by landing into the category "c" whereby an adult was present. But what if the parent had been in another room of the house and not within earshot. That would land us in the "d" category.

Think of the scary result in the case of the self-driving car. The youngster arrives home and rushes to find a penny. Before the parents get a chance to say hello to the child and welcome the youngster home, the kid is forcing a penny into an electrical socket. Yikes!

Speaking of kids, let's shift our attention to teenagers.

You probably know that teenagers will often perform daring feats that are unwise. If a parent tells them to do something, they might refuse to do it simply because it was an adult that told them what to do. If a fellow teenager tells them to do something, and even if it is highly questionable, a teenager might do it anyway.

What happens when AI provides questionable advice to a teenager?

Some teenagers might ignore the unsavory advice. Some might believe the advice because it came from a machine and they assume that the AI is neutral and reliable. Others might relish the advice due to the belief that they can act unethically and handily blame the AI for having prodded or goaded them into an unethical act.

Teens are savvy in such ways.

Suppose the AI driving system advises a teenager that is riding in the self-driving car to go ahead and use their parent's credit card to buy an expensive video game. The teen welcomes doing so. They knew that normally they were required to check with their parents before making any purchases on the family credit card, but in this case, the AI advised that the purchase be undertaken. From the teen's perspective, it is nearly akin to a Monopoly game get out of jail free card, namely just tell your parents that the AI told you to do it.

I don't want to get gloomy but there are much worse pieces of radically bad advice that the AI could spew to a teenager. For example, suppose the AI advises the teen that should cast open the car windows, extend themselves out of the autonomous vehicle, and wave and holler to their heart's content. This is a dangerous practice that I've predicted might become a viral sensation when self-driving cars first become relatively popular.

Why in the world would an AI system suggest an ill-advised stunt like that?

The easiest answer is that the AI is doing a text regurgitation, similar to the instance of Alexa and the penny in the electric socket saga. Another possibility is that the AI-generated the utterance, perhaps based on some other byzantine set of computations. Realize that today's AI has no semblance of cognition and no capacity for common sense. Whereas it would certainly strike you as a crazy thing for the AI to emit, the computational path that led to the utterance doesn't need to have any humanly sensible intentions.

Conclusion

In a world in which AI is going to be ubiquitous, we have to be on our alert about AI that interacts or in some fashion dovetails into coming in contact with children.

We can lean into the United Nations and its *Convention on the Rights of the Child (CRC)*, proffering a myriad of vital principles underlying the rights and safety of children, for which this is a cornerstone clause: "In all actions concerning children, whether undertaken by public or private social welfare institutions, courts of law, administrative authorities or legislative bodies, the best interests of the child shall be a primary consideration."

Can we get all of the varied stakeholders that surround everyday AI systems to be cognizant that AI and children matter?

It will be an uphill battle, that's for darned sure.

Needed efforts encompass:

- We need to increase awareness about the AI and children topic all told throughout society
- AI development methodologies must include the AI-for-kids considerations
- Laws need to take into account the concerns about AI for children
- Adoption of an AI labeling approach ought to be undertaken
- AI developers need to have AI-for-Kids Ethics on their minds and get training as needed
- Parents and guardians must come forward wanting AI-for-kids

disclosures
- Top executives have to take seriously and purposefully the matter of AI and children
- Etc.

As a final remark for now, whenever you talk about children and the future, a sage bit of wisdom ought to be in your mind at all times.

Here it is: *Children are the living messages we send to a time we will not see* (so said, John F. Kennedy).

Let's send our children into a future in which AI has beneficially shaped them and not misshapen them.

Please go ahead and make your solemn and ironclad pledge for that future aspiration, doing so today and before it is too late.

CHAPTER 10
AI ETHICS AND AI BIASES STANDARDS

Have you ever played fifty-two card pick-up?

It is not a game that you would normally willingly undertake. Here's why. Someone offers to you that it is an allegedly fun sport and if you take the sweet bait they then toss an entire deck of playing cards into the air and summarily onto the floor. The person then gives you a cheeky smile and tells you to go ahead and pick up the cards. That's the entire game.

Prankster!

I do have a somewhat thoughtful question to ask you about this.

Suppose that one of the cards slipped underneath a nearby sofa. When you had finished picking up all the cards, you would know that one was missing because there would only be fifty-one in your hand.

The question is, could you determine which card was missing?

I'm sure that you would immediately say that you could easily figure out which card was not in your hands. All you would have to do is put the deck into order. You know that a standard deck consists of four suits and that within each suit the cards are numbered from one to ten and then into Jack, Queen, and King.

You know this because a standard deck of playing cards is based on a standard.

Whoa, that statement might seem like one of those totally obvious assertions. Well, yes, of course, a standard playing deck is based on a standard. We all know that. My point is that by having a standard we can rely upon the standard when so needed.

Besides being able to deduce what card is missing from a deck, you can also readily play zillions of well-known card games with other people. Once someone is told the rules of a game, they are directly able to play because they already fully know what the deck consists of. You don't need to explain to them that the deck has four suits and variously numbered cards. They already know that to be the case.

Where am I going with this?

I am trying to take you down a path that is a vital means of making progress in the field of AI and especially the realm of AI Ethics and Ethical AI. You see, we need to try and come up with widespread and all-agreed upon standards about AI Ethics. If we can do so, it will enhance the ease of getting adoption of Ethical AI and demonstrably aim to improve the AI systems that keep getting pell-mell tossed into the marketplace (like an unnumbered and unordered deck of wild cards).

One particular segment or portion of AI Ethics that has been getting a lot of media attention consists of AI that exhibits untoward biases and inequities. You might be aware that when the latest era of AI got underway there was a huge burst of enthusiasm for what some now call *AI For Good.* Unfortunately, on the heels of that gushing excitement, we began to witness *AI For Bad.* For example, various AI-based facial recognition systems have been revealed as containing racial biases and gender biases.

Efforts to fight back against *AI For Bad* are actively underway. Besides vociferous *legal* pursuits of reining in the wrongdoing, there is also a substantive push toward embracing AI Ethics to righten the AI vileness. The notion is that we ought to adopt and endorse key Ethical AI principles for the development and fielding of AI doing so to undercut the *AI For Bad* and simultaneously heralding and promoting the preferable *AI For Good.*

In a moment, I'll share with you some overarching principles underlying AI Ethics.

There are lots of these kinds of lists floating around here and there. You could say that there isn't as yet a singular list of universal appeal and concurrence. That's the unfortunate news. The good news is that at least there are readily available AI Ethics lists and they tend to be quite similar. All told, this suggests that by a form of reasoned convergence of sorts that we are finding our way toward a general commonality of what AI Ethics consists of.

I bring this up to provide a foundation for my discussion herein that will focus on a particular segment or portion of the broader realm of AI Ethics, namely as mentioned earlier the specific element of AI biases. The reason too that I share this topic with you is that a newly released document by the National Institute of Standards and Technology (NIST) is trying to get us to inch our way toward a standard characterizing AI biases. The document is entitled *Towards A Standard For Identifying And Managing Bias In Artificial Intelligence* by authors Reva Schwartz, Apostol Vassilev, Kristen Greene, Lori Perine, Andrew Burt, and Patrick Hall, and was published by U.S. Department of Commerce, NIST Special Publication 1270, in March 2022.

We will be unpacking this handy and encouraging effort toward establishing what we mean by AI biases. The old saying is that you cannot manage that which you cannot measure. By having a standard that lays out the variety of AI biases, you can begin to measure and manage the AI biases scourge.

First, let's cover briefly some of the overall Ethical AI precepts to illustrate what ought to be a vital consideration for anyone crafting, fielding, or using AI.

For example, as stated by the Vatican in the *Rome Call For AI Ethics* and as I've covered in-depth, these are their identified six primary AI ethics principles:

- **Transparency:** In principle, AI systems must be explainable
- **Inclusion:** The needs of all human beings must be taken into consideration so that everyone can benefit, and all individuals can be offered the best possible conditions to express themselves and develop

- **Responsibility:** Those who design and deploy the use of AI must proceed with responsibility and transparency
- **Impartiality:** Do not create or act according to bias, thus safeguarding fairness and human dignity
- **Reliability:** AI systems must be able to work reliably
- **Security and privacy:** AI systems must work securely and respect the privacy of users.

As stated by the U.S. Department of Defense (DoD) in their *Ethical Principles For The Use Of Artificial Intelligence*, these are their six primary AI ethics principles:

- **Responsible:** DoD personnel will exercise appropriate levels of judgment and care while remaining responsible for the development, deployment, and use of AI capabilities.
- **Equitable:** The Department will take deliberate steps to minimize unintended bias in AI capabilities.
- **Traceable:** The Department's AI capabilities will be developed and deployed such that relevant personnel possesses an appropriate understanding of the technology, development processes, and operational methods applicable to AI capabilities, including with transparent and auditable methodologies, data sources, and design procedure and documentation.
- **Reliable:** The Department's AI capabilities will have explicit, well-defined uses, and the safety, security, and effectiveness of such capabilities will be subject to testing and assurance within those defined uses across their entire lifecycles.
- **Governable:** The Department will design and engineer AI capabilities to fulfill their intended functions while possessing the ability to detect and avoid unintended consequences, and the ability to disengage or deactivate deployed systems that demonstrate unintended behavior.

I've also discussed various collective analyses of AI ethics principles, including having covered a set devised by researchers that examined and condensed the essence of numerous national and international AI ethics tenets in a paper entitled "The Global Landscape Of AI Ethics Guidelines" (published in *Nature*), which led to this keystone list:

- **Transparency**
- **Justice & Fairness**
- **Non-Maleficence**
- **Responsibility**
- **Privacy**
- **Beneficence**
- **Freedom & Autonomy**
- **Trust**
- **Sustainability**
- **Dignity**
- **Solidarity**

As you might directly guess, trying to pin down the specifics underlying these principles can be extremely hard to do. Even more so, the effort to turn those broad principles into something entirely tangible and detailed enough to be used when crafting AI systems is also a tough nut to crack. It is easy to overall do some handwaving about what AI Ethics precepts are and how they should be generally observed, while it is a much more complicated situation in the AI coding having to be the veritable rubber that meets the road.

The AI Ethics principles are to be utilized by AI developers, along with those that manage AI development efforts, and even those that ultimately field and perform upkeep on AI systems. All stakeholders throughout the entire AI life cycle of development and usage are considered within the scope of abiding by the being-established norms of Ethical AI. This is an important highlight since the usual assumption is that "only coders" or those that program the AI is subject to adhering to the AI Ethics notions. As earlier stated, it takes a village to devise and field AI, and for which the entire village has to be versed in and abide by AI Ethics precepts.

Underlying many of those key AI Ethics precepts is the insidious nature of AI biases.

Just like a deck of cards, it sure would be nifty if we could somehow group together the AI biases into a set of "suits" or categories. Indeed, the NIST document proffers a suggested grouping.

Three major categories are being proposed:

1) **Systemic Biases**
2) **Statistical and Computational Biases**
3) **Human Biases**

Whether all AI biases fit neatly within one of those three categories is certainly something to be considered. You can assuredly argue that some AI biases fall into one, two, or all three categories at the same time. Furthermore, you might claim that more categories deserve to be mentioned, such as some fourth, fifth, sixth, or more series of groupings.

I hope that's what you are thinking because we need to get everyone involved in helping to shape these standards. If you are riled up with the way that these standards are first shaping up, I urge you to turn that energy into aiding the rest of us in making those budding standards as robust and complete as they can be carved into.

For now, we can take a closer look at the proposed three categories and see what kind of a hand we've been dealt with so far (yes, I am going to continue to use an analogy to a deck of playing cards, doing so throughout the entirety of this written piece, you can bet your bottom dollar on that not so hidden ace of a theme).

What is meant by referring to systemic biases?

Here's what the NIST document says: "Systemic biases result from procedures and practices of particular institutions that operate in ways which result in certain social groups being advantaged or favored and others being disadvantaged or devalued. This need not be the result of any conscious prejudice or discrimination but rather of the majority following existing rules or norms. Institutional racism and sexism are the most common examples" (note that this is merely a short excerpt and readers are encouraged to see the fuller explanation).

AI comes into the mix of systemic biases by providing a means of conveying and applying those biases in AI-based apps. Whenever you use an AI-infused piece of software, for all you know it might contain a slew of biases that are already baked into the system via the companies and industry practices that led to the making of the AI. As per the NIST study: "These biases are present in the datasets used in AI, and the institutional norms, practices, and processes across the AI lifecycle and in broader culture and society."

Next, consider the set of biases that are labeled as being statistical and computational biases.

The NIST document states this: "Statistical and computational biases stem from errors that result when the sample is not representative of the population. These biases arise from systematic as opposed to random error and can occur in the absence of prejudice, partiality, or discriminatory intent. In AI systems, these biases are present in the datasets and algorithmic processes used in the development of AI applications, and often arise when algorithms are trained on one type of data and cannot extrapolate beyond those data."

This type of statistical and computational bias is often cooked into an AI system that uses Machine Learning (ML) and Deep Learning (DL). Bringing up the hefty matter of contemporary ML/DL necessitates a related side tangent about what AI is and what ML/DL is.

Let's make sure we are on the same page about the nature of today's AI.

There isn't any AI today that is sentient. We don't have this. We don't know if sentient AI will be possible. Nobody can aptly predict whether we will attain sentient AI, nor whether sentient AI will somehow miraculously spontaneously arise in a form of computational cognitive supernova (usually referred to as the singularity).

The type of AI that I am focusing on consists of the non-sentient AI that we have today. If we wanted to wildly speculate about *sentient* AI, this discussion could go in a radically different direction. A sentient AI would supposedly be of human quality. You would need to consider that the sentient AI is the cognitive equivalent of a human. More so, since some speculate we might have super-intelligent AI, it is conceivable that such AI could end up being smarter than humans (for my exploration of super-intelligent AI as a possibility).

Let's keep things more down to earth and consider today's computational non-sentient AI.

Realize that today's AI is not able to "think" in any fashion on par with human thinking. When you interact with Alexa or Siri, the conversational capacities might seem akin to human capacities, but the reality is that it is computational and lacks human cognition. The latest era of AI has made extensive use of Machine Learning and Deep Learning, which leverage computational pattern matching. This has led to AI systems that have the appearance of human-like proclivities. Meanwhile, there isn't any AI today that has a semblance of common sense and nor has any of the cognitive wonderment of robust human thinking.

ML/DL is a form of computational pattern matching. The usual approach is that you assemble data about a decision-making task. You feed the data into the ML/DL computer models. Those models seek to find mathematical patterns. After finding such patterns, if so found, the AI system then will use those patterns when encountering new data. Upon the presentation of new data, the patterns based on the "old" or historical data are applied to render a current decision.

I think you can guess where this is heading. If humans that have been making the patterned upon decisions have been incorporating untoward biases, the odds are that the data reflects this in subtle but significant ways. Machine Learning or Deep Learning computational pattern matching will simply try to mathematically mimic the data accordingly. There is no semblance of common sense or other sentient aspects of AI-crafted modeling per se.

Furthermore, the AI developers might not realize what is going on either. The arcane mathematics in the ML/DL might make it difficult to ferret out the now hidden biases. You would rightfully hope and expect that the AI developers would test for the potentially buried biases, though this is trickier than it might seem. A solid chance exists that even with relatively extensive testing that there will be biases still embedded within the pattern matching models of the ML/DL.

You could somewhat use the famous or infamous adage of garbage-in garbage-out. The thing is, this is more akin to biases-in that insidiously get infused as biases submerged within the AI. The algorithm decision-making (ADM) of AI axiomatically becomes laden with inequities.

Not good.

This brings us squarely to the third category of the NIST set of three groupings, specifically the role of human biases in the emergence of AI biases. Here's what the NIST document indicated: "Human biases reflect systematic errors in human thought based on a limited number of heuristic principles and predicting values to simpler judgmental operations. These biases are often implicit and tend to relate to how an individual or group perceives information (such as automated AI output) to make a decision or fill in missing or unknown information. These biases are omnipresent in the institutional, group, and individual decision-making processes across the AI lifecycle, and in the use of AI applications once deployed."

You've now gotten a rapid-fire introduction to the three categories.

I'd like to share with you some additional food for thought as expressed in the NIST document. A chart in their narrative provides a useful summary of the key questions and considerations that underlie each of the three sets of AI biases. I list them here for your convenience of reference and edification.

#1: Systemic Biases

- Who is counted and who is not counted?
    - Issues with latent variables
    - Underrepresentation of marginalized groups

- What is important?
    - Automation of inequalities
    - Underrepresentation in determining utility function
    - Processes that favor the majority/minority
    - Cultural bias in the objective function (best for individuals vs best for the group)

- How do we know what is right?
    - Reinforcement of inequalities (groups are impacted more with higher use of AI)
    - Predictive policing more negatively impacted
    - Widespread adoption of ridesharing/self-driving cars/etc. may change policies that impact population based on use

#2: Statistical and Computational Biases

- Who is counted and who is not counted?
    - Sampling and selection bias
    - Using proxy variables because they are easier to measure
    - Automation bias

- What is important?
    - Likert scale (categorical to ordinal to cardinal)
    - Nonlinear vs linear
    - Ecological fallacy

- Minimizing the L1 vs. L2 norm
- General difficulty in quantifying contextual phenomena

- How do we know what is right?
  - Lack of adequate cross-validation
  - Survivorship bias
  - Difficulty with fairness

#3: Human Biases

- Who is counted and who is not counted?
  - Observational bias (streetlight effect)
  - Availability bias (anchoring)
  - McNamara fallacy

- What is important?
  - Groupthink leads to narrow choices
  - Rashomon effect leads to subjective advocacy
  - Difficulty in quantifying objectives may lead to McNamara fallacy

- How do we know what is right?
  - Confirmation bias
  - Automation bias

At this juncture of this weighty discussion, I'd bet that you are desirous of some illustrative examples that might showcase the three categories of AI biases. There is a special and assuredly popular set of examples that are close to my heart. You see, in my capacity as an expert on AI including the ethical and legal ramifications, I am frequently asked to identify realistic examples that showcase AI Ethics dilemmas so that the somewhat theoretical nature of the topic can be more readily grasped. One of the most evocative areas that vividly presents this ethical AI quandary is the advent of AI-based true self-driving cars. This will serve as a handy use case or exemplar for ample discussion on the topic.

Here's then a noteworthy question that is worth contemplating: *Does the advent of AI-based true self-driving cars illuminate anything about the three proposed categories of AI biases, and if so, what does this showcase?*

Allow me a moment to unpack the question.

Envision that an AI-based self-driving car is underway on your neighborhood streets and seems to be driving safely. At first, you had devoted special attention to each time that you managed to catch a glimpse of the self-driving car. The autonomous vehicle stood out with its rack of electronic sensors that included video cameras, radar units, LIDAR devices, and the like. After many weeks of the self-driving car cruising around your community, you now barely notice it. As far as you are concerned, it is merely another car on the already busy public roadways.

Probably the main reason right now that they might notice the autonomous vehicles is because of the irritation and exasperation factor. The by-the-book AI driving systems make sure the cars are obeying all speed limits and rules of the road. For hectic human drivers in their traditional human-driven cars, you get irked at times when stuck behind the strictly law-abiding AI-based self-driving cars.

That's something we might all need to get accustomed to, rightfully or wrongly.

Back to our tale.

We shall consider next how systemic biases might come to play in this context of self-driving cars.

Some pundits are very worried that self-driving cars will be the province of only the wealthy and the elite. It could be that the cost to use self-driving cars will be prohibitively expensive. Unless you've got big bucks, you might not ever see the inside of a self-driving car. Those that will be utilizing self-driving cars are going to have to be rich, it is purportedly contended.

As such, some disconcertingly exhort that a form of systemic bias will permeate the advent of AI-based self-driving cars. The overall autonomous vehicle industrial system as a whole will keep self-driving cars out of the hands of those that are poor or less affluent. This might not necessarily be by overt intent and just turns out that the only believed way to recoup the burdensome costs of having invented self-driving cars will be to charge outrageously high prices.

If you retort that today there are these self-driving car tryouts that are allowing the everyday person to use, thus it seems apparent that you don't need to be rich per se, the counterargument is that this is a kind of shell game as it were. The automakers and self-driving tech firms are supposedly willing to make it appear as though the cost will not be a substantive barrier. They are doing this for public relations purposes right now and will jack up the prices once they get the wrinkles figured out. A conspiracist might even claim that the "guinea pigs" as everyday persons are being perniciously used to enable the rich to ultimately get richer.

So, given that rather contentious matter, and putting my own two cents on this sordid topic, I do not believe that self-driving cars will be outpriced for everyday use.

Moving on, we can next consider the matter of AI-related statistical and computational biases.

Contemplate the seemingly inconsequential question of where self-driving cars will be roaming to pick up passengers. This seems like an abundantly innocuous topic. We will use the tale of the town or city that has self-driving cars to highlight the perhaps surprisingly potential specter of AI-related statistical and computational biases.

At first, assume that the AI was roaming the self-driving cars throughout the entire town. Anybody that wanted to request a ride in the self-driving car had essentially an equal chance of hailing one. Gradually, the AI began to primarily keep the self-driving cars roaming in just one section of town. This section was a greater money-maker and the AI system had been programmed to try and maximize revenues as part of the usage in the community.

Community members in the impoverished parts of the town were less likely to be able to get a ride from a self-driving car. This was because the self-driving cars were further away and roaming in the higher revenue part of the locale. When a request came in from a distant part of town, any request from a closer location that was likely in the "esteemed" part of town would get a higher priority. Eventually, the availability of getting a self-driving car in any place other than the richer part of town was nearly impossible, exasperatingly so for those that lived in those now resource-starved areas.

You could assert that the AI pretty much landed on a form of statistical and computational biases, akin to a form of proxy discrimination (also often referred to as indirect discrimination). The AI wasn't programmed to avoid those poorer neighborhoods. Instead, it "learned" to do so via the use of the ML/DL.

It was assumed that the AI would never fall into that kind of shameful quicksand. No specialized monitoring was set up to keep track of where the AI-based self-driving cars were going. Only after community members began to complain did the city leaders realize what was happening.

For the third category of human biases as related to AI biases, we turn to an example that involves the AI determining whether to stop for awaiting pedestrians that do not have the right-of-way to cross a street.

You've undoubtedly been driving and encountered pedestrians that were waiting to cross the street and yet they did not have the right-of-way to do so. This meant that you had discretion as to whether to stop and let them cross. You could proceed without letting them cross and still be fully within the legal driving rules of doing so.

Studies of how human drivers decide on stopping or not stopping for such pedestrians have suggested that sometimes the human drivers make the choice based on untoward biases. A human driver might eye the pedestrian and choose to not stop, even though they would have stopped had the pedestrian had a different appearance, such as based on race or gender.

Imagine that the AI-based self-driving cars are programmed to deal with the question of whether to stop or not stop for pedestrians that do not have the right-of-way. Here's how the AI developers decided to program this task. They collected data from the town's video cameras that are placed all around the city. The data showcases human drivers that stop for pedestrians that do not have the right-of-way and human drivers that do not stop. It is all collected into a large dataset.

By using Machine Learning and Deep Learning, the data is modeled computationally. The AI driving system then uses this model to decide when to stop or not stop. Generally, the idea is that whatever the local custom consists of, this is how the AI is going direct the self-driving car.

To the surprise of the city leaders and the residents, the AI was evidently opting to stop or not stop based on the age of the pedestrian. How could that happen?

Upon a closer review of the video of human driver discretion, it turns out that many of the instances of not stopping entailed pedestrians that had a walking cane of a senior citizen. Human drivers were seemingly unwilling to stop and let an aged person cross the street, presumably due to the assumed length of time that it might take for someone to make the journey. If the pedestrian looked like they could quickly dart across the street and minimize the waiting time of the driver, the drivers were more amenable to letting the person cross.

This got deeply buried into the AI driving system. The sensors of the self-driving car would scan the awaiting pedestrian, feed this data into the ML/DL model, and the model would emit to the AI whether to stop or continue. Any visual indication that the pedestrian might be slow to cross, such as the use of a walking cane, mathematically was being used to determine whether the AI driving system should let the awaiting pedestrian cross or not.

You could contend that this was a reliance on a preexisting human bias.

Conclusion

Some final thoughts for now.

There is a popular saying that you cannot change the cards that you are dealt and must instead learn how to adequately play with whatever hand you've been given.

In the case of AI biases, if we don't fervently get on top of establishing AI Ethics across the board and especially solidify the characterization of AI biases, the kinds of hands we are going to be dealt with will be overflowing with seedy unethical, and possibly unlawful stratum. We have to stop those cards from ever being dealt, to begin with. The valiant aim to create and promulgate Ethical AI standards is a crucial tool to combat the rising tsunami of upcoming *AI For Bad.*

You can decidedly take to the bank that rampant AI bias and unethical AI will be like a flimsy house of cards, imploding upon itself and likely being disastrous for all of us.

Let's play to win, doing so with suitably ethical AI.

CHAPTER 11
UNESCO HISTORIC AI ETHICS AGREEMENT

Be forewarned, there are more than you can shake a stick at.

Yes, indeed, there are so many AI Ethics guidelines popping up these days that you are perfectly right to be slightly vexed and ostensibly confused. What is going on, you might be wondering. The good news is that this is a healthy sign and something we can generally herald and cherish. Of course, there can sometimes be too much of a good thing, which I'll explain why in a moment.

First, we do in fact earnestly need a kind of NorthStar as it were of AI Ethics to aid in providing guardrails and insights for the advent of AI.

You might be aware that when the latest era of AI got underway there was a huge burst of enthusiasm for what some now call *AI For Good*. Unfortunately, on the heels of that gushing excitement, we began to witness *AI For Bad*. For example, various AI-based facial recognition systems have been revealed as containing racial biases and gender biases.

Efforts to fight back against *AI For Bad* are actively underway. Besides vociferous *legal* pursuits of reining in the wrongdoing, there is also a substantive push toward embracing AI Ethics to righten the AI vileness. The notion is that we ought to adopt and endorse key Ethical AI principles for the development and fielding of AI doing so to undercut the *AI For Bad* and simultaneously heralding and promoting the preferable *AI For Good*.

In a moment, I'll share with you some overarching principles underlying AI Ethics. There are lots of these kinds of lists floating around here and there. You could say that there isn't as yet a singular list of collective appeal and unmitigated concurrence (well, maybe kind of there is, which I'll be focusing on herein). The good news either way is that at least there are readily available AI Ethics lists and they tend to be quite similar. All told, this suggests that by a form of reasoned convergence of sorts that we are finding our way toward a general commonality of what AI Ethics consists of.

One of my favorite AI Ethics lists was released last year by the United Nations Educational, Scientific, and Cultural Organization (UNESCO). I would say it is appropriate and fair to express that this was a historic moment since the set of AI Ethics presented was adopted by nearly 200 member countries of the UN. As aptly stated by UNESCO about the dangers of AI: "We see increased gender and ethnic bias, significant threats to privacy, dignity and agency, dangers of mass surveillance, and increased use of unreliable Artificial Intelligence technologies in law enforcement, to name a few. Until now, there were no universal standards to provide an answer to these issues" (per the UNESCO posting entitled "193 Countries Adopt First-Ever Global Agreement On The Ethics Of Artificial Intelligence" on November 25, 2021).

You could reasonably argue that this AI Ethics elicitation by UNESCO is the closest thing that we have toward a truly universal and all-agreed Ethical AI stipulation. Some though prefer to describe the listing as a global normative framework. To them, the listing is useful as a backdrop, but it is not what they necessarily themselves wish to directly utilize per se.

Why so?

One viewpoint is that the UNESCO AI Ethics list is overly complicated and not easily digested (some would harshly say it uses the contortionist bloated language of diplomacy). As such, some have crafted their own Ethical AI listings and borrowed or aligned such declarations extensively with the UNESCO version.

Others had already created their AI Ethics guidelines before the UNESCO release, and upon close inspection decided that they were sufficiently in comport with the UNESCO set, thus there was no need to change their preexisting proprietary approach.

Frankly, some simply have that veritable *Not Invented Here* (NIH) mindset and have cantankerously opted to start from scratch when devising their AI Ethics principles. Or, perhaps beneficially, they want to feel a sense of pride and ownership by making their Ethical AI precepts specific to themselves. Another angle is that some pick an AI Ethics listing that has become popular in their industry or their particular niche, for which UNESCO is perhaps more broadly aimed.

And so on.

Those that are newbies to the AI Ethics realm are frequently unaware that the UNESCO AI Ethics listing exists. That's a shame. That's a darned shame. I hope to right that "wrong" by providing you herein with a tasty sampling of what the UNESCO agreement contains. Perhaps doing so will further whet your appetite to look into the AI Ethics arena all told.

For cynics among you that blather about AI Ethics lists as being nothing more than words on paper, I would fervently assert that we do need words on paper. Without some semblance of a structure or a plan, we are going to be forever lost amongst an increasingly vast and potentially endangering forest of untoward AI systems.

I relish a key quote by UNESCO Chief Audrey Azoulay that said this when the UNESCO AI Ethics principles were finally approved and published: "The world needs rules for artificial intelligence to benefit humanity. The Recommendation on the Ethics of AI is a major answer. It sets the first global normative framework while giving States the responsibility to apply it at their level. UNESCO will support its 193 Member states in its implementation and ask them to report regularly on their progress and practice" (as stated in the same UNESCO blog post noted above).

Let's cover briefly some of the overall Ethical AI precepts that I've previously discussed in my columns to herein illustrate what ought to be a vital consideration for anyone and everyone that is crafting, fielding, or using AI. We'll then take a peek at the UNESCO AI Ethics precepts.

As stated by the Vatican in the *Rome Call For AI Ethics*, these are their identified six primary AI ethics principles:

- **Transparency:** In principle, AI systems must be explainable.
- **Inclusion:** The needs of all human beings must be taken into consideration so that everyone can benefit, and all individuals can be offered the best possible conditions to express themselves and develop.
- **Responsibility:** Those who design and deploy the use of AI must proceed with responsibility and transparency.
- **Impartiality:** Do not create or act according to bias, thus safeguarding fairness and human dignity.
- **Reliability:** AI systems must be able to work reliably.
- **Security and privacy:** AI systems must work securely and respect the privacy of users.

As stated by the U.S. Department of Defense (DoD) in their *Ethical Principles For The Use Of Artificial Intelligence*, these are their six primary AI ethics principles:

- **Responsible:** DoD personnel will exercise appropriate levels of judgment and care while remaining responsible for the development, deployment, and use of AI capabilities.
- **Equitable:** The Department will take deliberate steps to minimize unintended bias in AI capabilities.
- **Traceable:** The Department's AI capabilities will be developed and deployed such that relevant personnel possesses an appropriate understanding of the technology, development processes, and operational methods applicable to AI capabilities, including with transparent and auditable methodologies, data sources, and design procedure and documentation.

- **Reliable:** The Department's AI capabilities will have explicit, well-defined uses, and the safety, security, and effectiveness of such capabilities will be subject to testing and assurance within those defined uses across their entire lifecycles.
- **Governable:** The Department will design and engineer AI capabilities to fulfill their intended functions while possessing the ability to detect and avoid unintended consequences, and the ability to disengage or deactivate deployed systems that demonstrate unintended behavior.

I've also discussed various collective analyses of AI ethics principles, including having covered a set devised by researchers that examined and condensed the essence of numerous national and international AI ethics tenets in a paper entitled "The Global Landscape Of AI Ethics Guidelines" (published in *Nature*), which led to this keystone list:

- **Transparency**
- **Justice & Fairness**
- **Non-Maleficence**
- **Responsibility**
- **Privacy**
- **Beneficence**
- **Freedom & Autonomy**
- **Trust**
- **Sustainability**
- **Dignity**
- **Solidarity**

As you might directly guess, trying to pin down the specifics underlying these principles can be extremely hard to do. Even more so, the effort to turn those broad principles into something entirely tangible and detailed enough to be used when crafting AI systems is also a tough nut to crack. It is easy to overall do some handwaving about what AI Ethics precepts are and how they should be generally observed, while it is a much more complicated situation in the AI coding having to be the veritable rubber that meets the road.

The AI Ethics principles are to be utilized by AI developers, along with those that manage AI development efforts, and even those that ultimately field and perform upkeep on AI systems. All stakeholders throughout the entire AI life cycle of development and usage are considered within the scope of abiding by the being-established norms of Ethical AI. This is an important highlight since the usual assumption is that "only coders" or those that program the AI is subject to adhering to the AI Ethics notions. As earlier stated, it takes a village to devise and field AI, and for which the entire village has to be versed in and abide by AI Ethics precepts.

Now that you are oriented toward the overall nature of AI Ethics precepts, let's next dig into the UNESCO formulation of AI Ethics principles.

Many lists of AI Ethics will start with a preamble that sets the stage for why the list is needed. The preamble is usually relatively short and just emphasizes that we need to be aiming toward producing AI that abides by human ethical values. As you might imagine, the UNESCO listing takes the concept of this to a whole higher level of embellishment.

Consider this rather grand opening remark of the UNESCO document: "Recognizing the profound and dynamic positive and negative impacts of artificial intelligence (AI) on societies, environment, ecosystems and human lives, including the human mind, in part because of the new ways in which its use influences human thinking, interaction and decision-making and affects education, human, social and natural sciences, culture, and communication and information," and furthermore, "Considering that AI technologies can be of great service to humanity and all countries can benefit from them, but also raise fundamental ethical concerns, for instance regarding the biases they can embed and exacerbate, potentially resulting in discrimination, inequality, digital divides, exclusion and a threat to cultural, social and biological diversity and social or economic divides; the need for transparency and understandability of the workings of algorithms and the data with which they have been trained; and their potential impact on, including but not limited to, human dignity, human rights and fundamental freedoms, gender equality, democracy, social, economic, political and cultural processes, scientific and engineering practices, animal welfare, and the environment and ecosystems" – they then proceed to layout the core AI Ethics precepts.

I don't want to belabor this steeply elaborated wording, though I do have to admit that this additional passage hits home for those that are keenly immersed in AI Ethics considerations, namely that their AI Ethics guidelines "approaches AI ethics as a systematic normative reflection, based on a holistic, comprehensive, multicultural and evolving framework of interdependent values, principles and actions that can guide societies in dealing responsibly with the known and unknown impacts of AI technologies on human beings, societies and the environment and ecosystems, and offers them a basis to accept or reject AI technologies. It considers ethics as a dynamic basis for the normative evaluation and guidance of AI technologies, referring to human dignity, well-being and the prevention of harm as a compass and as rooted in the ethics of science and technology."

A mouthful, filled with topnotch nourishment.

Moving on, here are the stated objectives or goals associated with the UNESCO AI Ethics precepts (quoting from the UNESCO document):

- To provide a universal framework of values, principles and actions to guide States in the formulation of their legislation, policies or other instruments regarding AI, consistent with international law;

- To guide the actions of individuals, groups, communities, institutions and private sector companies to ensure the embedding of ethics in all stages of the AI system life cycle;

- To protect, promote and respect human rights and fundamental freedoms, human dignity and equality, including gender equality; to safeguard the interests of present and future generations; to preserve the environment, biodiversity and ecosystems; and to respect cultural diversity in all stages of the AI system life cycle;

- To foster multi-stakeholder, multidisciplinary and pluralistic dialogue and consensus-building about ethical issues relating to AI systems;

- To promote equitable access to developments and knowledge in the field of AI and the sharing of benefits, with particular attention to the needs and contributions of LMICs, including LDCs, LLDCs and SIDS.

There is a bit of UN jargon contained within the document, such as the reference in that last bulleted point to LMICs (low- and middle-income countries), LDCs (least developed countries), LLDCs (landlocked developing countries), and SIDS (small island developing States). Do not let that dissuade you from reading and garnering value from the UNESCO material. Plus, snappily, we might as well all become familiar with the language of global finesse anyway, one might so advise.

Following the lengthy preamble, the initial list-oriented portion of the UNESCO document discusses the key values underlying the AI Ethics guidelines and consists of twenty-four pronouncements that are organized into these four categories:

Values

- Respect, protection and promotion of human rights and fundamental freedoms and human dignity
- Environment and ecosystem flourishing
- Ensuring diversity and inclusiveness
- Living in peaceful, just and interconnected societies

The next segment discusses the key principles underlying the AI Ethics guidelines and consists of nearly twenty-five pronouncements that are organized into these ten categories:

Principles

1) Proportionality and Do No Harm
2) Safety and Security
3) Fairness and Non-discrimination
4) Sustainability
5) Rights to Privacy and Data Protection
6) Human Oversight and Determination
7) Transparency and Explainability
8) Responsibility and Accountability
9) Awareness and Literacy
10) Multi-Stakeholder and Adaptive Governance and Collaboration

After covering those values and principles, the next section entails areas of policy action.

The notion of the policy actions is that advice is being given regarding how to try and operationalize the set of values and principles. I favor this kind of added material in any proffered AI Ethics precepts. Some of the Ethical AI lists are solely a dry and stark listing and lack any indication or recommendation about how to turn those cornerstone precepts into something tangibly workable. Regrettably, without a sense of operationalization, those that come upon an AI Ethics listing are bound to be unsure of what to do with the list.

AI Ethics has to be both words and deeds.

Here are the areas of policy action that UNESCO provides:

Policy Action Areas

- Policy Area 1: Ethical Impact Assessment
- Policy Area 2: Ethical Governance and Stewardship
- Policy Area 3: Data Policy
- Policy Area 4: Development and International Cooperation
- Policy Area 5: Environment and Ecosystems
- Policy Area 6: Gender
- Policy Area 7: Culture
- Policy Area 8: Education and Research
- Policy Area 9: Communication and Information
- Policy Area 10: Economy and Labour
- Policy Area 11: Health and Social Well-Being

You might now realize why some are overwhelmed by the UNESCO listing. If you are a company that is crafting AI systems and you want to quickly establish an AI Ethics basis for your efforts, the odds are that you are not especially tasked with broad strokes worldwide matters such as international cooperation, social well-being, and similar globally sobering and weighty matters. That is a bridge too far for your otherwise relatively narrow and focused AI activities.

As I earlier observed, please do not let the density and scope of the UNESCO AI Ethics concordance intimidate you from wading into the contents. I assure you that many meaty morsels are utterly applicable to companies of all sizes and shapes. Do a little unpacking of the wording and you'll find tremendously valued nuggets about essential Ethical AI considerations.

I'd like to share with you in some detail one of the elements that I think you'll find notably intriguing, namely Policy Area #1 on Ethical Impact Assessments.

I am a strong advocate of companies undertaking an AI Ethics Impact analysis of their AI-related activities. Sadly, not many firms are yet doing this. Once the proverbial mess hits the fan in terms of AI adoption, only then is there a sudden and usually panicked attempt at doing an AI Ethics Impact assessment. The problem with a belated attempt is that the horse is usually already out of the barn and the solutions to cope with the AI unethical dilemmas brewing become harder to solve and often much more expensive to contend with, including severe reputational harm to the brand of the firm and Pandora's box of potential legal troubles.

Better to be safe than sorry is the catchphrase for doing your AI Ethics Impact analyses upfront.

Various methodologies can be used when performing an AI Ethics Impact assessment. The UNESCO document doesn't lay out the specifics of such approaches but does at least emphasize the importance of doing the proper and timely groundwork. I've selected a few excerpts to illustrate the type of concerns and components that are listed regarding AI Ethics Impacts evaluations:

- "Member States should introduce frameworks for impact assessments, such as ethical impact assessment, to identify and assess benefits, concerns and risks of AI systems, as well as appropriate risk prevention, mitigation and monitoring measures, among other assurance mechanisms."

- "Member States and private sector companies and civil society should investigate the sociological and psychological effects of AI-based recommendations on humans in their decision-making autonomy."

- "Member States and business enterprises should implement appropriate measures to monitor all phases of an AI system life cycle, including the functioning of algorithms used for decision-making, the data, as well as AI actors involved in the process, especially in public services and where direct end-user interaction is needed, as part of ethical impact assessment."

- "The assessment should also establish appropriate oversight mechanisms, including auditability, traceability and explainability, which enable the assessment of algorithms, data and design processes, as well as include an external review of AI systems."

You can silently cross out the "Member States" phrasing and insert your company name if that will help to showcase how the pronouncements made about AI Ethics Impact assessments would be relevant to your particular firm or entity. I might add that the realm of AI Ethics does apply to both for-profit and non-profit entities, such that it doesn't matter whether you are in business for profit or a social enterprise since one way or another any devising or use of AI has to be undertaken in an Ethical AI manner.

No excuses, no exceptions.

At this juncture of this substantive discussion, I'd bet that you are desirous of some illustrative examples that might showcase the UNESCO AI Ethics guidelines.

There is a special and assuredly popular set of examples that are close to my heart. You see, in my capacity as an expert on AI including the ethical and legal ramifications, I am frequently asked to identify realistic examples that showcase AI Ethics dilemmas so that the somewhat theoretical nature of the topic can be more readily grasped. One of the most evocative areas that vividly presents this ethical AI quandary is the advent of AI-based true self-driving cars. This will serve as a handy use case or exemplar for ample discussion on the topic.

Here's then a noteworthy question that is worth contemplating: *Does the advent of AI-based true self-driving cars illuminate anything about the UNESCO AI Ethics guidelines, and if so, what does this showcase?*

Allow me a moment to unpack the question.

Envision that an AI-based self-driving car is underway on your neighborhood streets and seems to be driving safely. At first, you had devoted special attention to each time that you managed to catch a glimpse of the self-driving car. The autonomous vehicle stood out with its rack of electronic sensors that included video cameras, radar units, LIDAR devices, and the like. After many weeks of the self-driving car cruising around your community, you now barely notice it. As far as you are concerned, it is merely another car on the already busy public roadways.

Lest you think it is impossible or implausible to become familiar with seeing self-driving cars, I've written frequently about how the locales that are within the scope of self-driving car tryouts have gradually gotten used to seeing the spruced-up vehicles.. Many of the locals eventually shifted from mouth-gaping rapt gawking to now emitting an expansive yawn of boredom to witness those meandering self-driving cars.

Probably the main reason right now that they might notice the autonomous vehicles is because of the irritation and exasperation factor. The by-the-book AI driving systems make sure the cars are obeying all speed limits and rules of the road. For hectic human drivers in their traditional human-driven cars, you get irked at times when stuck behind the strictly law-abiding AI-based self-driving cars.

That's something we might all need to get accustomed to, rightfully or wrongly.

Back to our tale.

Contemplate the seemingly inconsequential question of where self-driving cars will be roaming to pick up passengers. This seems like an abundantly innocuous topic. We will use the tale of the town or city that has self-driving cars to highlight the perhaps surprisingly potential specter of AI-related biases.

At first, assume that the AI was roaming the self-driving cars throughout the entire town. Anybody that wanted to request a ride in the self-driving car had essentially an equal chance of hailing one. Gradually, the AI began to primarily keep the self-driving cars roaming in just one section of town. This section was a greater money-maker and the AI system had been programmed to try and maximize revenues as part of the usage in the community.

Community members in the impoverished parts of the town were less likely to be able to get a ride from a self-driving car. This was because the self-driving cars were further away and roaming in the higher revenue part of the locale. When a request came in from a distant part of town, any request from a closer location that was likely in the "esteemed" part of town would get a higher priority. Eventually, the availability of getting a self-driving car in any place other than the richer part of town was nearly impossible, exasperatingly so for those that lived in those now resource-starved areas.

You could assert that the AI pretty much landed on a form of statistical and computational biases, akin to a form of proxy discrimination (also often referred to as indirect discrimination). The AI wasn't programmed to avoid those poorer neighborhoods. Instead, it "learned" to do so via the use of the ML/DL.

It was assumed that the AI would never fall into that kind of shameful quicksand. No specialized monitoring was set up to keep track of where the AI-based self-driving cars were going. Only after community members began to complain did the city leaders realize what was happening.

The horse got out of the barn.

As I mentioned earlier, it is vital to upfront work on AI Ethics Impact assessments. Why didn't the city or town do their homework before they gave a green light for the use of self-driving cars on their public roadways? Why didn't the automaker or self-driving tech firm do their homework before they paraded their self-driving cars on the public roadways of that town or city?

It's a shame.

Conclusion

A memorable quote from the UNESCO document might be a fruitful way to conclude this discussion about AI Ethics: "AI technologies can deepen existing divides and inequalities in the world, within and between countries, and that justice, trust and fairness must be upheld so that no country and no one should be left behind, either by having fair access to AI technologies and enjoying their benefits or in the protection against their negative implications, while recognizing the different circumstances of different countries."

Benjamin Franklin was known for his famous quip that by failing to prepare, you are preparing to fail. We need to be adopting AI Ethics principles. We need to be acting on the gist of AI Ethics principles. And we need to be doing our homework beforehand and preparing mindful and useful AI Ethics Impacts assessments to make sure that we are prepared for what AI is going to do.

An ounce of prevention is worth a pound of cure, maybe especially so in the case of adopting AI.

CHAPTER 12
AI ETHICS AND AI RISK MANAGEMENT FRAMEWORK

We seem to be told repeatedly that taking risks is important in life.

If you look at any everyday listing of quotable quotes there is a preponderance of life hacks telling you to embrace risk. Take a chance and climb out on a limb. Set aside your constraining worries and fly free with the wonderment of risk. Risk is your friend. Risk makes the world go around. Simply stated, no risk, no gain.

Though these glowing encouragements about being a risk-taker seem sensible, somehow the counterbalancing and sobering thoughts about the downsides of risk are left unsaid. Risk can put you in jeopardy. Dire harms can occur from risky actions. Simply stated, risk is not risk-free.

General George Patton famously asserted that we should always be risk-minded via taking sufficiently *calculated* risks, which he characterized as being quite different from being rash. Thus, think beforehand about the risks that you are willing to absorb. Be aware of known risks and the potential of unknown risks. A person has got to know their limitations when it comes to risk and risk-taking.

I am bringing up the nature and scope of "risk" as a type of analytically describable phenomenon in order to highlight that when it comes to AI there is an increasing need to determine how risky our expanding adoption of AI is. AI is not risk-free. On the contrary, AI presents many sizable and scarily massive risks that require us all to take a deep breath and start seriously calculating what those risks are. We must have our eyes wide open and know about AI risks as we plunge headfirst into the pell-mell rush toward embracing AI.

Please realize that all of today's stakeholders are faced with AI risks.

For example, a firm that is crafting an AI system is taking a risk that the AI eventually could cause some form of substantive harm to those that use the AI system. The harm might be financial, psychological, or possibly physical harm that could injure or kill someone. Executives of the firm are likely to be held legally accountable for having devised and released the AI. AI developers that built the AI are bound to be held accountable. There are lots of hands that go into making and promulgating AI and they all can be considered jointly responsible and culpable for what they allowed to adversely occur.

Think of AI risk as something that floats along and attaches to all that have a touchpoint associated with the AI. Users of an AI system are taking on some amount of risk. They might be harmed by AI. Those that devised the AI are taking on some amount of risk associated with the harmful outcomes that their AI might produce. Risk is pervasive in the realm of AI and yet oftentimes seems completely neglected and generally woefully understated.

The bad news then is that not enough attention is going toward AI risks.

The good news is that a burgeoning appreciation of the vitalness of understanding and measuring AI risk is gaining speed. As a healthy sign of this awareness, we can take a look at the being formulated *AI Risk Management Framework (RMF)* that the National Institute of Standards and Technology (NIST) is undertaking. I'll be quoting herein from the draft document dated March 17, 2022. There are various meetings underway to further refine and expand the document. A semi-finalized version known as AI RMF 1.0 is targeted to be issued in January 2023.

Before I jump into the existing draft of the AI RMF, I would like to emphasize that anyone genuinely interested in AI Ethics ought to be especially keeping track of what the AI RMF consists of.

Besides staying on top of the draft, you might also consider getting involved with the drafting effort and aid in the formulation of the AI Risk Management Framework all told (note that the NIST is undertaking public workshops that welcome such input). You indeed can help make history.

Let's briefly explore an important mash-up that exists between AI Ethics and AI risks. AI risks are integral to the utility of Ethical AI. You could readily claim that AI risk is immersed throughout all AI Ethics principles or precepts. A convenient mental model would be to envision a spreadsheet of sorts whereby the principles of AI Ethics as the horizontal elements (the columns) and AI risk is a vertical component (rows) that weave in and throughout the horizontals.

Speaking of AI risks brings up the varying nuance of what manner of AI one is alluding to. Despite those blaring headlines about the proclaimed human-like wonders of AI, there isn't any AI today that is sentient. We don't know if sentient AI will be possible. Nobody can aptly predict whether we will attain sentient AI, nor whether sentient AI will somehow miraculously spontaneously arise in a form of computational cognitive supernova (usually referred to as the singularity).

The type of AI that I am focusing on herein consists of the non-sentient AI that we have today.

If we wanted to wildly speculate about *sentient* AI, this discussion could go in a radically different direction. A sentient AI would supposedly be of human quality. You would need to consider that the sentient AI is the cognitive equivalent of a human. More so, since some speculate we might have super-intelligent AI, it is conceivable that such AI could end up being smarter than humans.

Let's keep things more down to earth and consider today's computational non-sentient AI.

Realize that today's AI is not able to "think" in any fashion on par with human thinking. When you interact with Alexa or Siri, the conversational capacities might seem akin to human capacities, but the reality is that it is computational and lacks human cognition. The latest era of AI has made extensive use of Machine Learning (ML) and Deep Learning (DL), which leverage computational pattern matching. This has led to AI systems that have the appearance of human-like proclivities. Meanwhile, there isn't any AI today that has a semblance of common sense and nor has any of the cognitive wonderment of robust human thinking.

ML/DL is a form of computational pattern matching. The usual approach is that you assemble data about a decision-making task. You feed the data into the ML/DL computer models. Those models seek to find mathematical patterns. After finding such patterns, if so found, the AI system then will use those patterns when encountering new data. Upon the presentation of new data, the patterns based on the "old" or historical data are applied to render a current decision.

I think you can guess where this is heading. If humans that have been making the patterned upon decisions have been incorporating untoward biases, the odds are that the data reflects this in subtle but significant ways. Machine Learning or Deep Learning computational pattern matching will simply try to mathematically mimic the data accordingly. There is no semblance of common sense or other sentient aspects of AI-crafted modeling per se.

Furthermore, the AI developers might not realize what is going on either. The arcane mathematics in the ML/DL might make it difficult to ferret out the now hidden biases. You would rightfully hope and expect that the AI developers would test for the potentially buried biases, though this is trickier than it might seem. A solid chance exists that even with relatively extensive testing that there will be biases still embedded within the pattern matching models of the ML/DL.

You could somewhat use the famous or infamous adage of garbage-in garbage-out. The thing is, this is more akin to biases-in that insidiously get infused as biases submerged within the AI. The algorithm decision-making (ADM) of AI axiomatically becomes laden with inequities. Not good.

You might be aware that when the latest era of AI got underway there was a huge burst of enthusiasm for what some now call *AI For Good.* Unfortunately, on the heels of that gushing excitement, we began to witness *AI For Bad.* For example, various AI-based facial recognition systems have been revealed as containing racial biases.

Efforts to fight back against *AI For Bad* are actively underway. Besides vociferous *legal* pursuits of reining in the wrongdoing, there is also a substantive push toward embracing AI Ethics to righten the AI vileness. The notion is that we ought to adopt and endorse key Ethical AI principles for the development and fielding of AI doing so to undercut the *AI For Bad* and simultaneously heralding and promoting the preferable *AI For Good.*

I've also discussed various collective analyses of AI ethics principles, including having covered a set devised by researchers that examined and condensed the essence of numerous national and international AI ethics tenets in a paper entitled "The Global Landscape Of AI Ethics Guidelines" (published in *Nature*),, which led to this keystone list:

- **Transparency**
- **Justice & Fairness**
- **Non-Maleficence**
- **Responsibility**
- **Privacy**
- **Beneficence**
- **Freedom & Autonomy**
- **Trust**
- **Sustainability**
- **Dignity**
- **Solidarity**

As you might directly guess, trying to pin down the specifics underlying these principles can be extremely hard to do. Even more so, the effort to turn those broad principles into something entirely tangible and detailed enough to be used when crafting AI systems is also a tough nut to crack. It is easy to overall do some handwaving about what AI Ethics precepts are and how they should be generally observed, while it is a much more complicated situation in the AI coding having to be the veritable rubber that meets the road.

The AI Ethics principles are to be utilized by AI developers, along with those that manage AI development efforts, and even those that ultimately field and perform upkeep on AI systems. All stakeholders throughout the entire AI life cycle of development and usage are considered within the scope of abiding by the being-established norms of Ethical AI. This is an important highlight since the usual assumption is that "only coders" or those that program the AI are subject to adhering to the AI Ethics notions. As earlier stated, it takes a village to devise and field AI, and for which the entire village has to be versed in and abide by AI Ethics precepts.

I mentioned earlier herein that AI risk is a matter that intersects across all of the AI Ethics precepts. To help fully exhibit that semblance, consider a rewording of the key AI Ethics principles to illuminate the AI risk matter:

- **Transparency and associated AI Risks**
- **Justice & Fairness and associated AI Risks**
- **Non-Maleficence and associated AI Risks**
- **Responsibility and associated AI Risks**
- **Privacy and associated AI Risks**
- **Beneficence and associated AI Risks**
- **Freedom & Autonomy and associated AI Risks**
- **Trust and associated AI Risks**
- **Sustainability and associated AI Risks**
- **Dignity and associated AI Risks**
- **Solidarity and associated AI Risks**

Before we unpack this, let's consider what the word "risk" means.

I say this because risk as a catchword has different meanings depending upon whom you are speaking with. In exploring this facet, I will also bring up another NIST document that you should consider studying if you are going to get into the AI RMF, namely that there is an overall NIST Risk Management Framework (RMF) that covers broadly Information Technology systems and risk management, having been in place for a while. The AI RMF is essentially an instantiation of the broader RMF (you might cheekily say that the AI RMF is the son or daughter of the all-told RMF).

Per the overall NIST RMF, here is a definition of risk: "Risk is a measure of the extent to which an entity is threatened by a potential circumstance or event. Risk is also a function of the adverse impacts that arise if the circumstance or event occurs, and the likelihood of occurrence. Types of risk include program risk; compliance/regulatory risk; financial risk; legal risk; mission/business risk; political risk; security and privacy risk (including supply chain risk); project risk; reputational risk; safety risk; strategic planning risk."

The NIST AI RMF draft defines risk this way: "Risk is a measure of the extent to which an entity is negatively influenced by a potential circumstance or event. Typically, risk is a function of 1) the adverse impacts that could arise if the circumstance or event occurs; and 2) the likelihood of occurrence. Entities can be individuals, groups, or communities as well as systems, processes, or organizations."

Digging deeper and perhaps muddying the waters, the *Stanford Encyclopedia of Philosophy* handily points out that risk is often couched in five different connotations:

1) Risk is an unwanted event that may or may not occur
2) Risk is the *cause* of an unwanted event that may or may not occur
3) Risk is the *probability* of an unwanted event that may or may not occur
4) Risk is the *statistical expectation value* of an unwanted event that may or may not occur
5) Risk is the fact that a decision is made under conditions of known probabilities

For now, let's collegially agree that we are going to within this discussion treat the notion of what risk is in a generalized manner as per the aforementioned NIST RMF and NIST AI RMF definitions and not get stuck on the tortuous variations. I trust then that you are comfortable with my above foundation of having settled for the time being the contextual meaning of AI and the meaning of risk.

An AI risk management framework is a means of ferreting out the risks of AI, along with hopefully managing those risks.

According to the AI RMF, here is the formal purpose or aspiration of the AI Risk Management Framework being formulated: "An AI Risk Management Framework (AI RMF, or Framework) can address challenges unique to AI systems. This AI RMF is an initial attempt to describe how the risks from AI-based systems differ from other domains and to encourage and equip many different stakeholders in AI to address those risks purposefully. This voluntary framework provides a flexible, structured, and measurable process to address AI risks throughout the AI lifecycle, offering guidance for the development and use of trustworthy and responsible AI."

The NIST also realizes that an AI RMF as a proposed standard has to be readily useable, be updated as technology advances, and embody other core criteria: "A risk management framework should provide a structured, yet flexible, approach for managing enterprise and societal risk resulting from the incorporation of AI systems into products, processes, organizations, systems, and societies. Organizations managing an enterprise's AI risk also should be mindful of larger societal AI considerations and risks. If a risk management framework can help to effectively address and manage AI risk and adverse impacts, it can lead to more trustworthy AI systems."

Some of you that are a bit skeptical might be questioning why we need an AI RMF versus just relying on the generalized RMF that is already readily available. Aren't we simply reinventing the wheel? The answer is no, we are not reinventing the wheel. A wheel is customizable to a particular need. A reasonable person would likely acknowledge that there are wheels of all different kinds of shapes and sizes.

The wheel on an airplane is undoubtedly quite different from the wheel that is on a child's tricycle. Sure, they are both wheels, but they are devised differently and ergo have different characteristics and can rightfully be examined distinctly too.

The AI RMF document expresses a similar sentiment: "Risks to any software or information-based system apply to AI; that includes important concerns related to cybersecurity, privacy, safety, and infrastructure. This framework aims to fill the gaps related specifically to AI."

In the existing version of the AI RMF draft, they define four stakeholder groups:

- AI System Stakeholders
- Operators and Evaluators
- External Stakeholders
- General Public

The bulk of the attention about AI risk usually goes toward the AI system stakeholders. That makes sense. These are the stakeholders that are involved in the conceiving of, designing, building, and fielding AI. In addition, we can include those that acquire or license AI for use. We tend to view those stakeholders as the highly visible parties that did the heavy lifting in shepherding the AI system into existence and fostered its deployment.

You might not have equally thought of or considered instrumental the AI operators and evaluators. As stated in the AI RMF, the AI operators and evaluators do this: "Operators and evaluators provide monitoring and formal/informal test, evaluation, validation, and verification (TEVV) of system performance, relative to both technical and socio-technical requirements." They are crucial to AI and also within the band of AI risks.

External stakeholders would encompass a wide array of entities including trade groups, advocacy groups, civil society organizations, and others. The general public consists of consumers and others that experience the risk associated with untoward AI.

You might be wondering how much risk is tolerable when it comes to AI.

Sorry to say that there is no particular number or assigned value that we can give to the amount of tolerable or acceptable risk that we might find worthwhile or societally permissible. For those of you that want a standardized designated numeric indication, you'll need to temper that desire by this notable point in the AI RMF draft: "The AI RMF does not prescribe risk thresholds or values. Risk tolerance – the level of risk or degree of uncertainty that is acceptable to organizations or society – is the context and use case-specific."

A recommended methodology by the AI RMF for examining and governing AI risk is depicted as consisting of base steps labeled as Map, Measure, and Manage. The Map function frames the risks of an AI system. The Measure function encompasses the tracking and analysis of AI risk. The Manage function makes use of the Map and Measure functions to then try and minimize adverse impacts while maximizing the benefits of the AI. According to the draft AI RMF, the later versions of the standard will include a Practice Guide as a companion to showcase examples and practices of using the AI RMF.

In the broader NIST RMF standard, there is an embellished set of seven steps that coincide with doing an overarching IT and systems risk management effort. I've found those seven steps handy:

The seven steps are (quoting from the NIST RMF standard):

1. Prepare to execute the RMF from an organization- and a system-level perspective by establishing a context and priorities for managing security and privacy risk.

2. Categorize the system and the information processed, stored, and transmitted by the system based on an analysis of the impact of loss.

3. Select an initial set of controls for the system and tailor the controls as needed to reduce risk to an acceptable level based on an assessment of risk.

4. Implement the controls and describe how the controls are employed within the system and its environment of operation.

5. Assess the controls to determine if the controls are implemented correctly, operating as intended, and producing the desired outcomes with respect to satisfying the security and privacy requirements.

6. Authorize the system or common controls based on a determination that the risk to organizational operations and assets, individuals, other organizations, and the Nation is acceptable.

7. Monitor the system and the associated controls on an ongoing basis to include assessing control effectiveness, documenting changes to the system and environment of operation, and conducting risk assessment.

At this juncture of this weighty discussion, I'd bet that you are desirous of some illustrative examples that might showcase the nature of AI risks. There is a special and assuredly popular set of examples that are close to my heart. You see, in my capacity as an expert on AI including the ethical and legal ramifications, I am frequently asked to identify realistic examples that showcase AI Ethics dilemmas so that the somewhat theoretical nature of the topic can be more readily grasped. One of the most evocative areas that vividly presents this ethical AI quandary is the advent of AI-based true self-driving cars. This will serve as a handy use case or exemplar for ample discussion on the topic.

Here's then a noteworthy question that is worth contemplating: *Does the advent of AI-based true self-driving cars illuminate anything about AI risks, and if so, what does this showcase?*

Allow me a moment to unpack the question.

As a human driver, you are a finely tuned risk calculator.

That's right, when you are driving a car you are in real-time tasked with figuring out the risks that a pedestrian might suddenly dart into the street, or that a car ahead of you will unexpectedly slam on its brakes. There is a decidedly murky haziness and fuzziness in the driving situations that we face.

You try to make as best an evaluation of the risks involved at every moment of driving and you then have to bear the consequences of your assessments. Lamentedly, there are about 40,000 car crash fatalities each year in the United States alone and about 2.5 million related injuries. Sometimes you cut things pretty close and escape a bad situation by the skin of your teeth. Other times you misjudge and bump against something or collide with someone.

You are ordinarily mentally updating the risk aspects as the driving effort is underway. Imagine the simple case of a bunch of kids aiming to jaywalk. At first, you might rate the risk of their jaywalking and get struck as being quite high. But then you notice that a nearby adult is prodding them not to jaywalk, and thus the risk of the kids intruding out into the street and getting run down is lessened. Note though that the risk did not drop to zero risk, since they can still opt to enter the roadway.

There is a well-known risk-related standard in the automotive realm known as the Automotive Safety Integrity Level (ASIL) risk classification scheme, based on an official document referred to as ISO 26262.

When determining risk while driving, here's an equation that provides a means to get your arms around risk aspects:

- Risk = Severity x (Exposure x Controllability)

Let's explore the formula and its components.

Severity is important to consider when ascertaining risk while driving since you might be heading toward a brick wall that will end up causing you and your passengers to be injured or killed (a notably high severity outcome) while hitting some discarded soda cans on the freeway might be relatively low in severity. Formally per the ISO standard, severity is a measure of the potential harm that can arise and is categorized into (S0) No injuries, (S1) Light and moderate injuries, (S2) Severe injuries, (S3) Life-threatening and fatal injuries.

Exposure is whether the chances of the incident occurring are substantial versus being unlikely as to you being exposed to the matter (i.e., the state of being in an operational situation of a hazardous nature). Per the ISO standard, exposure can be divided into (E0) negligible, (E1) very low, (E2) low, (E3) medium, and (E4) high.

Controllability refers to the capability of being able to maneuver the car to avoid a pending calamity. This can range from avoiding the situation entirely or merely skirting it, or that no matter what you do there is insufficient means to steer, brake, or accelerate and avert the moment. The ISO standard indicates controllability can be divided into (C0) generally controllable, (C1) simply controllable, (C2) normally controllable, and (C3) difficult or uncontrollable.

By combining the three factors of severity, exposure, and controllability, you can arrive at an indication of the risk assessment for a given driving situation. Presumably, we do this in our heads, cognitively, though how we actually do so and whether we even use this kind of explicit logic is debatable since no one really knows how our minds work in this capacity.

Do not be misled by the seemingly mathematical formula and construe that the matter of deriving risk while driving is somehow entirely clear-cut. There is a tremendous amount of judgment that goes into how you as a human classify the exposure, the severity, and the controllability.

This deriving of driving risk is hard for humans. Trying to craft AI to do likewise is also extraordinarily difficult. Notably, a core capability of an AI driving system entails having to make algorithm-based decisions (ADM) about driving risks. You might be surprised to know that many of the AI driving systems today do not undertake the calculating and assessing of driving risk robustly. Generally, very crude and highly simplified approaches are used. Whether this will scale up to widespread adoption of self-driving cars is an open question. For more about this dilemma, tied with a famous thought experiment known as the Trolley Problem.

Another concern is that the AI driving systems are often programmed in a byzantine way and the portions that deal with driving risk aspects are buried deep within a morass of code. There is little transparency about how a particular automaker or self-driving tech firm has opted to program the driving risk capacities of their AI system. There is a likelihood that we will see regulatory and public scrutiny come to bear once self-driving cars become more prevalent.

Recall that the AI Risk Management Framework defined four stakeholder groups, for which self-driving cars can be readily viewed:

- **AI System Stakeholders** -- Automakers and self-driving tech firms
- **Operators and Evaluators** – Fleet operators
- **External Stakeholders** – City leaders, regulators, etc.
- **General Public** – Pedestrians, bicyclists, etc.

The automakers and self-driving tech firms should be examining the risks associated with the AI that they are developing and fielding in self-driving cars. A mainstay of AI risk would be in the AI driving system elements, though there are other uses of AI in autonomous vehicles and driverless cars.

The expectation is that there will be fleet operators that will be in charge of running large sets of self-driving cars for use by the public. Those fleet operators are typically supposed to keep the autonomous vehicles in proper drivable shape and make sure that the self-driving cars are safe for use. Their focus is mainly aimed at the hardware and less so on dealing with the onboard software.

In any case, they too should be considering the AI risks associated with self-driving cars and their operational uses.

Wherever self-driving cars are approved for public use, the odds are that various city, state, and at times federal levels of approval and possibly oversight will be undertaken. There are also various existing laws and newly enacted laws that govern how self-driving cars can be deployed onto public roadways.. These public-minded stakeholders should also be examining the AI risks associated with self-driving cars.

As long as self-driving cars are placed on public highways and byways, the general public also should be thinking about the AI risks involved. Pedestrians are at risk of a self-driving car ramming into them. The same for bicyclists. All other roadway users are potentially vulnerable to AI risks entwined within the use of autonomous vehicles in any given locale.

Conclusion

We need to get more attention to AI risks. Having a standardized AI risk management framework will provide a handy tool for ascertaining AI risks. The odds are too that the expanding use of AI Ethics guidelines will carry along the need for determining AI risks, doing so as part and parcel of abiding by the precepts of Ethical AI.

I began this discussion by pointing out that General Patton said we should be explicitly calculating risk. He also famously exhorted that people should always do more than what is required of them.

I implore you to consider that even if you are not being required to examine AI risks, you should earnestly go beyond the norm and strive to do so. Let's all face up to AI risks and make sure that we don't climb out on a precarious societal perch that we cannot get safely back from.

CHAPTER 13
AI ETHICS
AND
AI ACCIDENTS

Do you perchance know someone that seems to be particularly accident-prone?

Seems like we all do.

Perhaps the person is that type that is apt to slip on a banana peel or knock over a precious vase in your living room. They are a human magnet for accidents of one kind or another. It could be so bad that you are even loath to be near them at times. You might get the ominous overflow or suffer the inglorious aftermath of one of their unsavory accidents.

But maybe we are being overly harsh when suggesting that anyone is more so predisposed to accidents than others are. An argument could be made that accidents can happen to any of us. We are all subject to the possibility of committing or getting embroiled in an accident. The best of us included.

Let's pile on top of this discussion an additionally vexing question.

Are accidents inevitable?

In other words, no matter how hard we might try to prevent accidents, it could inextricably be that nonetheless there is still a chance of and an ultimate certainty that accidents will occur. You can seek to protect the world from accidents. That seems indubitably prudent. But one way or another, accidents will still rear their ugly head.

As they say, accidents are waiting to happen.

It might be helpful to clarify what is meant by referring to some event as being appropriately labeled as an accident. The usual dictionary definition is that an accident is a type of incident that occurs unexpectedly and unintentionally, for which there is an unfortunate result that consists of a semblance of damage or injury.

Mindfully unpack that definition.

The said incident is unexpected. This implies that we did not seem to realize that the accident itself would arise.

The said incident is unintentional. This suggests that we should rule out the circumstances wherein somebody intentionally sought to have the incident occur. If a prankster places a banana peel on the floor where they know an unlucky and unsuspecting innocent will step, you would be hard-pressed to assert that the person tripping over it had suffered an accident. They were instead tricked and insidiously led into a trap.

The definition also includes the criterion that the result is unfortunate. An accident in this light must lead to a sour outcome. The person that accidentally knocked over a vase has cracked and possibly damaged the relished item beyond repair. The owner of the vase is harmed by the loss of value. The person that ran into the vase might now owe the owner for the loss. Heaven forbid that anyone might have gotten cut or scrapped by the breaking of the vase.

For sake of equal balance, we might want to note that there are also so-called "good" accidents. A person could find themselves in great fortune or accrue some other vital benefit due to the result of an accident. One of the most oft-cited examples consists of Sir Alexander Fleming and his acclaimed discovery of penicillin. The story goes that he was a bit careless in his laboratory and upon returning from a two-week vacation he found a mold on one of his culture plates. Reportedly, he said this about the matter: "One sometimes finds what one is not looking for. When I woke up just after dawn on Sept. 28, 1928, I certainly didn't plan to revolutionize all medicine by discovering the world's first antibiotic, or bacteria killer. But I guess that was exactly what I did."

We shall set aside the favorable accidents and focus herein on the dismal accidents. The frown face version of accidents is where those adverse outcomes can be especially life-threatening or have onerous results. As much as possible, the downside accidents we want to minimize (and, of course, the upside accidents we'd like to maximize, if that is feasible to do, though I'll cover that smiley face variant in a later column).

I'd like to slightly reword the earlier question about the inevitability of accidents. So far, we have kept our attention on accidents that occur in the particular instance of a singular person. There is no doubt that accidents can also impact a multitude of people all at once. This can be particularly encountered when people are immersed in a complex system of one sort or another.

Get yourself ready for a variant of the previously floated question.

Are system accidents inevitable?

We should mull this over.

Suppose a factory floor is laid out to make parts for cars. Those that designed the factory are let's say extremely concerned about worker accidents that might occur. Factory workers are required to wear helmets at all times. Signs in the factory exhort to watch out for accidents and be mindful in your work. All manner of precautions is taken to avert accidents from happening.

In this system, we might hope that nobody will ever incur an accident. Do you believe that there is zero chance of an accident happening? I would dare suggest that no reasonable thinker would bet that the chance of an accident is zero in this case. The odds might be really low of an accident happening, yet we still know and assume that despite all the precautions there is still a modicum of risk that an accident will take place.

All of this points to the idea that in a system of sufficient complexity we are bound to believe that accidents will still occur, regardless of how hard we try to prevent them. We are reluctantly backing ourselves into the stipulation that system accidents are indeed inevitable. A grandiose statement of this caliber might have a caveat that the system would have to be of some threshold of complexity such that it is essentially impossible to cover all the bases to prevent accidents totally.

You have now been neatly step-by-step introduced to a broadly outlined theory about accidents that can be labeled as Normal Accidents or the Normal Accident Theory (NAT). Here is a handy description by researchers that have examined this notion: "At a large enough scale, any system will produce 'normal accidents'. These are unavoidable accidents caused by a combination of complexity, coupling between components, and potential harm. A normal accident is different from more common component failure accidents in that the events and interactions leading to normal accident are not comprehensible to the operators of the system" (as stated in "Understanding and Avoiding AI Failures: A Practical Guide" by Robert Williams and Roman Yampolskiy, *Philosophies* journal).

The reason I've brought you to the land of so-called *normal accidents* is that we might need to carefully apply this theory to something that is gradually and inevitably becoming ubiquitous in our society, namely the advent of Artificial Intelligence (AI).

Let's dig into this.

Some people falsely assume that AI is going to be perfection. AI systems will not make mistakes and will not get us into trouble, the speculation goes. All you need to do is make sure that those AI developers do a good enough job, and voila, AI will never do anything that could be construed as accidental or begetting an accident.

Not so fast on that hypothetical belief. If you are willing to buy into the theory of *normal accidents*, any AI of any substantive complexity is going to inevitably bring about an accident. Regardless of how much late-night tinkering those AI developers do to prevent an accident, the AI will surely at some point in time be embroiled in an accident. That is the way the cookie crumbles. And there's no respite by crying in our spilled milk about it.

Ponder the mashup of AI and the conceptual tenets of *normal accidents.*

Envision that we have an AI system that controls nuclear weapons. The AI has been carefully crafted. Every conceivable check and balance has been coded into the AI system. Are we safe from an AI-based accident that might occur? Those that support the normal accidents viewpoint would say that we are not quite as safe as might be assumed. Given that the AI is likely to be especially complex, a normal accident is silently waiting in there to someday emerge, perhaps at the worst possible moment.

The gist of those thorny questions and qualms is that we must be on our toes that AI is bound to be accident-laden, and humankind has to do something sensible and proactive about the dangers that can ensue. As you will see in a moment or two, this is a looming consideration when it comes to using AI, and the field of AI Ethics and Ethical AI is wrestling quite a bit about what to do.

Before we go down a rabbit hole, let's make sure we are on the same page about the nature of AI. There isn't any AI today that is sentient. We don't have this. We don't know if sentient AI will be possible. Nobody can aptly predict whether we will attain sentient AI, nor whether sentient AI will somehow miraculously spontaneously arise in a form of computational cognitive supernova (usually referred to as the singularity).

The type of AI that I am focusing on consists of the non-sentient AI that we have today. If we wanted to wildly speculate about *sentient* AI, this discussion could go in a radically different direction.

A sentient AI would supposedly be of human quality. You would need to consider that the sentient AI is the cognitive equivalent of a human giving you advice. More so, since some speculate we might have super-intelligent AI, it is conceivable that such AI could end up being smarter than humans. All told these scenarios would ratchet up the assessment of the source.

Let's keep things more down to earth and consider today's computational non-sentient AI.

Realize that today's AI is not able to "think" in any fashion on par with human thinking. When you interact with Alexa or Siri, the conversational capacities might seem akin to human capacities, but the reality is that it is computational and lacks human cognition. The latest era of AI has made extensive use of Machine Learning (ML) and Deep Learning (DL), which leverages computational pattern matching. This has led to AI systems that have the appearance of human-like proclivities. Meanwhile, there isn't any AI today that has a semblance of common sense and nor has any of the cognitive wonderment of robust human thinking.

You might be aware that when the latest era of AI got underway there was a huge burst of enthusiasm for what some now call *AI For Good.* Unfortunately, on the heels of that gushing excitement, we began to witness *AI For Bad.* For example, various AI-based facial recognition systems have been revealed as containing racial biases and gender biases.

Efforts to fight back against *AI For Bad* are actively underway. Besides vociferous *legal* pursuits of reining in the wrongdoing, there is also a substantive push toward embracing AI Ethics to righten the AI vileness. The notion is that we ought to adopt and endorse key Ethical AI principles for the development and fielding of AI doing so to undercut the *AI For Bad* and simultaneously heralding and promoting the preferable *AI For Good.*

All told, a general hope is that by establishing a sense of AI Ethics precepts we will at least be able to increase societal awareness of what AI can both beneficially do and can adversely produce too. I've extensively discussed various collective analyses of AI ethics principles, including having covered a set devised by researchers that examined and condensed the essence of numerous national and international AI ethics tenets in a paper entitled "The Global Landscape Of AI Ethics Guidelines" (published in *Nature*), and that my coverage explores at **the link here**, which led to this keystone list:

- **Transparency**
- **Justice & Fairness**
- **Non-Maleficence**
- **Responsibility**
- **Privacy**
- **Beneficence**
- **Freedom & Autonomy**
- **Trust**
- **Sustainability**
- **Dignity**
- **Solidarity**

As you might directly guess, trying to pin down the specifics underlying these principles can be extremely hard to do. Even more so, the effort to turn those broad principles into something entirely tangible and detailed enough to be used when crafting AI systems is also a tough nut to crack. It is easy to overall do some handwaving about what AI Ethics precepts are and how they should be generally observed, while it is a much more complicated situation in the AI coding having to be the veritable rubber that meets the road.

The AI Ethics principles are to be utilized by AI developers, along with those that manage AI development efforts, and even those that ultimately field and perform upkeep on AI systems. All stakeholders throughout the entire AI life cycle of development and usage are considered within the scope of abiding by the being-established norms of Ethical AI. This is an important highlight since the usual assumption is that "only coders" or those that program the AI are subject to adhering to the AI Ethics notions.

As earlier stated, it takes a village to devise and field AI, and for which the entire village has to be versed in and abide by AI Ethics precepts.

We might need to add to the vaunted AI Ethics listings that we need to explicitly be considering and taking overt action to prevent or at least stridently mitigate AI-based *normal accidents* that might occur. Those that develop AI need to do their best on that front. Those that deploy AI need to do likewise. Those that use or are somehow subject to AI should be wary and on their guard for the possibility of AI accidents that seemingly are going to arise.

You might be tempted to think that enough precautions can be built into the AI that the chances of an accident should drop to zero. For those that are techies, the usual hubris is that if a piece of tech can generate a problem, another piece of tech can surely solve the problem. Just keep tossing more and more tech until the problem goes away.

Well, those that have studied systems-oriented accidents would tend to disagree and politely retort to the presumed techie pomposity by proffering a standpoint known as the Swiss Cheese Model (SCM): "In the SCM, the layers of safety are modeled as slices of cheese with holes in them representing weak points in each layer of safety. Over time, holes change shape and move around. Eventually, no matter how many slices of cheese (layers of safety) there are, the holes will align allowing a straight shot through all of the slices of cheese (an accident occurs)" (per the earlier cited paper by Robert Williams and Roman Yampolskiy).

I don't want to get bogged down into this side tangent about whether or not there is a guaranteed way to program AI to entirely and always avert any chance of an accident. There is all manner of mathematical and computational proving approaches that are being tried. I think it is reasonable and fair to declare that we do not today have a scalable working method nor technologies that can ironclad guarantee such a zero chance, plus we definitely are saddled with tons upon tons of AI that is being pell-mell produced that we know for sure has not sought to abide by such practices.

That latter point is crucial since even if we can concoct something in an AI lab, scaling that to the zillions of wild and carefree AI efforts underway and that will continue to emerge is a knotty issue and not likely solved even if a computational proving machine silver bullet existed.

Another point that I believe merits a brief mention consists of AI that is turned into doing untoward acts as a result of malicious human actors. I am not going to place those instances into the realm of AI accidents. Remember that the opening discussion suggested that the dictionary definition of an accident was an incident of an *unintentional* nature. If a human cybercrook manages to get an AI system to do bad things, I don't classify that AI as experiencing an accident. I trust that you will go along with that presumption.

An interesting question comes up as to how much of various AI untoward actions can be attributed to purely an AI accident versus a cybercriminal's devious act. According to some of the existing AI incidents reporting databases, it appears that the AI accidents happen more so than the maliciously spurred incidents, though you have to take that notion with a hefty dose of salt. I say this because there is a great temptation to not report when an AI system was attacked, and perhaps be somewhat more willing to report when an AI accident occurs.

There is an extremely important caveat we need to discuss concerning AI accidents.

Using the catchphrase "AI accidents" is generally undesirable and going to create quite a mess for us all, meaning for all of society. When a human perchance has an accident, we often shrug our shoulders and are sympathetic to the person that had the accident. We seem to treat the word "accident" as though it means that no one is responsible for what happened.

Let's take the example of getting into a car accident. One car swings wide at a right turn and accidentally rams into another car that was going straight ahead. Shucks, it was just an accident and accidentally happened. Those that weren't involved in the incident are perhaps going to let the matter slide if the event is couched in terms of merely being an accident that happened.

I have a feeling though that if you were in the car that got struck, you would not be so sympathetic to the driver that made the overly wide turn. Your opinion would certainly be that the other driver was a lousy driver and that either an ostensibly illegal or unwise driving act led to the car crash. By labeling the incident as an "accident" the driver that was stuck is now at a somewhat disadvantage since the appearance is that it all occurred by happenstance alone, rather than via the hands of the driver that messed up.

In fact, the word "accident" is so filled with varying connotations that by and large, the government statistics on car crashes refer to the matter as car collisions or car crashes, rather than making use of the phrase car accidents. A car collision or a car crash does not seem to have any implications about how the incident came to be. Meanwhile, the phrasing of a "car accident" almost leads us to think that it was a quirk of fate or somehow outside the hands of humankind.

You can abundantly see how this connotational consideration comes to play when referring to AI accidents. We don't want AI developers to hide behind the connotational shield that the AI just accidentally caused someone harm. The same goes for those that deploy AI. You could argue that the phrasing of "AI accidents" is almost an anthropomorphizing of AI that will mislead society into allowing the humans that were behind the scenes of the AI to escape accountability.

I am going to henceforth herein use the catchphrase of AI accidents, but I do so reluctantly and only because it is the conventional way of referring to this phenomenon. Attempts to word this differently tend to be regrettably more bloated and not as easily read.

Please make sure to interpret the catchphrase in a manner that does not cause you to look the other way and fail to realize that the humans underlying the AI are culpable when AI goes awry.

To help illustrate the likely confusion or misleading aspects of referring to AI as incurring accidents we can return to my remarks about knocking over a vase. Consider this example of AI doing so: "This problem has to do with things that are done by accident or indifference by the AI. A cleaning robot knocking over a vase is one example of this. Complex environments have so many kinds of 'vases' that we are unlikely to be able to program in a penalty for all side effects" (per the paper by Robert Williams and Roman Yampolskiy).

An AI system that is put into use in a household and then "accidentally" knocks over a vase would seem to suggest that nobody ought to be blamed for this adverse action of the AI. It was just an accident, one might lamentedly decry. On the other hand, we should rightfully ask why the AI system wasn't programmed to handle the vase circumstance in general. Even if the AI developers didn't anticipate a vase per se as being within the scope of the objects that could be encountered, we can certainly question why there wasn't some overarching object avoidance that would have kept the AI system from knocking over the vase (thus, the AI might not admittedly classify the vase as a vase, but still could have avoided it as a detectable object to be avoided).

I have predicted and continue to predict that we are gradually heading toward a humongous legal battle over the emergence of AI systems that get themselves into "AI accidents" and cause some form of harm. Up until now, society has not reacted in any sizable way to legally pushback at AI that is shoveled out into the marketplace and produces adverse consequences, either by intent or unintentionally. Today's AI bandwagon that has become a goldrush of half-baked AI makers and those that hurriedly enact the AI deployment are getting lucky right now and remain relatively untouched by civil lawsuits and criminal prosecutions.

The AI-stoked legal backlash is coming to come, sooner or later.

Moving on, how are we to try and cope with the inevitability of so-called AI accidents?

One thing we can do right away is try to anticipate how AI accidents might occur. By anticipating the AI accidents, we can at least seek to devise means to curtail them or minimize their likelihood of occurring. Furthermore, we can attempt to put in place guardrails so that when an AI accident does happen, the chances of demonstrative harm are lessened.

A helpful set of factors that were described in the earlier cited research article *Understanding and Avoiding AI Failures: A Practical Guide* includes these properties (as quoted from the research paper):

- The system which is affected by the outputs of the AI.
- Time delay between AI outputs and the larger system, system observability, level of human attention, and ability of operators to correct for malfunctioning of the AI.
- The maximum damage possible by malicious use of the systems the AI controls.
- Coupling of the components in proximity to the AI and complexity of interactions.
- Knowledge gap of AI and other technologies used and the energy level of the system.

At this juncture of this hefty discussion, I'd bet that you are desirous of some illustrative examples that might further elucidate the AI accidents topic. There is a special and assuredly popular set of examples that are close to my heart. You see, in my capacity as an expert on AI including the ethical and legal ramifications, I am frequently asked to identify realistic examples that showcase AI Ethics dilemmas so that the somewhat theoretical nature of the topic can be more readily grasped. One of the most evocative areas that vividly presents this ethical AI quandary is the advent of AI-based true self-driving cars. This will serve as a handy use case or exemplar for ample discussion on the topic.

Here's then a noteworthy question that is worth contemplating: *Does the advent of AI-based true self-driving cars illuminate anything about the advent of so-called AI accidents and if so, what does this showcase?*

Allow me a moment to unpack the question.

Envision that an AI-based self-driving car is underway on your neighborhood streets and seems to be driving safely. At first, you had devoted special attention to each time that you managed to catch a glimpse of the self-driving car. The autonomous vehicle stood out with its rack of electronic sensors that included video cameras, radar units, LIDAR devices, and the like. After many weeks of the self-driving car cruising around your community, you now barely notice it. As far as you are concerned, it is merely another car on the already busy public roadways.

Lest you think it is impossible or implausible to become familiar with seeing self-driving cars, I've written frequently about how the locales that are within the scope of self-driving car tryouts have gradually gotten used to seeing the spruced-up vehicles. Many of the locals eventually shifted from mouth-gaping rapt gawking to now emitting an expansive yawn of boredom to witness those meandering self-driving cars.

Probably the main reason right now that they might notice the autonomous vehicles is because of the irritation and exasperation factor. The by-the-book AI driving systems make sure the cars are obeying all speed limits and rules of the road. For hectic human drivers in their traditional human-driven cars, you get irked at times when stuck behind the strictly law-abiding AI-based self-driving cars.

That's something we might all need to get accustomed to, rightfully or wrongly.

Back to our tale.

One day, the self-driving car gets into an accident.

While making a right turn, the AI driving system swung the autonomous vehicle widely and a human-driven car was struck. The human-driven car was proceeding straight ahead in the proper lane of traffic. There was no particular opportunity for the human driver to swerve or avoid getting hit. In addition, there was no warning or indication by the self-driving car that it was going to widely make the right turn.

Is this an accident?

We can certainly say that it is encompassed within the rubric of being an AI accident. The basis for such an assertion is that there was an AI driving system at the wheel of the self-driving car. Somehow, for whatever reasons, the AI opted to make a wide swing when taking a right turn. The result led to the self-driving car hitting a human-driven car.

Recall the earlier discussion about the connotations associated with the word "accident" and see how such undertones come to play in this scenario. Also, remember that we discussed the case of a human driver making a wide right turn and running into a fellow human-driven car. We realized that the notion of this act being an "accident" is misleading and confounding. The human driver that made the wide swing could hide behind the idea that an accident merely occurred that was seemingly by happenstance or the vagaries of fate.

Instead of labeling the scenario as an "AI accident" in the case of the AI-based self-driving car going wide and hitting the human-driven car, perhaps we should say that it was a car crash or car collision involving a self-driving car and a human-driven car. We can then dispense with the vacuous confusion of it being an accident of unknowable means.

What do you think the public reaction to the incident would be?

Well, if the automaker or self-driving tech firm can stick with the labeling of the matter as an accident, they might be able to skirt around the potential backlash from the community at large.

A sense of sympathy about accidents all told would possibly flow over onto the particular circumstance..

If the situation is plainly described as a car crash or car collision, perhaps that might then allow for the realization that someone or something is perhaps to blame for the incident. A knee-jerk reaction might be that the AI is to be held responsible. The thing is, until or if we ever decide to anoint AI as having a semblance of legal personhood, you are not going to be able to pin the responsibility on the AI per se.

We can inspect the AI driving system to try and figure out what led to the seeming inappropriate driving and the subsequent car crash. That doesn't though imply that the AI is going to be held accountable. The responsible parties include the AI developers, the fleet operator of the self-driving car, and others. I include others too since there is a possibility that the city might be held partially responsible for the design of the corner where the turn took place. In addition, suppose a pedestrian was darting off the corner and the AI driving system opted to avoid the person and yet then got enmeshed into the car crash.

And so on.

Conclusion

We would want to know what the AI was computationally calculating and what it had been programmed to do. Did the AI do as was coded? Maybe the AI encountered a bug or error in the programming, which doesn't excuse the actions but provides more of a clue to how the crash came about.

What kind of AI guardrails were programmed into the AI driving system? If there were guardrails, we would want to figure out why they seemed to not prevent the car crash. Maybe the AI driving system could have come to a halt rather than making the turn. We would want to know what alternatives the AI computationally assessed during the course of the incident.

Besides getting to the bottom of the particular incident, another rightful qualm is whether the AI driving system has a flaw or other embedded aspect that will do similar kinds of adverse acts. In essence, this incident might be a telltale indicator of more to come. How were computer-based simulations of driving situations used to try and anticipate this type of AI driving system prompting? Was there sufficient roadway driving tests to have ferreted out the AI issues that might have led to the car crash?

This scenario highlights a contentious conundrum that is facing the emergence of AI-based self-driving cars.

It goes like this.

On the one hand, there is a societal desire to adopt self-driving cars expeditiously due to the hope that AI driving systems will be as safe or possibly safer than human drivers. In the United States alone, we currently have nearly 40,000 human fatalities annually due to car crashes and about 2.5 million human injuries. Analyses suggest that a sizable portion of those car crashes are attributable to human error such as driving while intoxicated, driving while distracted, etc.

AI driving systems won't drink and drive. They won't need rest and they won't get worn out while at the wheel. The assumption is that by establishing self-driving cars as a viable mode of transportation, we can reduce the number of human drivers. This in turn should mean that we'll reduce summarily the number of annual human fatalities and injuries from car crashes.

Some pundits have said that we will end up with zero fatalities and zero injuries, and those self-driving cars will supposedly be uncrashable, but this is an altogether absurd and utterly false set of expectations.

In any case, assume that we are going to have some amount of car crashes that self-driving cars get involved in. Assume too that those car crashes will have some amount of fatalities and injuries.

The question that is being agonized over is whether we as a society are willing to tolerate any such instances at all. Some say that if even one fatality or one injury happens as a result of true self-driving cars, the whole kit and kaboodle should be closed down.

The countervailing viewpoint is that if the lives saved are reducing the annual counts, we should be continuing to encourage the advent of self-driving cars and not react in such an illogical manner. We will need to accept the premise that some amount of fatalities and injuries will still exist, even with self-driving cars, and yet realize that the annual count if being decreased suggests that we are on the right path.

Of course, some argue that we should not have self-driving cars on our public roadways until they are either cleared for such use as a result of extensive and exhaustive computer-based simulations or as via private closed-track testing. The counterargument is that the only viable and fastest way to get self-driving cars going is by using public roadways and that any delays in adopting self-driving cars are going to otherwise allow the horrendous counts of the human-driven car crashing to continue. I've covered in greater length this debate in my columns and urge readers to look at those discussions to get the full sense of the perspectives on this controversial matter.

Let's wrap things up for now.

AI accidents are going to happen. We must resist the impulse to construe an AI accident as seemingly *accidental* and ergo falsely let the makers and those that deploy AI be categorically off-the-hook.

There is an added twist that I leave you with as a final intriguing thought for your day.

The comedian Dane Cook reportedly told this joke about car accidents: "A couple of days back, I got into a car accident. Not my fault. Even if it's not your fault, the other person gets out of their car and looks at you like it's your fault: Why did you stop at a red light and let me hit you doing 80!"

Where the twist comes to the fore is the possibility that an AI system might opt to insist that when an AI accident occurs involving that particular AI, the AI touts that the incident was the fault of the human and assuredly not the fault of the AI. By the way, this could be abundantly true and the human might be trying to scapegoat the AI by claiming that it was the fault of the AI.

Or maybe the AI is trying to scapegoat the human.

You see, the AI that we devise might be tricky that way, either by accident or not.

CHAPTER 14
AI ETHICS
AND
ALEXA ISSUES

A recent incident involving the AI-based conversational interactive system known as Alexa provides keen insights into the importance of AI Ethics and the need to abide by Ethical AI precepts. Let's take a close look at what happened.

A recent news report indicated that via a household Echo Dot, Alexa urged a 10-year-old girl to go ahead and try a dangerous experiment that could have had unimaginable consequences. The experiment consisted of telling the girl to plug a phone charger halfway into a wall outlet so as to leave the prongs partially exposed. The Alexa voiced instruction further stated that a penny should then be touched upon the exposed prongs.

DO NOT DO THIS!

The result can be catastrophic.

Luckily, the mother was listening to Alexa with the girl (her daughter) and countermanded the AI-based system instruction by telling the girl to not proceed with the commanded indication. Whew, another of life's many perils that managed to be skirted around, thank goodness.

No one got hurt.

Of course, had the girl been alone and abided by Alexa, the story could have turned out much differently. Indeed, any youngster might readily fall victim to the Alexa instruction. One supposes that even an adult might possibly try out the instruction, though presumably adults would be astute enough to know this is a wildly hazardous experiment and should not be attempted.

I'm sure you are abundantly puzzled as to why in the world would Alexa provide such a risky and unwarranted set of instructions.

Was it a bug or error in the AI programming?

Nope.

Was it a hack by some nefarious hacker that sought to bring about a bit of outrageous evildoing?

Nope.

Turns out that Alexa came up with this craziness by simply culling through its large database and searching the web, looking for something to provide as a "challenge" for the girl as based on a simple verbal request by her in seeking to undertake an interesting challenge that might be fun to do.

You see, the girl and her mother were indoors and relishing some quiet time together (the weather outside was seasonally unpleasant). They had already asked for a physical challenge from Alexa that turned out to be quite comical and joyous, namely, Alexa indicated to lay down on the floor, hold a shoe on one foot, and try to roll over. This had been a howl of an enjoyable activity for the mother and daughter (revered quality bonding time).

Upon the girl asking for another physical related challenge as a follow-up, the electrical fate-tempting instruction was issued by Alexa. In a brief instant, the setting in the household went from one of frolicking joy to utter seriousness.

The mother realized immediately that any such endeavor could produce a severe electrical shock, could potentially start a fire, could result in the loss of a finger or hand, and otherwise was a categorically outrageously bad idea.

Let's dig more deeply into how Alexa came up with this "gem" of an idea (note my heavy sarcasm, plus please make sure that you don't try this scary prong-and-penny challenge).

Turns out that a year ago there was a widely popular online social media viral challenge that entailed this prong-and-penny venture. You might have seen it, especially on TikTok. Gradually, thankfully, the challenge subsided amid the short attention span of the Internet. People moved on to other likely insipid challenges (ones that perchance are less perilous, I hope).

You might be familiar with the common refrain that the Internet never forgets. In that sense, it is akin to the proverbial elephant that never forgets. Items that get posted on the Internet can potentially rear their ugly heads repeatedly, time not being a barrier and nor inattention. When you might least expect it, foul outdated junk can pop up and ruin your day.

So, Alexa used its AI search techniques to discover physical related challenges that had been previously posted and landed upon the prong-and-penny challenge. This was then dutifully shoveled out to the Echo Dot and into the waiting ears of the 10-year-old and the mother.

This might seem stridently unconscionable that the team that developed and maintains Alexa has allowed such a dangerous piece of posted flotsam to be resurfaced and regurgitated to unsuspecting Alexa users. A youngster would ostensibly have little basis to gauge that this instruction is foolhardy and potentially injurious.

In fact, you could reasonably argue that the AI ought to have some capability to assess the instructions that are being vocalized. I say this because many people, both kids and adults, often tend to take the utterances from a disembodied robot-like device as though it is entirely safe and well checked.

The irony is that if you had a stranger call you or come to your door and tell you to do the penny-and-prong challenge, nearly everyone would instantly reject the idea and be highly suspicious. Not so with the Alexa or similar such device that sits in your kitchen, in your living room, in your bedrooms, and is fully available throughout the presumed sanctity of your home.

What makes this even more deceptive is that the vocalizing AI device is "right" some or much of the time. If you ask what year Washington crossed the Delaware River, you get the right answer. If you ask what the capital of New York is, you get the right answer. And so on.

After a while, you are lulled into believing that the vocalizing AI is always correct, always watchful, always respectful. In the case of the mother and daughter, the fact that they had gotten the shoe holding challenge would undoubtedly have bolstered the assumption that the system was able to choose sensible and innocent challenges for use in the most innocuous of settings.

Allow me to clarify that none of this is a knock on Alexa per se and also that any such AI vocalizing system could readily do exactly the same kind of miscuing. To its credit, the Alexa team has reportedly updated the system to no longer voice the prong-and-penny challenge after having been alerted to the matter.

That being said, do not fall into the trap that this means that some other nutty challenge won't be picked up and broadcast out to those using these AI vocalizing systems. You would be much wiser to assume that there are going to be many and ongoing instances of this caliber.

Another frightening element is that this was not just a factual question-and-answer type of scenario. Suppose you asked what the population of Idaho was. An incorrect answer would not likely be life-threatening. The aspect that this was a provided challenge, essentially a set of instructions, makes it really disconcerting. Children are taught to follow instructions, and the authoritative AI vocalizing system is bound to be perceived as an authority to be obeyed.

Again, as a bit of an aside, there is a sheen of irony that a youngster might doubt an adult that gives them an instruction while giving much more credence and obedience to an automated system of a convincing nature that uses AI to have the appearance of something even better than a customary adult (possibly more so than their beloved parents!).

You can certainly envision that some 10-year-old slightly rebellious youngsters might opt to debate the prong-and-penny instructions with their parents. The parent says don't do it. The youngster insists that if the AI says it should be undertaken, it must be safe to do so. The parent sternly states don't do it. Regrettably, the youngster might nod yes, and then later on, when alone in their room, decide to try it anyway, figuring the parent is overprotective and clueless about the latest hip things for kids to do.

I trust that you get the overall gist that you need to be extremely careful about using any of the AI vocalizing systems and make sure that your kids do not overinflate what the AI is capable of.

Some parents refuse to allow such systems into their homes. That might seem like a prudent precaution, but of course, the kids can nonetheless access such systems on their parent-provided smartphones that the kids have with them at all times. Welcome to the planet of no-win.

All told, this is a proverbial Pandora's box that underpins the latest and greatest high-tech and you need to face up to the reality that Pandora is not going back into that little box. Pandora is out, ready, and here to stay.

Where else might this same kind of AI vocalizing provide potent dangers?

I'm glad you asked.

A handy lesson from this circumstance of the prong-and-penny AI vocalized challenge can be reapplied to the advent of AI-based self-driving cars.

Here's an intriguing question that is worth pondering: *What should we be worried about concerning AI vocalization systems as part of the advent of AI-based self-driving cars?*

You get into an AI-based self-driving car and decide to go for a ride. As an adult, you probably are savvy enough to be wary of any AI vocalizations that seem off base. Use that assumption for the moment, but we'll soon recant it and see why.

A teenager gets into an AI-based self-driving car to get a lift to school. The parents normally use their human-driven car to take their teen to the campus, but this morning the parents are busy and are fine with having the teen make use of a self-driving car instead.

I realize that some of you might be insisting that only a rotten parent would ever let their offspring ride in a self-driving car without the presence of the parent or some other adult. This is in fact going to be an emerging problem or ethical dilemma of sorts. A human-driven car always has an adult present since an adult is required for driving the car (well, to be clearer, a licensed driver is either an adult or nearly so).

Since there isn't any human driver needed for a true self-driving car, you can readily let your offspring ride in a self-driving car without any adult supervision. This seems out of the question to you right now because you aren't used to having self-driving cars pervasively cruising all around us. Once self-driving cars are commonly in use, I assure you that people are going to let their kids ride without any adults along for the ride.

Anyway, go with the flow herein and agree that there is a notable chance that teens (and even younger) will be riding in self-driving cars without any in-car adult presence.

I have led you to this setting to bring up the AI vocalization considerations.

Envision that the AI being used to drive the self-driving car also has other duties. These duties include asking passengers where they want to go. Plus, the duties encompass asking what preferences the rider has about the use of air conditioning, heating, lighting, music, and a slew of other ambiance-related facets.

A teen riding to school is perchance bored during the drive and asks the AI for something fun to do. The AI system searches a database and the web to discover something that has been previously posted and proclaimed to be fun.

Get yourself ready for what I am about to tell you.

Are you ready?

Imagine that the AI tells the teen to go ahead and open the windows of the self-driving car, stick their head out, wave their arms, and scream out obscenities.

Wait for a second, you are assuredly thinking, this is crazy and certainly there is no kind of AI that would ever instruct a teen to do such a wanton and dangerous thing. The teen could spark a road rage incident. The teen could inadvertently get their arms banged up by another vehicle that comes adjacent to the self-driving car. Etc.

Turns out (let's pretend), this was an online viral social media challenge that had been found by the AI when searching for fun things to do while riding inside a car. The AI opted to grab this gem and share it with the teen.

Do you think the teen might abide by the AI-provided instruction?

I'm willing to bet that some teens would do so.

In a manner of comparison, this is nearly identical to the case of the prong-and-penny challenge. In this allied instance, the AI blindly searched for a fun in-car activity and then provided it to the passenger.

You have to keep in mind that there isn't any kind of AI today that has a commonsense facility, not at least in the semblance of common sense that we humans have. If an adult told a teen to do something like this, you would rightfully be darned irked at the adult. The adult ought to have more common sense than to tell a teen to do this perilous antic.

Not so with AI.

The lack of common sense is a serious concern about where AI is going and how it is going to be deployed. You could say that AI is currently like a box of chocolates, whereby you never know what you are going to get.

Sure, there are lots of ways to try and programmatically bound the AI to keep it from going off the rails. The problem is that as the AI gets more advanced at doing the things we like to have done, the lack of a common-sense capability is going to increasingly become apparent. And, worse still, increasingly lead us into dark hallways and compromising dead ends.

For those of you that are only mildly convinced and shrug your shoulders about the "nonconformist" instruction for the teen to wave their arms outside of the self-driving car (it seems harmless, you implore), I am happy to amp up the frightfulness for you.

Imagine that the AI finds a viral social media challenge that urged riders to climb out the window of the car and surf on top of the vehicle. Certainly, you must acknowledge the inherent and sober riskiness of that kind of "fun and games" related to a moving self-driving car that might be barreling down a freeway at 65 miles per hour.

This is decidedly a harmful suggested challenge.

One quick retort is that the AI driving system would seemingly detect that the rider is climbing outside of the autonomous vehicle and dutifully bring the self-driving car to a cautious halt.

Don't hold your breath on that assumption and nor bet your life on it (nor the lives of non-adults).

A human driver would almost certainly realize when a rider is doing such a crazy act. The human driver would presumably yell at the passenger to get back into the vehicle. We would assume that the human driver would try to as safely as possible to bring the car to a halt and do so without tossing the surf-riding passenger into nearby traffic.

This kind of capability is not yet built into most of the existing AI driving systems. The developers already have their hands full with trying to get the AI to simply drive from point A to point B (doing so without getting into a car crash of one kind or another). Developing code to also detect that a rider is climbing out a car window and opting to ride on the exterior of the autonomous vehicle is not in the cards for right now.

You might say that this seemingly oddball circumstance would be rated as an edge case or outlier type of concern. Nobody in their right mind would try to climb out and ride atop a self-driving car, goes the dubious developers about whether this is a low priority or high priority addition to the AI capabilities. The automakers and AI self-driving car developers already have a ton of other higher priority tasks to be undertaken. Those items that get placed on the edge case list are deemed low priority facets that someday (maybe) the AI developers will devote some attention to.

I'll tackle another retort that some of you might be exhorting in your mind.

All that needs to be done is prevent the AI from telling riders about any kind of challenges or similar instructions.

That seems simple enough. Case closed.

I would like to remind you of one little thing you are overlooking.

Smartphones.

A teen gets into a self-driving car to go to school. The AI driving system asks some questions about the driving request, and otherwise, the AI is as quiet as a clam. No challenges, no instructions, nothing else is uttered by the in-car AI.

Meanwhile, the teen pulls out their handy dandy smartphone. By using a few clicks here and there, the teen brings up a social media viral challenge about climbing out of the car and surfing on the top of it.

The rest of the sordid tale is the same as before.

Conclusion

There is a quite important aspect that I want to further emphasize about all of this.

The AI was not hacked. The AI did not have a bug or error in it.

I mention this because the easy way to sidestep the overarching issue is to try and lay the problem at the feet of a hacker or of a hidden bug that regrettably surfaced at the worst of times. All of those possibilities are indeed possible, mind you, but that's not the nature of this herein discussion.

Today's AI is being incessantly anthropomorphized as though it has human-like qualities, such as embodying common sense and ergo won't be telling people to do stupid and life-endangering acts. Sorry to tell you that this is an utter falsity and you've got to resist the alluring temptation to assume such conditions exist.

AI is not your friend. It doesn't have your best interests at heart. Today's AI is a bunch of programming and devised and divined by humans that develop and field such systems.

Keep your guard up, and somehow, someway, teach your kids to likewise be on their guard, for the sake of their safety and their lives.

That is a New Year's resolution that I hope you will take to heart.

CHAPTER 15
AI ETHICS TUNING KNOBS

AI systems are being churned out at quite a rapid pace, meanwhile, there are considerable qualms about whether such AI will exhibit ethical behavior.

There is a rising tide of concern about AI ethics.

How so?

Consider a real-world example.

Suppose an AI application is developed to assess car loan applicants.

Using Machine Learning (ML) and Deep Learning (DL), the AI system is trained on a trove of data and arrives at some means of choosing among those that it deems are loan worthy and those that are not.

The underlying Artificial Neural Network (ANN) is so computationally complex that there are no apparent means to interpret how it arrives at the decisions being rendered. Also, there is no built-in explainability capability and thus the AI is unable to articulate why it is making the choices that it is undertaking (note: there is a movement toward including XAI, explainable AI components to try and overcome this inscrutability hurdle).

Upon the AI-based loan assessment application being fielded, soon thereafter protests arise by some that assert they were turned down for their car loan due to an improper inclusion of race or gender as a key factor in rendering the negative decision.

At first, the maker of the AI application insists that they did not utilize such factors and professes complete innocence in the matter.

Turns out though that a third-party audit of the AI application reveals that the ML/DL is indeed using race and gender as core characteristics in the car loan assessment process. Deep within the mathematically arcane elements of the neural network, data related to race and gender were intricately woven into the calculations, having been dug out of the initial training dataset provided when the ANN was crafted.

That is an example of how biases can be hidden within an AI system.

And it also showcases that such biases can go otherwise undetected, including that the developers of the AI did not realize that the biases existed and were seemingly confident that they had not done anything to warrant such biases being included.

People affected by the AI application might not realize they are being subjected to such biases. In this example, those being adversely impacted perchance noticed and voiced their concerns, but we are apt to witness a lot of AI that no one will realize they are being subjugated to biases and therefore not able to ring the bell of dismay.

Various AI Ethics principles are being proffered by a wide range of groups and associations, hoping that those crafting AI will take seriously the need to consider embracing AI ethical considerations throughout the life cycle of designing, building, testing, and fielding AI.

I've previously discussed the AI Ethics principles that the Vatican released, and those of the U.S. Department of Defense,, and have also described those of the OECD, which consist briefly of these five core precepts::

1) Inclusive growth, sustainable development, and well-being
2) Human-centered values and fairness
3) Transparency and explainability
4) Robustness, security, and safety
5) Accountability

We certainly expect humans to exhibit ethical behavior, and thus it seems fitting that we would expect ethical behavior from AI too.

Since the aspirational goal of AI is to provide machines that are the equivalent of human intelligence, being able to presumably embody the same range of cognitive capabilities that humans do, this perhaps suggests that we will only be able to achieve the vaunted goal of AI by including some form of ethics-related component or capacity.

What this means is that if humans encapsulate ethics, which they seem to do, and if AI is trying to achieve what humans are and do, the AI ought to have an infused ethics capability else it would be something less than the desired goal of achieving human intelligence.

You could claim that anyone crafting AI that does not include an ethics facility is undercutting what should be a crucial and integral aspect of any AI system worth its salt.

Of course, trying to achieve the goals of AI is one matter, meanwhile, since we are going to be mired in a world with AI, for our safety and well-being as humans we would rightfully be arguing that AI had better darned abide by ethical behavior, however that might be so achieved.

Now that we've covered that aspect, let's take a moment to ponder the nature of ethics and ethical behavior.

Do humans always behave ethically?

I think we can all readily agree that humans do not necessarily always behave in a strictly ethical manner.

Is ethical behavior by humans able to be characterized solely by whether someone is in an ethically binary state of being, namely either purely ethical versus being wholly unethical?

I would dare say that we cannot always pin down human behavior into two binary-based and mutually exclusive buckets of being ethical or being unethical. The real-world is often much grayer than that and we at times are more likely to assess that someone is doing something ethically questionable, but it is not purely unethical, nor fully ethical.

In a sense, you could assert that human behavior ranges on a spectrum of ethics, at times being fully ethical and ranging toward the bottom of the scale as being wholly and inarguably unethical.

In-between there is a lot of room for how someone ethically behaves.

If you agree that the world is not a binary ethical choice of behaviors that fit only into truly ethical versus solely unethical, you would therefore also presumably be amenable to the notion that there is a potential scale upon which we might be able to rate ethical behavior.

This scale might be from the scores of 1 to 10, or maybe 1 to 100, or whatever numbering we might wish to try and assign, maybe even including negative numbers too.

Let's assume for the moment that we will use the positive numbers of a 1 to 10 scale for increasingly being ethical (the topmost is 10), and the scores of -1 to -10 for being unethical (the -10 is the least ethical or in other words most unethical potential rating), and zero will be the midpoint of the scale.

Please do not get hung up on the scale numbering, which can be anything else that you might like. We could even use letters of the alphabet or any kind of sliding scale. The point being made is that there is a scale and we could devise some means to establish a suitable scale for use in these matters.

The twist is about to come, so hold onto your hat.

We could observe a human and rate their ethical behavior on particular aspects of what they do. Maybe at work, a person gets an 8 for being ethically observant, while perhaps at home they are a more devious person and they get a -5 score.

Okay, so we can rate human behavior.

Could we drive or guide human behavior by the use of the scale?

Suppose we tell someone that at work they are being observed and their target goal is to hit an ethics score of 9 for their first year with the company. Presumably, they will undertake their work activities in such a way that it helps them to achieve that score.

In that sense, yes, we can potentially guide or prod human behavior by providing targets related to ethical expectations.

I told you a twist was going to arise, and now here it is.

For AI, we could use an ethical rating or score to try and assess how ethically proficient the AI is.

In that manner, we might be more comfortable using that particular AI if we knew that it had a reputable ethical score.

And we could also presumably seek to guide or drive the AI toward an ethical score too, similar to how this can be done with humans, and perhaps indicate that the AI should be striving towards some upper bound on the ethics scale.

Some pundits immediately recoil at this notion.

They argue that AI should always be a +10 (using the scale that I've laid out herein). Anything less than a top ten is an abomination and the AI ought to not exist.

Well, this takes us back into the earlier discussion about whether ethical behavior is in a binary state.

Are we going to hold AI to a "higher bar" than humans by insisting that AI always be "perfectly" ethical and nothing less so?

This is somewhat of a quandary due to the point that AI overall is presumably aiming to be the equivalent of human intelligence, and yet we do not hold humans to that same standard.

For some, they fervently believe that AI must be held to a higher standard than humans. We must not accept or allow any AI that cannot do so.

Others indicate that this seems to fly in the face of what is known about human behavior and begs the question of whether AI can be attained if it must do something that humans cannot attain.

Furthermore, they might argue that forcing AI to do something that humans do not undertake is now veering away from the assumed goal of arriving at the equivalent of human intelligence, which might bump us away from being able to do so as a result of this insistence about ethics.

Round and round these debates continue to go.

Those on the must-be topnotch ethical AI are often quick to point out that by allowing AI to be anything less than a top ten, you are opening Pandora's box. For example, it could be that AI dips down into the negative numbers and sits at a -4, or worse too it digresses to become miserably and fully unethical at a dismal -10.

Anyway, this is a debate that is going to continue and not be readily resolved, so let's move on.

If you are still of the notion that ethics exists on a scale and that AI might also be measured by such a scale, and if you also are willing to accept that behavior can be driven or guided by offering where to reside on the scale, the time is ripe to bring up tuning knobs.

Ethics tuning knobs.

Here's how that works.

You come in contact with an AI system and are interacting with it.

The AI presents you with an ethics tuning knob, showcasing a scale akin to our ethics scale earlier proposed.

Suppose the knob is currently at a 6, but you want the AI to be acting more aligned with an 8, so you turn the knob upward to the 8.

At that juncture, the AI adjusts its behavior so that ethically it is exhibiting an 8-score level of ethical compliance rather than the earlier setting of a 6.

What do you think of that?

Some would bellow out balderdash, hogwash, and just unadulterated nonsense.

A preposterous idea or is it genius?

You'll find that there are experts on both sides of that coin.

Perhaps it might be helpful to provide the ethics tuning knob within a contextual exemplar to highlight how it might come to play.

Here's a handy contextual indication for you: *Will AI-based true self-driving cars potentially contain an ethics tuning knob for use by riders or passengers that use self-driving vehicles?*

Let's unpack the matter and see.

Some believe that a self-driving car should always strictly obey the speed limit.

Imagine that you have just gotten into a self-driving car in the morning and it turns out that you are possibly going to be late getting to work. Your boss is a stickler and has told you that coming in late is a surefire way to get fired.

You tell the AI via its Natural Language Processing (NLP) that the destination is your work address.

And, you ask the AI to hit the gas, push the pedal to the metal, screech those tires, and get you to work on-time.

But it is clear cut that if the AI obeys the speed limit, there is absolutely no chance of arriving at work on-time, and since the AI is only and always going to go at or less than the speed limit, your goose is fried.

Better luck at your next job.

Whoa, suppose the AI driving system had an ethics tuning knob.

Abiding strictly by the speed limit occurs when the knob is cranked up to the top numbers like say 9 and 10.

You turn the knob down to a 5 and tell the AI that you need to rush to work, even if it means going over the speed limit, which at a score of 5 it means that the AI driving system will mildly exceed the speed limit, though not in places like school zones, and only when the traffic situation seems to allow for safely going faster than the speed limit by a smidgeon.

The AI self-driving car gets you to work on-time!

Later that night, when heading home, you are not in as much of a rush, so you put the knob back to the 9 or 10 that it earlier was set at.

Also, you have a child-lock on the knob, such that when your kids use the self-driving car, which they can do on their own since there isn't a human driver needed, the knob is always set at the topmost of the scale and the children cannot alter it.

How does that seem to you?

Some self-driving car pundits find the concept of such a tuning knob to be repugnant.

They point out that everyone will "cheat" and put the knob on the lower scores that will allow the AI to do the same kind of shoddy and dangerous driving that humans do today. Whatever we might have otherwise gained by having self-driving cars, such as the hoped-for reduction in car crashes, along with the reduction in associated injuries and fatalities, will be lost due to the tuning knob capability.

Others though point out that it is ridiculous to think that people will put up with self-driving cars that are restricted drivers that never bend or break the law.

You'll end-up with people opting to rarely use self-driving cars and will instead drive their human-driven cars. This is because they know that they can drive more fluidly and won't be stuck inside a self-driving car that drives like some scaredy-cat.

As you might imagine, the ethical ramifications of an ethics tuning knob are immense.

In this use case, there is a kind of obviousness about the impacts of what an ethics tuning knob foretells.

Other kinds of AI systems will have their semblance of what an ethics tuning knob might portend, and though it might not be as readily apparent as the case of self-driving cars, there is potentially as much at stake in some of those other AI systems too (which, like a self-driving car, might entail life-or-death repercussions).

Conclusion

If you really want to get someone going about the ethics tuning knob topic, bring up the allied matter of the Trolley Problem.

The Trolley Problem is a famous thought experiment involving having to make choices about saving lives and which path you might choose. This has been repeatedly brought up in the context of self-driving cars and garnered acrimonious attention along with rather diametrically opposing views on whether it is relevant or not.

In any case, the big overarching questions are will we expect AI to have an ethics tuning knob, and if so, what will it do and how will it be used.

Those that insist there is no cause to have any such device are apt to equally insist that we must have AI that is only and always at the upmost of ethical behavior.

Is that a Utopian perspective or can it be achieved in the real world as we know it?

Only my crystal ball can say for sure.

CHAPTER 16

AI ETHICS
AND
AI TECHNICAL DEBT

One aspect of AI Ethics that is seldom being discussed consists of the facets underlying so-called AI Technical Debt. The notion is that many AI systems are being devised that are on borrowed time as to their technological underpinnings and that inevitably a form of "debt" is going to need to be paid. The same can be said of a corresponding semblance of AI Ethics debt. Let's jump into the matter.

Getting in over your head.

That's what often happens when people take on debt.

Shakespeare famously warned us about the dangers of going into debt, stating that "neither a borrower nor a lender is; for loan doth oft lose both itself and friend." For some people that become swamped by debt, they find themselves sinking into an all-encompassing abysmal abyss. The debt sorely and adversely impacts them, their loved ones, their friends and acquaintances, and otherwise bodes for indubitably rotten tidings.

Sometimes, a person is oblivious to their mounting debt.

I know that seems nearly impossible to imagine. What can happen is that the person starts making zillions of charges on their credit cards and they meanwhile delude themselves into not realizing there will ultimately be unfavorable consequences. The piper though will eventually need to be paid.

Credit card agencies often make life especially easy for those that wantonly are apt to spend. Charge this, charge that, and it all seems like free money. You have a seemingly endless credit limit, so why not keep spending. Little or no thought goes toward how this is going to get paid for.

Some people realize what they are doing but are insidiously hooked on spending recklessly. It is said to at times be like a gambling addiction. They might overtly know that what they are doing is racking up a debt that they can never afford to repay. Turns out that the urge to go into debt is seemingly greater than the stopping forces to prevent it.

More variations arise.

Some people know they are getting themselves into a lot of debt and do so straightforwardly. They are anticipating that the money being borrowed will provide a sizable payoff. Taking on debt could be highly profitable, and there are lots of instances where this has been a proven strategy.

They say that at times the debt rainbow can lead to a pot of gold at the end. That's at least the grand hope unless of course the payoff never happens.

Oopsie.

Why all this talk about debt?

Because there is another kind of debt that few know about, a type of debt that arises in the software development realm and has been coined as *technical debt.*

To be clear, technical debt can arise in any engineering or technological endeavor. I'm going to focus on the nature of technical debt in the context of software systems. Please do though keep in mind that the same notions can be applied to lots of other tech-oriented contexts.

Here's how technical debt in software arises.

A software engineer is working night and day on a programming project. It is a hard-fought battle. A timeline has been established for getting the code done and put into production by the end of the month. This is a ridiculous deadline and the programmer is at their wit's end as to how the coding can be finished by that rapidly approaching date.

Most seasoned programmers are used to these kinds of scenarios, which seem to happen overly frequently. Rather than receiving a deadline that is based on what can be done, there is a tendency for others to assign deadlines simply based on other whims that have nothing to do with the actual programming required. Get things done by this date is the mantra, regardless that the date was plucked from thin air or based on a dreamy whimsy.

Anyway, a programmer is apt to decide that to meet the deadline will require doing a bit of flimflam on the coding. Good programming practices dictate that you ought to build in error handling so that your code will be resilient and able to handle gotchas that occur once the program is put into use.

Nice idea, but that's going to get placed aside, for now, the hectic programmer decides. The programmer doubts there are many errors in the code and thus the error handling won't especially ever be needed. So, skip it, for now.

Score a foul point for the entry of technical debt into this scenario.

In essence, the program has taken on a form of debt. The debt is a future cost that for the moment seems worthwhile. Put off for today that which can be dealt with at some later unspecified date.

Nobody will presumably notice the debt for now. It is hidden from view. The programmer knows about it. Whether the managers overseeing the project know about it is another question. Sometimes they do, and they encourage the debt, aiming to attain the touted and prized deadline on time.

Sometimes the debt is only known to those that are creating it. Others that are presently unaware will on a later occasion find out to their dismay that such debt is laden inside the code.

Returning to the scenario, the programmer determines that omitting the error handling is not going to be enough of a jettison to reach the deadline. Something else has to be tossed over the side of this boat. After giving the matter some pronounced thought, the programmer stops documenting the code and goes into a heads-down mode of churning out lines upon lines of code.

Yes, that's another kind of technical debt that has been added to this mounting stack or heap.

The programmer figures that since they personally produced the code and ergo know the code by heart, there is no need to document it. No need to write down what the code does. No need to proffer inline explanations. The programmer believes that the code is so transparent and so obvious that anyone coming along to later update or modify the code will immediately understand it. Plus, documentation is not much fun and won't aid in meeting the deadline of having a running app that works.

For those of you that aren't programmers, you might not realize this is a rather common refrain by some alleged purists of coding. They don't want to mar their code with commentary, nor waste their precious mind on doing something considered mundane. The thing is, these same programmers will often curse themselves later on when called back to revise their prior code since they no longer remember what was in their minds when they generated the code.

In addition, any programmer that has ever had to take over someone else's code will undoubtedly tell you that it can be a nightmare to try and divine what the other programmer was trying to do. The code itself is insufficient to showcase what the purpose is. Without some documentation, albeit even meager or scant documentation, the code can be an enigma that either takes an excessive amount of time and effort to figure out or sometimes you end up having to summarily chuck out the code and start anew.

We've now got two variants of technical debt in this situation. There is a lack of error handling as one form of technical debt. The other technical debt is the paucity of documentation.

You might be tempted to assume that this is marginally any semblance of debt. It seems like nothing of great consequence is being owed.

Sorry, that's akin to playing the odds at the roulette wheel.

Let's assume that those incurred technical debts are able to allow the programmer to attain the end of the month deadline. Hurray! The deadline was achieved and all are happy and delightfully pleased with the now underway app.

Lurking though in the shadows is the ominous technical debt.

Imagine that after the app is in use for a week or two, when all of a sudden, the code reaches an unexpected error. Yikes! Without the error handling capabilities, the app has no provision about what to do. The app shuts down each time that the error occurs.

People using the app are furious.

What the heck is going on with this crazy app. One minute it seems to be working just fine, and the next moment it inexplicably closes down. Carping about this bizarre behavior spreads quickly across the vastness of social media and the Internet. Those that at first hailed the app as a tremendous breakthrough are now warning that you cannot count on it. At the worst of times, it can get flakey and die on you.

You see, the debt is now being paid, rather involuntarily one might say.

The cost to pay this technical debt could be enormous. Perhaps the app is no longer used by anyone and languishes as a useless or haphazard app that should be avoided entirely.

On top of that, whoever developed the app and fostered it into becoming available could face reputational ruin. You might anticipate lawsuits too, assuming that those using the app might believe that they suffered some form of losses due to the flakiness of the app.

In short, the cost to cover this technical debt might be many times more than the perceived debt value at the time it was initially incurred.

We can go further and make this a rather sad tale of woe. A different programmer is quickly brought in to resurrect the app. Upon looking at the code, the programmer is dismayed and taken aback that there is absolutely no documentation. The code is inscrutable. It is going to take weeks or maybe months to decipher this murky mound of enigmatic code.

The technical debt of not having documentation now rears its ugly head. This was not apparent by those that were earlier running the app as they had only encountered the other technical debt (i.e., the error handling technical debt).

As a rule of thumb, some technical debt will be readily witnessed or experienced, while other kinds of technical debt can remain hidden and elusive.

There is also the concept of garnering interest on technical debt, similar to incurring interest on financial debt. Suppose the programmer that is brought in to modify the code can successfully do so, and meanwhile doesn't document what they are doing. You could say that the technical debt associated with the lack of documentation is growing in interest or being further piled onto.

One other aspect to be aware of is that technical debt can happen at any stage of software development. I've focused for the moment on code debt, which is ostensibly the most popularly discussed instance of software technical debt.

You can also have software design debt. That's when you scrimp or incur technical debt during the design stage or phase of developing a system. This happens quite frequently, whereby there is angst to move right away into coding and so the design efforts are shortchanged. The shortchanged design elements are a form of technical design debt that will someday need to be repaid.

Another stage or phase of software technical debt consists of testing debt.

Developers do this all the time. When deadlines are nearing, the seemingly easiest thing to do is shorten or narrow the amount of testing that is going to be done. There is that infamous Silicon Valley mindset that it is best to move fast and break things. This includes a willingness to forgo extensive testing and just let the end-users become the testers.

That can be sensible or it can be a horrendous choice.

If an application is going to be used in simple ways and not be a life-or-death matter, you can potentially get away with piles of technical debt. Those that use the app might shrug off the problems of the app. They might be excited to be able to use the app, perhaps being in a beta group that gets access sooner than others.

The problem is that any life-or-death software that has technical debt is like a ticking timebomb. Depending upon the nature of the software technical debt involved, the consequences of that underlying debt might cause notable damages or harm.

One area that is already starting to encounter the throes of technical debt includes AI-based systems. I refer to this as *AI technical debt*. Though you might be assuming that AI systems are surely developed with the utmost of heightened stringent controls and capabilities, you'd be sadly and utterly mistaken. Indeed, as I've often pointed out, the pell-mell rush toward crafting AI systems has regrettably led to a goldrush that is ridden with software that is unreliable, poorly tested, and waiting to fail.

Let's then combine the overall software technical debt aspects and the AI goldrush, tying this amalgamation to matters entailing real-time life-or-death types of systems.

Where can such facets converge?

Answer: *AI-based self-driving cars.*

That might seem surprising, perhaps shocking to some. Well, get used to it. There is AI technical debt right now being incurred in the development of AI self-driving cars.

The piper will someday need to be repaid.

This is an alarming realization when you somberly consider that the future of cars consists of AI-based true self-driving cars. There isn't a human driver involved in a true self-driving car. Keep in mind that true self-driving cars are driven via an AI driving system. There isn't a need for a human driver at the wheel, and nor is there a provision for a human to drive the vehicle.

Here's an intriguing question that is worth pondering: *How might AI technical debt potentially undermine the advent of AI-based true self-driving cars?*

There is AI technical debt aplenty amidst the AI driving systems and related code of today's budding self-driving cars.

First, some estimates are that there could be around 100 million lines of code or more that exist to empower and enable the capabilities of a self-driving car. This includes proprietary code that a particular automaker or self-driving tech firm has devised for their self-driving cars. Also included are the reams and reams of third-party code, such as the use of open-source code that is intermixed into the AI driving systems and other components.

Scarily, many firms are unaware of how much AI technical debt they are sitting atop.

This is somewhat akin to those people that take on financial debt and aren't aware that they are doing so. It just kind of happens. Debt is incurred and not noted or tracked. The same can be said for some of the AI development groups and their amazing efforts to craft AI driving systems. They are incurring AI technical debt here and there, right and left, above and below, yet there isn't an explicit effort toward noting that it is piling up.

Where might this AI technical debt reside?

One of the most significant arenas consists of the AI underlying the sensory suite and all of its machinations.

The sensors for self-driving cars are crucial. By and large, sensors are being used that encompass real-time video cameras, radar, LIDAR, ultrasonic detection, thermal imagining, and so on (the choice of which kinds of sensors to use is highly variable and differs from firm to firm).

The sensors are essentially the eyes and ears of the AI driving system. During a driving journey, data is streaming into the sensors and being computationally analyzed. A significant means of doing the needed computational pattern matching consists of utilizing Machine Learning (ML) and Deep Learning (DL). Besides analyzing the data directly, there is also the need to perform Multi-Sensor Data Fusion (MSDF), bringing together the data and seeking to align and triangulate the interpretations of the driving scene.

Hidden within all of the complex code for these sensory uses is all manner of AI technical debt.

Some of the debt has been incurred by a rush to pull together the AI driving system and try to get a self-driving car up and going for tryouts. Some of the debt exists as a result of putting a myriad of AI developers to the task of developing the code, stretching the skills of novice AI developers, or pushing to the brink the skills of savvy AI developers. In addition, this is at times being undertaken without rigorous tracking and software coding practices being set up and observed.

I've described previously that the AI development efforts for self-driving cars can be given an overly wide berth and allowed to do their "magic" without the typical rigors expected of similar real-time life-or-death systems of this nature.

There are relatively few self-driving car makers that are directly watching out for AI technical debt.

What they all need to do is take a comprehensive inventory of their enormous efforts and figure out where that AI technical debt is potentially lurking. This can be painstaking and painful to do. Finger-pointing and all manner of unsightly blame-game exhortations can arise.

The easier path is to just wait and see what happens.

Note too that the AI technical debt can arise throughout each of the stages or phases of a self-driving car and its life cycle. It could be that there are design debt aspects that have yet to be uncovered, perhaps only gaining visibility once the self-driving car is underway on roadway trials. That's a bad time to be running into the skulking technical debt.

Conclusion

There are numerous additional twists and turns (I'll mention just a few more, given the space limitations herein).

Though the AI technical debt can be demonstratively bad, it can also be somewhat of a "necessity" in some cases, though this comes with a big caveat. If an AI team is at least aware of where the technical debt is being incurred, they can consider the tradeoffs of allowing it to exist. They can try to minimize the dangers of the debt. They can seek to reduce the amount of debt-related technical interest that will be accrued.

What should not happen is the outright hiding of any mounting AI technical debt. Trying to keep say upper management in the dark about the technical debt is going to be unseemly in the end, for everyone involved. Pressures to meet deadlines or to keep costs tapped down are certainly primal urges to go ahead and allow technical debt to soak into the AI driving system.

Lamentedly, those that are outspoken can find themselves internally blacklisted for decrying the generation of software technical debt, as per my discussion about the potential for whistleblowers to start appearing in the self-driving cars industry.

All told, if an existing self-driving car development effort isn't already on top of the AI technical debt phenomena, it is time to do something about it.

Better late than never.

And remember the immortal words of Benjamin Franklin in his 1758 treatise entitled *The Way To Wealth*: "The second vice is lying, and the first is running in debt."

Good old Ben knew what he was talking about back then, and which still applies in today's state-of-the-art AI-infused self-driving cars emergent world. This is undeniably sage wisdom worthy of posting on the cubicle walls of contemporary AI developers and their managers.

CHAPTER 17
AI ETHICS
AND
AI MALCISIOUS TAKEOVER

One aspect of AI Ethics that seems to be inadequately explored consists of the somewhat sci-fi spurred notion that AI will potentially exert a malicious takeover of humankind. Since this comes up with some frequency as a voiced concern, we can give the matter its due attention and do so in the real-world context of self-driving cars. Let's take a close look at this.

There are a lot of movies and TV shows that depict a mass control takeover of self-driving cars.

This seems to be on our minds.

For quite good reasons.

If a malicious evildoer was somehow able to take command of Autonomous Vehicles (AVs) such as self-driving cars, the outcome could be disastrous. This almost goes without saying. The usual portrayal in films is that the villain opts to have cars crash into each other. Well, that's just for starters. The self-driving cars are rammed into anything that isn't nailed down, and by gosh also steer into and collide with objects that are ostensibly nailed down too.

Humans riding inside self-driving cars are harmed. Humans in nearby conventional cars are harmed. Pedestrians are harmed. The gist is that self-driving cars under the command of a baddie will become a frightening and seemingly unstoppable destructive force.

How would you avoid becoming prey?

The key would seem to be staying off the roadways.

By keeping yourself indoors, it is highly unlikely that a devilishly directed self-driving car could reach you. Sure, one supposes that the autonomous vehicle could be instructed to try and ram your house.

We already know that this happens today from time to time when a human driver loses control of the wheel and swerves into a domicile (thus, it occurs at the direct hands of the human driver). Perhaps if several self-driving cars were directed to this malevolent task, it might become endangering. The odds are though that being indoors would be sufficiently protective.

We would need to abundantly curtail our travel activities.

Anyone on a bicycle becomes a potential target. Driving a conventional car is also going to be a target. Armored trucks would be a target, plus if they were self-driving capable, they could be added to the arsenal of the wrongdoer.

Pedestrians could potentially sprint from spot to spot, going through narrow passages that a self-driving car could not traverse. That won't be much satisfaction for trying to go from any given point A to point B on any long-distance basis. We would be essentially trapped in our nearest domains and be unable to do any extensive traveling.

When you see these kinds of portrayals, one question that some ask entails the matter of the vehicles running out of gas. Wouldn't self-driving cars eventually run out of gas? And if so, they would become useless paperweights. Without the fuel needed to be underway, any such self-driving car that is empty would no longer be much of a threat to anyone.

This might seem like a means of overcoming the feared invasion of the overlord-snatched AI-based self-driving cars, but regrettably, there is a catch. You see, there are plans afoot of trying to make refueling for self-driving cars an unmanned chore. A self-driving car pulls up to a gas pump or charging station, and an automated robotic arm makes sure that the hose connects with the vehicle.

You would certainly want this if we had a lot of everyday self-driving cars on our roadways.

Suppose you owned a self-driving car. Rather than having to take it over to the gas station or charging station to keep refueling the darned thing, you would just send it there on its own. In fact, assuming that you are likely using the self-driving car as ridesharing or ride-hailing vehicle, making you some extra dough, you would merely indicate to the AI driving system that whenever there is idle time and nothing else to do, route over to the nearest fueling station and get stocked up.

I realize this seems to be a disappointment for those hoping that it was the Achilles heel of self-driving cars that are surreptitiously overtaken by awful people.

You might say that another angle on how to stop this incursion would be that those self-driving cars are bound to eventually have something go awry since they are still cars when it comes down to it. A tire might blow out. The engine might conk out. Some kind of mechanical failure or breakage has got to ultimately arise.

There is some goods news and bad news on that front.

First, the bad news is that it is generally presumed that self-driving cars are going to be kept in a rather pristine shape. Those that own and run their self-driving cars are going to want to keep the maintenance at tiptop condition. The logic is somewhat obvious. If you are using your self-driving car to make money by providing rides, the time spent in a repair facility is lost income. To avoid extended stays in a repair shop, you'd better keep the vehicle in the best possible order.

This implies that upon the takeover of self-driving cars, the vehicles will most likely be in great shape and able to go quite a while before things start to fall apart. That's the bad news about pinning your hopes on the breakage vulnerability.

The good news somewhat is that eventually wear-and-tear would occur, and assuming that nobody will be willing to then fix up a self-driving car, we'll have those vehicles sloppily stuck and completely out of sorts. They will come to a grinding halt of their own accord, gradually and inevitably. Of course, we would be living in fear and uncertainty until that day arrived.

Here's yet another believed way to deal with those wayward self-driving cars.

You sneak up to a self-driving car. In your hands, you have a USB memory stick or equivalent. Upon getting into the vehicle, you plug in the device. It contains some form of programming that can undercut the existing programming. This will allow you to get the AI driving system to no longer be under the command or spell of the mastermind.

Aha, humanity and goodness will triumph once again.

Hold on for a second, there are problems with that proposed solution.

Sneaking up on a self-driving car could be a challenging affair.

Most self-driving cars are chockful of handy sensors such as video cameras, radar, LIDAR, ultrasonic units, thermal imaging, and the like. We can most likely assume that the takeover of the self-driving car has kept those sensory devices intact and underway. Without the use of those sensors, the AI driving system can't do much in terms of ascertaining where to drive the car (as a side note, the use of maps could be resorted upon, though this could be undermined in various ways by those trying to prevent the now-blinded self-driving cars from getting around readily).

The evildoer would presumably have the AI driving system be on constant alert for anyone approaching the vehicle, and then have the self-driving car skirt away (or try to drive at the person). The idea of trying to secretly get into a self-driving car in this takeover scenario is rather outstretched. I'm not saying that it cannot be done and simply emphasizing that it would be difficult to successfully achieve.

Even if you did get into the vehicle, the other problem is that your effort to reprogram the AI driving system might not be feasible.

Think of it this way.

If self-driving cars could easily be reprogrammed by merely getting into the vehicle and installing a memory stick or other programming tool, this would be a huge and dangerous exposure for all self-driving cars. It would imply that anybody riding in a self-driving car can pretty much willy-nilly change the AI driving system.

It is hoped and generally anticipated that there will be rigorous cybersecurity protections included in self-driving cars. This is intended to avert the odds of someone doing the very thing that we are now suggesting is wanted. Most of the time, we won't want someone to be able to take such an act. In the rare and so far fictional notion of a mass takeover, we might regret that we built such impenetrable protections, but meanwhile, it makes indubitable sense to have them.

For those of you that perchance know something about cybersecurity, you know that it is an ongoing cat and mouse game. As such, even if self-driving cars are well-protected from such an attack, there is still the chance of finding a way around the fortress of barriers and blockages. One guesses that if a mass takeover occurred, and upon virtually bringing together the most notable of cybersecurity experts and potential good-oriented hackers, perhaps a means could be figured out to make this USB memory stick containing an AI driving system reprogramming become a reality.

Remember though that getting into the car would be a challenge unto itself.

Plus, imagine that you were trying to go to every self-driving car and do this corrective action. We don't know how many self-driving cars we might eventually have on our roadways, so the number is still unknown. On the other hand, there are about 250 million conventional cars in the United States alone.

Some predict that by and large, we will gradually wean ourselves away from conventional cars. If that happens, we might end up with the same number of self-driving cars, namely on the order of 250 million or so.

There are arguments about the number of self-driving cars that we will need.

Since most conventional cars are only used about 5% or less of their available time (sitting parked about 95% or more of the time), we might not need the same number of self-driving cars due to the built-in AI driving system and that they can operate 24x7. Some believe we can have a lot fewer self-driving cars to make up for the eventual junking of all those conventional cars.

Other experts suggest that our demand to use self-driving cars will skyrocket as we realize how convenient they are. This suggests we all might go for journeys in cars more so than we do today. Ergo, it is conceivable that we might need just as many self-driving cars as the number of today's conventional cars, or perhaps even more self-driving cars will be desired.

The key point is that trying to go to each and every self-driving car to insert the antidote, as it were, would be laborious and seemingly impractical.

That doesn't end the case for trying to do the AI driving system reprogramming. There is another potential avenue.

Self-driving cars will be making use of OTA (Over-The-Air) electronic communication capabilities. This is akin to what happens when you get your laptop or smartphone updated. It is expected that self-driving cars will connect to the cloud of the fleet owner or operator, doing so to get updates to the onboard software. In addition, the self-driving car can upload data to the cloud. This might include the status of the vehicle, along with the sensory data collected during a driving journey.

I think you know where I am heading.

Rather than having to physically get into each self-driving car, perhaps we could exploit the OTA to try and change the AI driving system. All we would need to do is get the OTA to willingly download some patches that we had put together. This might either turn the AI driving system back into what it was supposed to be doing or maybe we have it be blanked out entirely. The approach of blanking out the AI driving system would seem the more assured approach to stop the evildoer takeover, though this also means that the vehicle becomes a doorstop.

Turns out that there are lots of twists and turns now that we've introduced the OTA aspects into this scenario. The beauty of using OTA is that we could presumably do so massively across the gamut of self-driving cars that have been villainously overtaken. Rather than trying to physically go to each self-driving car by hand, we can on a widespread basis electronically communicate the presumed remedy that we've hurriedly crafted.

Sounds good, and a relief that the matter is seemingly settled.

Not so fast.

There are plenty of gotchas and holes in that corrective scheme.

One aspect that we've not yet discussed is how in the heck did the takeover happen to begin with? In other words, we took at face value that somehow the maniac mastermind has been able to take over self-driving cars. Let's explore that overthrow and then return to considering how to undo or overtake the overtaking.

As already suggested, one approach would be to physically get into a self-driving car and use some immediate means to try and reprogram the AI driving system, doing so for evildoer purposes rather than to correct whatever an evildoer has already done. There are a variety of ways that this in-car invasion could be approached. One would hope that the cybersecurity of the AI driving system has been mindfully constructed and will not be especially readily breached. That's not to say it cannot necessarily be flouted, only that it will be hard to do.

Of course, the laborious chore of going from self-driving car to self-driving car would seem not very expedient if the fiend is aiming to perform a mass takeover. The alternative would be to use the OTA. Yes, the same OTA that is purposely included by the automaker or self-driving tech firm for aiding in making desired updates could be sneakily used for wicked intent.

The OTA provides an opportunity for badness. If a crook can somehow plant something into the cloud of the self-driving car fleet, there is a chance of getting that distributed out and into the self-driving cars via the OTA. This might occur by hiding the untoward element inside an otherwise accepted and everyday update going down to the autonomous vehicles. Or it could consist of a special update package that convinces the OTA mechanism that everything is okay and the element should be sent out.

As might be evident, the OTA is a dual-edged sword.

Then again, maybe it is a tri-edged sword.

Here's why.

The OTA is normally used to send approved updates that are downloaded and installed into the AI driving system. There is the chance that a malicious code leverages the OTA and gets downloaded and installed. And there is the possibility of using the OTA to correct or delete the malicious code. Perhaps that's at least three sides of the sword, though we could continue this line of thought indefinitely and continue the cat and mouse game indefinitely.

Since the OTA is the drawbridge that connects the fortress to the rest of the world, there needs to be a lot of protection about allowing the drawbridge to be used. For those automakers and self-driving tech firms, they do not want the drawbridge to be used by those devilish intruders.

Meanwhile, the devilish intruder would likely not only realize that their best shot would be to exploit the OTA drawbridge, but they also might decide to try and cut off the drawbridge after successfully making an invasion. Either burn the drawbridge to the ground and stop any further OTA or try to alter the drawbridge so that only they can continue to make use of it.

We need to also bring up another crucial factor.

Not all self-driving cars will be the same.

A particular automaker might choose to develop or select a self-driving stack of code that befits their specific brands and makes of self-driving cars. When you see a self-driving car that is made by company X, the odds are that the software and systems running onboard are quite different from the self-driving cars made by company Y. The same can be generally said about the OTA being used.

The reason this is notable in the case of a mass takeover of self-driving cars is that it is going to be somewhat harder to intrude across all variants of self-driving cars. An evildoer might focus on a particular set of self-driving cars made by company X. Whether they can do the same against the self-driving cars of company Y is not necessarily assured.

What this means is that it might not be a mass per se, and only a subset of self-driving cars that the maniacal takeover occurs. Suppose that we had a city with hundreds of self-driving cars made by company X, and other hundreds of self-driving cars made by company Y. It could be that only the company X self-driving cars are part of the takeover, while an attempt to overrun the company Y was rebuffed or not even tried at all.

This might not be of much solace if there are millions upon millions of those company X self-driving cars out on our public roadways. You could say that only those company X self-driving cars are being conquered, but that still is a potentially large number of autonomous vehicles and ostensibly dangerous to have in the takeover column.

Conclusion

Much more can be examined in this doom-and-gloom scenario.

When or if such a mass takeover were to occur, one key question is whether the self-driving cars would now have wholly contained whatever their foul mission is to be, or would they rely upon the OTA or some other form of electronic communication to get instructions during their adverse takeover journeys.

In essence, one approach involves infusing the AI driving system with whatever bad acts it is supposed to undertake, and then try to break off any further electronic communications. Another approach involves seeking to communicate on a mass basis to direct the self-driving cars while they are in this deranged takeover mode. This allowance for communicating though becomes a point of potential weakness in the takeover plot since it can possibly be used to disrupt or ultimately nullify the malevolent scheme.

Makes your head spin at all of the trickery involved.

Not wanting to further be glum, but there is a similar chance of doing the same kind of mass takeover for cars that are not self-driving cars. Those vehicles that are at Level 2 and Level 3 are bound to eventually have OTA. Everything we've just discussed applies to Level 2 and Level 3 and has an added variation. Since Level 2 and Level 3 presume that a human driver is available at the wheel, this means that the programmed takeover could end up becoming a struggle between the human driver and the automation.

You might be thinking that the solution to nearly all of this would be to have a big red button or an on-off switch inside all cars that could be used to turn off the automation. Some pundits are pushing for this arguable solution.

Okay, so where does this leave us?

For those that are devising self-driving cars (and pretty much any automotive vehicles containing advanced automation), the importance of establishing rigorous cybersecurity protections is paramount.

That is a tall order. There is a myriad of ways to undercut the computer system security of an automobile. Lots and lots of possible attack vectors and vulnerable paths exist.

Discussing the notion of a mass takeover seems like a crying wolf to some. Those skeptics ought to also take into account the role of nation-states as it pertains to self-driving cars. The purpose herein was not to suggest that a mass takeover will of necessity happen. The intent is to awaken the awareness of what all automakers and self-driving tech firms need to be doing, namely devoting a tremendous amount of energy, expertise, and devoted attention to securing their automation from cyberattacks.

In the rush to try and deploy self-driving cars onto the roadways, seeking to have those vehicles safely proceed from point A to point B, it can be easy to lose sight of the cybersecurity considerations. Those leading the existent self-driving car efforts are at times preoccupied with the point A to point B tryouts (naturally so), and not equally garnering focus on the cybersecurity elements. Sadly, some even have that "we'll worry about it later" perspective, figuring they have plenty of time to one day get the cybersecurity in place for their AI driving systems.

Let's not allow the strident pursuit of self-driving cars to become a vulnerability by undervaluing or being distracted from the concerns and dangers that are looming from those evildoers that would seek to do malicious cyberhacking on a mass sized basis.

The veritable hand wringing on this topic is well worth the stress and abject worry, mark my words.

CHAPTER 18

AI ETHICS AND AI FORBIDDEN KNOWLEDGE

An intriguing aspect that AI Ethics is only starting to explore consists of the possibility that AI efforts could reveal disastrous forbidden knowledge. We need to explore this notion and grapple with the ramifications, preferably doing so before the genie is already out of the bottle. Let's take a close look at the matter.

I have a vexing question for you.

Are there things that we must not know?

This is an age-old question.

Some assert that there is the potential for knowledge that ought to not be known. In other words, there are ideas, concepts, mental formulations, and other at times tangible and yet somewhat intangible facets of knowledge that if we should become aware of that knowledge it could be our downfall. The discovery or invention of some new innovation or way of thinking could be unduly dangerous. It would be best to not go there, as it were, and avoid ever landing into such knowledge.

A common means to refer to such knowledge is to coin it as forbidden knowledge.

The typical basis for wanting to forbid the discovery or emergence of so-called forbidden knowledge is that the adverse consequences are overwhelming. By overwhelming, the emphasis is that even if the knowledge was possibly helpful and had merits, the end result is so devastating and undercutting that the bad side outweighs the good that could be derived from the knowledge.

It is conceivable that there might be knowledge that is so bad that it has no good possibilities at all. Thus, rather than trying to balance or weigh the good versus the bad, the knowledge has no counterbalancing effects. It is just plain bad. This would seem to be harder to try and declare as worthy of consideration in such an extreme case.

We are usually though faced with the matter of knowledge that has both the good and the bad as to how it might be utilized or employed. This then leads to a dogged debate about whether the bad is so bad that it outweighs the good. On top of this, there is the unrealized bad and the unrealized good, which could be differentiated from the realized bad and the realized good (in essence, the knowledge might be said to be either good or bad, though this is purely conceptual and not put into real-world conditions to attest or become realized as such).

The most familiar reference to forbidden knowledge is likely evoked via the Garden of Eden and the essence of forbidden fruit.

A contemporary down-to-earth example often discussed about forbidden knowledge consists of the atomic bomb. Some suggest that the knowledge devised or invented to ultimately produce a nuclear bomb provides a quite visible and overt exemplar of the problems associated with knowledge. Had the knowledge about being able to attain an atomic bomb never been achieved, there presumably would not be any such device. In debates about the topic, it is feasible to take a resolute position favoring the attainment of an atomic bomb and there are equally counterbalancing contentions sternly disfavoring this attainment.

One perplexing problem about forbidden knowledge encompasses knowing beforehand the kind of knowledge that might end up in the forbidden category. This is a bit of a Catch-22 or circular type of puzzle. You might discover knowledge and then ascertain it ought to be forbidden, but the cat is kind of out of the bag due to the knowledge having been already uncovered or rendered. Oopsie, you should have in advance decided to not go there and therefore have avoided falling into the forbidden knowledge zone.

On a related twist, suppose that we could beforehand declare what type of knowledge is to be averted because it is predetermined as forbidden. Some people might accidentally discover the knowledge, doing so by happenstance, and now they've again potentially opened Pandora's box. Meanwhile, there might be others that regardless of being instructed to not derive any such stated forbidden knowledge, do so anyway.

This then takes us to a frequently used retort about forbidden knowledge, namely, if you don't seek the forbidden knowledge there is a chance that someone else will, and you'll be left in the dust because they got there first. In that preemptive viewpoint, the claim is that it is better to go ahead and forage for the forbidden knowledge and not get caught behind the eight ball when someone else beats you to the punch.

Round and round we can go.

The main thing that most would agree to is that knowledge is power.

The alluded to power could be devastating and destroy others, possibly even leading to the self-destruction of the wielder of the knowledge. Yet there is also the potential for knowledge to be advantageous and save humanity from other ills.

Maybe we ought to say that knowledge is powerful. Despite that perhaps obvious proclamation, we might also add that knowledge can decay and gradually become outdated or less potent. Furthermore, since we are immersing ourselves herein into the cauldron of the love-it or hate-it knowledge conundrum, knowledge can be known and yet undervalued, perhaps only becoming valuable at a later time and in a different light.

There is a case to be made that humankind has a seemingly irresistible allure toward more and more knowledge.

Some philosophers suggest you are unlikely to be able to bottle up or stop this quest for knowledge. If that's the manner of how humanity will be, this implies that you must find ways to control or contain knowledge and give up on the belief that we can altogether avoid landing into forbidden knowledge.

There is a relatively new venue prompting a lot of anxious hand wringing pertaining to forbidden knowledge, namely the advent of Artificial Intelligence (AI).

Here's the rub.

Suppose that we are able to craft AI systems that make use of knowledge about how humans can think. There are two major potential gotchas.

First, the AI systems themselves might end up doing good things and they also might end up doing bad things. If the bad outweighs the good, maybe we are shooting our own foot by allowing AI to be put into use.

Secondly, perhaps this could be averted entirely by deciding that there is forbidden knowledge about how humans think, and we ought to not discover or reveal those mental mechanisms. It is the classic stepwise logic that step A axiomatically leads to step B. We won't need to worry about AI systems (step B), if we never allow the achievement of step A (figuring out how humans think and then imparting that into computers), since the attainment of AI would presumably not arise.

In any case, there is inarguably a growing concern about AI.

Plenty of efforts are underway to promulgate a semblance of AI Ethics, meaning that those developers and indeed all stakeholders that are conceiving of, building, and putting into use an AI system needs to consider the ethical aspects of their efforts. AI systems have been unveiled and placed into use that is replete with all sorts of notable concerns, including incorporating unsavory biases and other problems.

All told, one bold and somewhat stark argument is that the pursuit of AI is being underpinned or stoked by the discovery and then exploitation of forbidden knowledge.

Be aware that many would scoff at this allegation.

There are those deeply immersed in the field of AI that would laugh that there is anything in the entirety of AI to date that constitutes potential forbidden knowledge. The technology and technological elements are relatively ho-hum, they would argue. You would be hard-pressed to pinpoint what AI-related knowledge that is already known comes anywhere near the ballpark of forbidden knowledge.

For those that concur with that posture, there is the reply that it might be future knowledge that we have not yet attained that is the upcoming forbidden kind, and for which we are heading pell-mell down that path. Thus, they would concede that we haven't arrived at forbidden knowledge at this juncture, but this is an insidious distractor due to the aspect that it masks or belies our qualms entailing the possibility that it lays in wait at the next turn.

One area where AI is being actively used is to create Autonomous Vehicles (AVs).

We are gradually seeing the emergence of self-driving cars and can expect self-driving trucks, self-driving motorcycles, self-driving drones, self-driving planes, self-driving ships, self-driving submersibles, etc.

Today's conventional cars are eventually going to give way to the advent of AI-based true self-driving cars. Self-driving cars are driven via an AI driving system. There isn't a need for a human driver at the wheel, and nor is there a provision for a human to drive the vehicle.

Here's an intriguing question that has arisen: *Might the crafting of AI-based true self-driving cars take us into the realm of discovering forbidden knowledge, and if so, what should be done about this?*

The crux here is whether or not there is forbidden knowledge lurking within the existing and ongoing efforts to achieve AI-based true self-driving cars. We'll begin by considering the status of the existent efforts and then shift into speculation about the future of such efforts.

Per the earlier discussion about whether there is forbidden knowledge that has already perchance been revealed or discovered via the efforts toward today's AI systems all told, the odds seem stacked against such a notion at this time, and likewise the same could be said about the pursuit of self-driving cars. Essentially, there doesn't seem to be any forbidden knowledge per se that has been discovered or revealed during the self-driving cars development journey so far, at least with respect to the conventional wisdom about what forbidden knowledge might entail.

One could try to argue that it is premature to reach such a conclusion and that we might, later on, realize that forbidden knowledge was indeed uncovered or invented, and we just didn't realize it. That is a rabbit hole that we'll not go down for now, though you are welcome to keep that presumption at hand if so desired.

That covers the present, and ergo we can turn our attention to the future.

Generally, the efforts underway today have been primarily aimed at achieving Level 4, and the hope is that someday we will go beyond Level 4 and attain Level 5. To get to a robust Level 4, most would likely say that we can continue the existing approaches.

Not everyone would agree with that assumption. Some believe that we will get stymied within Level 4. Furthermore, the inability to produce a robust Level 4 will ostensibly preclude us from being able to attain Level 5. There is a contingent that suggests we need to start over and set aside the existing AI approaches, which otherwise are taking us down a dead-end or blind alley. An entirely new way of devising AI for autonomous vehicles is needed, they would vehemently argue.

There is also a contingent that asserts the Level 4 itself is a type of dead-end. In brief, those proponents would say that we will achieve a robust Level 4, though this will do little good towards attaining Level 5. Once again, their view is similar to the preceding remark that we will need to come up with some radically new understandings about AI and the nature of cognitive acumen in order to get self-driving cars into the Level 5 realm.

Aha, it is within that scope of having to dramatically revisit and revamp what AI is and how we can advance significantly in the pursuit of AI that the forbidden knowledge question can reside. In theory, perhaps the only means of attaining Level 5 will be to strike upon some knowledge that we do not yet know and that for which bodes for falling within the realm of forbidden knowledge.

To some, this seems farfetched.

They would emphatically ask; just what kind of knowledge are you even talking about?

Here's their logic. Humans are able to drive cars. Humans do not seem to need or possess forbidden knowledge as it relates to the act of driving a car. Therefore, it seems ridiculous on the face of things to claim or contend that the only means to get AI-based true self-driving cars, for which they would be driven on an equal basis as human drivers can drive, would require the discovery or invention of whatever might be construed as forbidden knowledge.

Seems like pretty ironclad logic.

The retort is that humans have common-sense reasoning. With common-sense reasoning, we seem to know all sorts of things about the world around us. When we drive a car, we intrinsically make use of our common-sense reasoning. We take for granted that we do have a common-sense reasoning capacity, and similarly, we take for granted that it integrally comes to the fore when driving a car.

Attempts to create AI that can exhibit the equivalent of human common-sense reasoning have made ostensibly modest or some would say minimal progress (to clarify, those pursuing this line of inquiry are to be lauded, it's just that no earthshattering breakthroughs seem to have been reached and none seem on the immediate horizon). Yes, there are some quite fascinating and exciting efforts underway, but when you measure those against the everyday common-sense reasoning of humans, there is no comparison. They are night and day. If this were a contest, the humans win hands down, no doubt about it, and the AI experimental efforts encompassing common-sense reasoning are mere playthings in contrast.

You might have gleaned where this line of thought is headed.

The belief by some is that until we crack open the enigma of common-sense reasoning, there is little chance of achieving a Level 5, and perhaps also this will hold back the Level 4 too. It could be that a secret ingredient of sorts for autonomous vehicles is the need to figure out and include common-sense reasoning into AI-based driving and piloting systems.

If you buy into that logic, the added assertion is that maybe within the confines of how common-sense reasoning takes place is a semblance of forbidden knowledge. On the surface, you would certainly assume that if we knew entirely how common-sense reasoning works, there would not appear to be any cause for alarm or concern. The act of employing common-sense reasoning does not seem to necessarily embody forbidden knowledge.

The twist is that perhaps the underlying cognitive means that gives rise to the advent of common-sense reasoning is where there is forbidden knowledge. Some deep-rooted elements in the nature of human thought and how we form common sense and undertake common-sense reasoning are possibly a type of knowledge that will be shown as crucial and a forbidden knowledge formulation.

Conclusion

Wow, that's quite a bit of pondering, contemplation, and (some would say) wild thinking.

Maybe so, but it is a consideration that some would wish that we gave at least some credence toward and devoted attention to. There is the angst that we might find ourselves by happenstance stumbling into forbidden knowledge on these voracious self-driving cars quests.

For however you might emphasize that having AI-based true self-driving cars will be a potential blessing, proffering mobility-for-all and leading to reducing the number of car crash-related fatalities, there is a sneaking suspicion that it will not be all-good. The catch or trap could be that there is some kind of forbidden knowledge that will get brought to the eye and we will inevitably kick ourselves that we didn't see it coming.

The next time you are munching on a delicious apple, give some thought to whether self-driving cars might be forbidden fruit.

We are on the path to taking a big bite, and we'll have to see where that takes us.

CHAPTER 19

AI ETHICS AND EXPLAINABLE AI

A core principle of AI Ethics is that AI systems are supposed to be transparent, allowing us to ascertain whether the AI is operating in an equitable and unbiased manner. Generally, one of the ways in which AI transparency is being devised consists of crafting AI that is able to explain itself. This is usually referred to as Explainable AI (XAI). Let's take a close look at the matter.

Our lives are filled with explanations.

You go to see your primary physician due to a rather sore shoulder. The doctor tells you to rest your arm and avoid any heavy lifting. In addition, a prescription is given. You immediately wonder why you would need to take medication and also are undoubtedly interested in knowing what the medical diagnosis and overall prognosis are.

So, you ask for an explanation.

In a sense, you have just opened a bit of Pandora's box, at least with regards to the nature of the explanation that you might get. For example, the medical doctor could rattle a lengthy and jargon-filled indication of shoulder anatomy and dive deeply into the chemical properties of the medication that has been prescribed. That's probably not the explanation you were seeking.

It used to be that physicians did not expect patients to ask for explanations. Whatever was said by the doctor was considered somewhat sacrosanct. The very nerve of asking for an explanation was tantamount to questioning the veracity of a revered medical opinion.

Some doctors would gruffly tell you to simply do as they have instructed (no questions permitted) or might utter something rather insipid like your shoulder needs help and this is the best course of action. Period, end of story.

Nowadays, medical doctors are aware of the need for viable explanations. There is specialized "bedside" training that takes place in medical schools. Hospitals have their own in-house courses. Upcoming medical doctors are graded on how they interact with patients. And so on.

Though that certainly has opened the door toward improved interaction with patients, it does not necessarily completely solve the explanations issue.

Knowing how to best provide an explanation is both art and science. You need to consider that there is the explainer that will be providing the explanation, and there is a person that will be the recipient of the explanation.

Explanations come in all shapes and sizes.

A person seeking an explanation might have in mind that they want a fully elaborated explanation, containing all available bells and whistles. The person giving the explanation might in their mind be thinking that the appropriate explanation is short and sweet. There you have it, an explanation mismatch brewing right before our eyes.

The explainer might do a crisp explanation and be happily satisfied with their explanation. Meanwhile, the person receiving the explanation is entirely dissatisfied. At this point, the person that received the explanation could potentially grit their teeth and just figure that this is all they are going to get. They might silently walk away and be darned upset, opting to not try and fight city hall, as it were, and merely accede to the minimal explanation proffered.

Perhaps the person receiving the explanation decides they would like to get a more elaborated version. They might stand their ground and ask for a more in-depth explanation. Now we need to consider what the explainer is going to do. The explainer might believe that the explanation was more than sufficient, and see no need to provide any additional articulation.

The explainer might be confused about why the initial explanation was not acceptable. Maybe the person receiving the explanation wasn't listening or had failed to grasp the meaning of the words spoken. At this juncture, the explainer might therefore decide to repeat the same explanation that was just given and do so to ensure that the person receiving the original explanation really understood what was said.

You can likely anticipate that this is about to spiral out of control.

The person that is receiving this "elaborated" explanation is bound to ascertain that it is merely the same explanation and has been repeated, nearly verbatim. That's insulting! The person receiving the explanation now believes they are being belittled by the explainer. Either this person will hold their own tongue and give up trying to get an explanation, or try hurtling insults about how absurd an explanation the explanation was.

It can devolve into a messy affair, that's for sure.

The overarching point is that there is a delicate dance between the explainer and the providing of an explanation, along with the receiver and the desired nature of an explanation.

We usually take for granted these aspects. In other words, you rarely see an explainer ask what kind of explanation someone wants to have. Instead, the explainer launches into whatever semblance of an explanation that they assume the person would find useful. Rushing into providing an explanation can have its benefits, though it can also start an unsightly verbal avalanche that is going to take down both the explainer and the person receiving the explanation.

Some suggest that the explainer ought to start by inquiring about the type of explanation that the other person is seeking. This might include asking what kind of background the other person has, such as in the case of a medical diagnosis whether the other person is familiar with medical terminology and the field of medicine. There might also be a gentle inquiry as to whether the explanation should be done in one large fell swoop or possibly divided into bite-sized pieces. Etc.

The difficulty with that kind of pre-game formation is that sometimes the receiver doesn't want to go through that gauntlet. They just want an explanation (or so they say). Trying to do a preamble is likely to irritate that receiver and they will feel as though the explanation is being purposely delayed. This could even smack of hiding of the facts or some other nefarious basis for delaying the explanation.

All told, we usually expect to get an explanation when we ask for one, and not have to go through a vast checklist beforehand.

Another twist to all of this entails the interactive dialogue that can occur during explanations.

The manner of explanations is not necessarily done in a one-breath fashion from start to end. Instead, it is more likely that during the explanation, the receiver will interrupt and ask for clarification or have questions that arise. This is certainly a sensible aspect. If the explanation is going awry, why have it go on and on, wherein instead the receiver can hopefully tailor or reshape the direction and style of the explanation.

For example, suppose that you are a medical professional and have gone to see a medical doctor about your sore shoulder. Imagine that the doctor doing the diagnosis does not realize that the patient is a fellow medical specialist. In that case, the explanation offered is likely to be aimed at a presumed non-medical knowledge base and proceed in potentially simplistic ways (with respect to medical advice). The person receiving the explanation would undoubtedly interrupt and clarify that they know about medicine and the explanation should rightfully be readjusted accordingly.

You might be tempted to believe that explanations can be rated as being either good or bad. Though you could take such a perspective, the general notion is that explanations and their beauty are in the eye of the beholder. One person's favored explanation might be a disastrous or terrible one for someone else. That being said, there is still a modicum of a basis for assessing explanations and comparing them to each other.

We can add a twist on that twist.

Suppose you receive an explanation and believe it to be a good one.

Later on, you learn something else regarding the matter and realize that the explanation was perhaps incomplete. Worse still, it could be that the explanation was intentionally warped to give you a false impression of a given situation. In short, an explanation can be used to purposely create falsehoods.

That's why getting an explanation is replete with problems. We oftentimes assume that if we ask for an explanation, and if it seems plausible, this attests that the matter is well-settled and above board. The thing is, an explanation can be distorted, either by design or by happenstance and lead us into a false sense of veracity or truthfulness at hand.

Another angle to explanations deals with asking for an explanation versus being given an explanation when it has not been requested. An explainer might give you an explanation outright because they assume you want one, whereas maybe you possibly don't want and nor care for getting an explanation and are satisfied to just continue on. At that point, if you disrupt the explanation, the explainer might be taken aback.

More twisting turns can arise.

Why all this talk about explanations?

Because of AI.

The increasing use of Artificial Intelligence (AI) in everyday computer systems is taking us down a path whereby the computer makes choices and we the humans have to live with those decisions. If you apply for a home loan, and an AI-based algorithm turns you down, the odds are that all you'll know is that you did not get the loan. You won't have any idea about why you were denied the loan.

Presumably, had you consulted with a human that was doing the loan granting, you might have been able to ask them to explain why you got turned down.

Note that this is not always the case, and it could be that the human would not be willing or able to explain the matter. The loan granting person might shrug their shoulders and say they have no idea why you were turned down, or they might tell you that company policy precludes them from giving you an explanation.

Ergo, I am not suggesting that just because a human is in the loop you will necessarily get an explanation. Plus, as repeatedly emphasized earlier, the explanation might be rather feeble and altogether useless. For example, the loan granting person might tell you that you were denied because you were turned down for the loan.

Say what?

Yes, that is a non-explanation explanation under the wink-wink fakery cloak of being an explanation.

In any case, there is a big hullabaloo these days that AI systems ought to be programmed to provide explanations for whatever they are undertaking.

This is known as Explainable AI (XAI).

XAI is growing quickly as an area of keen interest. People using AI systems are going to likely expect and somewhat demand that they get an explanation provided to them. Since the number of AI systems is rapidly growing, there is going to be a huge appetite for having a machine-produced explanation about what the AI is doing.

The rub is that oftentimes the AI is arcane and not readily amenable to generating an explanation.

Take as an example the use of Machine Learning (ML) and Deep Learning (DL). These are computational pattern matching algorithms that examine data and try to ferret out mathematical patterns. Sometimes the inner computational aspects are complex and do not lend themselves to being explained in any everyday human-comprehensible and logic-based way.

This means that the inherent design of the AI is by its structure not intrinsically set up for providing explanations. In that case, there are usually attempts to add on an XAI component. This XAI either probes into the AI and tries to ferret out what took place, or it sits aside from the AI and has been preprogrammed to provide explanations based on what is assumed has occurred within the mathematically enigmatic mechanisms.

Some assert that you ought to build the XAI into the core of whatever AI is being devised. Thus, rather than bolting onto the AI some afterthought about producing explanations, the design of the AI from the ground-up should encompass a proclivity to produce explanations.

Amidst all of that technological pondering, there are the other aspects of what constitutes an explanation. If you revisit my earlier comments about how explanations tend to work, and the variability depending upon the explainer and the person receiving the explanation, you can readily see how difficult it might be to programmatically produce explanations.

The cheapest way to go involves merely having pre-canned explanations. A loan granting system might have been set up with five explanations for why a loan was denied. Upon your getting turned down for the loan, you get shown one of those five explanations. There is no interaction. There is no particular semblance that the explanation is fitting or suitable to you in particular.

Those are the pittance explanations.

A more robust and respectable XAI capability would consist of generating explanations on the fly, in real-time, and do so based on the particular situation at hand. In addition, the XAI would try to ascertain what flavor or style of explanation would be suitable for the person receiving the explanation.

And this explainer feature ought to allow for fluent interaction with the person getting the explanation. The receiver should be able to interrupt the explanation, getting the explainer or XAI to shift to other aspects or reshape the explanation based on what the person indicates.

Of course, those are the same types of considerations that human explainers should also take into account. This brings up the fact that doing really good XAI is harder than it might seem. In a manner of speaking, you are likely to need to use AI within the XAI in order to be able to simulate or mimic what a human explainer is supposed to be able to do (though, as we know, not all humans are adept at giving explanations).

Shifting gears, you might be wondering what areas or applications could especially make use of XAI.

One such field of endeavor entails Autonomous Vehicles (AVs). We are gradually going to have autonomous forms of mobility, striving toward a mobility-for-all mantra. There will be self-driving cars, self-driving trucks, self-driving motorcycles, self-driving submersibles, self-driving drones, self-driving planes, and the rest.

You might at first thought be puzzled as to why AVs might need XAI. We can use self-driving cars to showcase how XAI is going to be a vital element for AVs.

The question is this: *In what way will Explainable AI (XAI) be important to the advent of AVs and as showcased via the emergence of self-driving cars?*

First, be aware that many of the existing self-driving car tryouts have very little if any semblance of XAI in them.

The initial belief was that people would get into a self-driving car, provide their destination, and be silently whisked to that locale. There would be no need for interaction with the AI driving system. There would ergo be no need for an explanation or XAI capability.

We can revisit that assumption by considering what happens when you use ridesharing and have a human driver at the wheel.

There are certainly instances wherein you get into an Uber or Lyft vehicle and there is stony silence for the entirety of the trip. You've likely already provided the destination via the ride-request app. The person driving is intently doing the driving and ostensibly going to that destination. No need to chat. You can play video games on your smartphone and act as though there isn't another human in the vehicle.

That's perfectly fine.

Imagine though that during the driving journey, all of a sudden, the driver decides to go a route that you find unexpected or unusual. You might ask the driver why there is a change in the otherwise normal path to the destination. They would hopefully prompt an explanation from the human driver.

There you go, I just said it, the notion of an explanation has come up in the context of driving a car.

Indeed, there are lots of situations in which a passenger is likely to seek an explanation from a driver.

We'll cover a few of those in a moment.

Now, in this ridesharing example, it could be that the human driver gives you no explanation or provides a flimsy explanation. Humans do that. In theory, a properly done XAI will provide an on-target explanation, though this can be challenging to do. Maybe the human driver tells you that there is construction taking place on the main highway, and to avoid a lengthy delay, an alternative course is being undertaken.

You might be satisfied with that explanation. On the other hand, perhaps you live in the area and are curious about the nature of the construction taking place. Thus, you ask the driver for further details about the construction. In a sense, you are interacting with an explainer and seeking additional nuances or facets about the explanation that was being provided.

Okay, put on your self-driving car thinking-cap and consider what a passenger might want from an XAI.

A self-driving car is taking you to your home.

The normal path that would be used is unexpectedly diverted from the AI driving system. You are likely to want to ask the AI why the driving journey is altering from your expected traversal. Many of the existing tryouts of self-driving cars would not have any direct means of having the AI explain this matter, and instead, you would need to connect with a remote agent of the fleet operator that oversees the self-driving cars.

In essence, rather than building the XAI, the matter is shunted over to a remote human to explain what is going on. This is something that won't be especially scalable. In other words, once there are hundreds of thousands of self-driving cars on our roadways, the idea of having the riders always needing to contact a remote agent for the simplest of questions is going to be a huge labor cost and a logistics nightmare.

There ought to be a frontline XAI that exists with the AI driving system.

Assume that a Natural Language Processing (NLP) interface is coupled with the AI driving system, akin to the likes of Alexa or Siri. The passenger interacts with the NLP and can discuss common actions such as asking to change the destination midstream, or ask to swing through a fast-food eatery drive-thru, and so on.

In addition, the passenger can ask for explanations.

Suppose the AI driving system has to suddenly hit the brakes. The rider in the self-driving car might have been watching an especially fascinating cat video and not be aware of the roadway circumstances. After getting bounced around due to the harsh braking action, the passenger might stridently and anxiously ask why the AI driving system made such a sudden and abrasive driving action.

You would want the AI to immediately provide such an explanation. If the only possible way to get an explanation involved seeking a remote agent, envision what that might be like. There you are, inside the self-driving car, and it has just taken radical action, but you have no idea why it did so. You have to press a button or somehow activate a call to a remote agent. This might take a few moments to engage.

Once the remote agent is available (assuming that one is readily available), they might begin the dialogue with a usual canned speech, such as welcome to the greatest of all self-driving cars. You, meanwhile, have been sitting inside this self-driving car, which is still merrily driving along, and yet you have no clue why it out-of-the-blue hit the brakes.

The point here is that by the time you engage in a discussion with the human remote operator, a lot of time and driving aspects could have occurred. During that delay, you are puzzled, concerned, and worried about what the AI driving system might crazily do next.

If there was an XAI, perhaps you would have been able to ask the XAI what just happened. The XAI might instantly explain that there was a dog on the sidewalk that was running toward the self-driving car and appeared to be getting within striking distance. The AI driving system opted to do a fast-braking action. The dog got the idea and safely scampered away.

A timely explanation, and one that then gives the passenger solace and relief, allowing them to settle back into their seat and watch more of those videos about frisky kittens and adorable puppies.

Conclusion

There are lots and lots of situations that can arise when riding in a car and for which you might desire an explanation. The car is suddenly brought to a halt. The car takes a curve rather strongly. The car veers into an adjacent lane without a comfortable margin of error. The car takes a road that you weren't expecting to be on. Seemingly endless possibilities exist. In that case, if indeed XAI is notably handy for self-driving cars, you might be wondering why it isn't especially in place already.

Well, admittedly, for those AI developers under intense pressures to devise AI that can drive a car from point A to point B, doing so safely, the aspect of providing machine-generated explanations is pretty low on their priority list. They would fervently argue that it is a so-called edge or corner case. It can be gotten to when the sunshine of having achieved sufficiently self-driving cars has been achieved.

Humans that are riding in AVs of all kinds are going to want to have explanations. A cost-effective and immediately available means of providing explanations entails the embodiment of XAI into the AI systems that are doing the autonomous piloting. One supposes that if you are inside a self-driving car and it is urgently doing some acrobatic driving maneuver, you might be hesitant to ask what is going on, in the same manner, that you might worry that you would be distracting a human driver that was doing something wild at the wheel.

Presumably, a well-devised XAI won't be taxing on the AI driving system and thus you are free to engage in a lengthy dialogue with the XAI. In fact, the likeliest question that self-driving cars are going to get is how does the AI driving system function. The XAI ought to be readied to cope with that kind of question.

The one thing we probably should not expect XAI to handle will be those questions that are afield of the driving chore. For example, asking the XAI to explain the meaning of life is something that could be argued as out-of-bounds and above the paygrade of the AI. At least until the day that AI does become sentient, then you can certainly ask away.

CHAPTER 20
AI ETHICS AND ASIMOV ROBOTIC LAWS

When discussing AI Ethics, perhaps the most visible forms of AI that spur an ethical discussion entail robots. Generally, robots can be considered as a subset of AI in that a "smart" robot would contain an AI system that undertakes the "thinking" aspects of the robot. Of course, robots can vary significantly in terms of their cognition-like capabilities. In any case, any look at robots and robotics is nearly obligated to consider the famous Asimov robotics laws. These carry demonstrative Ethical AI questions and considerations. Let's jump into the matter.

Those robots and their wild and crazy ways.

Advances in Artificial Intelligence (AI) will continue to spur widespread adoption of robots into our everyday lives. Robots that once seemed so expensive that they could only be afforded for heavy-duty manufacturing purposes have gradually come down in cost and equally been reduced in size. You can consider that Roomba vacuum cleaner in your home to be a type of robot, though we still do not have the ever-promised home butler robot that was supposed to take care of our daily routine chores.

Perhaps one of the most well-known facets about robots is the legendary set of three rules proffered by writer Isaac Asimov. His science fiction tale entitled *The Three Laws* was published in 1942 and has seemingly been unstoppable in terms of ongoing interest and embrace.

Here are the three rules that he cleverly devised:

1) A robot may not injure a human being or, through inaction, allow a human being to come to harm,

2) A robot must obey the orders given it by human beings except where such orders would conflict with the First Law,

3) A robot must protect its own existence as long as such protection does not conflict with the First or Second Law.

Though he referred to these as laws, please know that they are ostensibly are not actual laws per se.

One viewpoint about laws is the notion of laws of nature. Those three rules are not laws of nature as there is nothing about them that somehow is determinable as being inexorably imbued via nature or required by the course of nature. Those rules are manmade and humanity discretionary. They can be observed and obeyed, or they can be completely disregarded, whichever we might choose to so abide.

Another perspective on laws is the aspect of mankind derived regulations and stipulations. Our revered Constitution is an indication of laws, something that we as a society have opted to try and live within. In that way of consideration, you could argue that Asimov was proposing laws that we ought to put onto our legal books as sensible to have in an era of robots that might be wandering amongst us.

His three rules are not yet embodied directly into our laws and we'll have to see whether it eventually makes sense to codify them explicitly accordingly. You might find of interest that there is a great deal of angst and attention right now on how to best govern the latest AI systems and we might find ourselves leaning heavily into Asimov's three rules.

When you read Asimov's remarks about robots, you might want to substitute the word "robot" for simply the overarching moniker of AI. I say this because you are likely to otherwise narrowly interpret his three rules as though they apply only to a robot that happens to look like us, conventionally having legs, arms, a head, a body, and so on.

Not all robots are necessarily so arranged.

Some of the latest robots look like animals. Perhaps you've seen the popular online videos of robots that are four-legged and appear to be a dog or a similar kind of creature. There are even robots that resemble insects. They look kind of creepy but nonetheless are important as a means to figure out how we might utilize robotics in all manner of possibilities.

A robot doesn't have to be biologically inspired. A robotic vacuum cleaner does not particularly look like any customary animal or insect. You can expect that we will have all sorts of robots that look quite unusual and do not appear to be based solely on any living organism.

Anyway, amongst the variety of robots that we are going to see emerging, the Asimov three rules are quite helpful, regardless of what kind of robot it is and what it might look like. I know it seems perhaps a bit of a stretch of the imagination, but the lowly robotic vacuum can be a candidate for abiding by the three rules. Yes, presumably, your swirling robotic vacuum in your home should not try to harm you and ought to do what it can to avoid doing so.

Some robots are readily in front of our eyes and yet we do not think of them as robots.

One such example is the advent of AI-based true self-driving cars.

A car that is being driven by an AI system can be said to be a type of robot. The reason you might not think of a self-driving car as a robot is that it does not have that walking-talking robot sitting in the driver's seat. Instead, the computer system hidden in the underbody or trunk of the car is doing the driving. This seems to escape our attention and thus the vehicle doesn't readily appear to be a kind of robot, though indeed it is.

In case you are wondering, there are encouraging efforts underway to create walking-talking robots that would be able to drive a car.

Imagine how that would shake-up our world.

Right now, the crafting of a self-driving car involves modifying the car to be self-driving. If we had robots that could walk around, sit down in a car, and drive the vehicle, this would mean that *all* existing cars could essentially be considered self-driving cars (meaning that they could be driven by such robots, rather than having a human drive the car). Instead of gradually junking conventional cars for the arrival of self-driving cars, there would be no need to devise a wholly-contained self-driving car and we would rely upon those meandering robots to be our drivers.

At this time, the fastest or soonest path to having self-driving cars is the build-it into the vehicle approach. Some believe there is a bitter irony in this approach. They contend that these emergent self-driving cars are going to inevitably be usurped by those walking-talking robots. In that sense, the self-driving car of today will become outdated and outmoded, giving way to once again having conventional driving controls so that either the vehicle can be driven by a human or be driven by a driving robot.

As an added twist, there are some that hope we will be so far along on adopting self-driving cars that we will not use independent robots to drive our cars.

Here's the logic.

If a robot driver is sitting at the wheel, this suggests that the conventional driving controls are still going to be available inside a car. This also implies that humans will still be able to drive a car, whenever they wish to do so. But the belief is that the AI driving systems, whether built-in or as part of a walking-talking robot, will be better drivers and reduce the incidences of drunk driving and other adverse driving behaviors. In short, a true self-driving car will not have any driving controls, precluding a walking-talking robot from driving (presumably) and precluding (thankfully, some assert) a human from driving.

This leads to the thinking that maybe the world will have completely switched to true self-driving cars and though a walking-talking driving robot might become feasible, things will be so far along that no one will turn back the clock and reintroduce conventional cars.

That seems somewhat like wishful (or possibly wistful) thinking.

One way or another, the central goal seems to be to take the human driver out of the equation.

This brings up another crucial and sometimes overlooked point about robots, namely that they can be put into positions of effort that entail life or death activities. Your home robotic vacuum cleaner is unlikely to be a life-or-death decision-maker. Meanwhile, a self-driving car, one that has the AI driving system built-in, or even a robot driver, would undeniably be in a life-or-death posture of ascertaining the fate of humans.

Each day that you get behind the wheel of a car, you are a life-or-death decision-maker, whether you realize it or recognize that this is so. With a bad turn of the steering wheel, you can get killed. Plus, you can end-up killing others, whether by veering into another car or possibly hitting pedestrians. There is life-or-death entirely surrounding the act of driving.

That might seem rather doom-and-gloom, but it is a harsh reality that needs to be emphasized.

This is also why the moment when you help your teenager learn to drive is more than just some simple bonding time. The instant that you put your beloved newbie driver at the driving controls, the specter of life-or-death suddenly becomes quite pronounced. The teenage driver usually also senses this heavy-duty, and you can see that some are reluctant to take on such a hefty burden.

Since it is life-or-death on the line, it is conceivable that we should consider applying Asimov's three rules in the use case of self-driving cars (it would seem inconceivable to not do so, as suggested by *The Princess Bride*).

Here is today's intriguing question: *Do the Asimov three laws of robots apply to AI-based true self-driving cars, and if so, what should be done about it?*

Let's briefly take a look at each of Asimov's three rules and see how they might apply to true self-driving cars.

First, there is the rule that a robot or AI driving system (in this case) shall not injure a human, either doing so by overt action and nor by its inaction.

That's a tall order when sitting at the wheel of a car.

Here's why.

A self-driving car is driving down a street and keenly sensing the surroundings. Unbeknownst to the AI driving system, a small child is standing between two parked cars, hidden from view and hidden from the sensory range and depth of the self-driving car. The AI is driving at the posted speed limit. All of a sudden, the child steps out into the street.

Some people assume that a self-driving car will never run into anyone since the AI has those state-of-the-art sensory capabilities and won't be a drunk driver. Unfortunately, in the kind of scenario that I've just posited, the self-driving car is going to ram into that child. I say this because the law of physics is paramount over any dreamy notions of what an AI driving system can do.

If the child has appeared seemingly out of nowhere and now is say a distance of 15 feet from the moving car, and the self-driving car is going at 30 miles per hour, the stopping distance is around 50 to 75 feet, which means that the child could readily get struck.

No two ways about that.

And this would mean that the AI driving system has just violated Asimov's first rule.

The AI has injured a human being. Keep in mind that I'm stipulating that the AI would indeed invoke the brakes of the self-driving car and do whatever it could to avoid the ramming of the child. Nonetheless, there is insufficient time and distance for the AI to avoid the collision.

Now that we've shown the impossibility of always abiding by Asimov's first rule in terms of strictly adhering to the rule, you could at least argue that the AI driving system *attempted* to obey the rule. By having used the brakes, it would seem that the AI driving system tried to keep from hitting the child, plus the impact might be somewhat less severe if the vehicle was nearly stopped at the time of impact.

What about the other part of the first rule that states there should be no inaction that could lead to the harm of a human?

One supposes that if the self-driving car did not try to stop, this kind of inaction might fall within that realm, namely once again being unsuccessful at observing the rule. We can add a twist to this. Suppose the AI driving system was able to swerve the car, doing so sufficiently to avoid striking the child, but meanwhile, the self-driving car goes smack dab into a redwood tree. There is a passenger inside the self-driving car and this person gets whiplash due to the crashing action.

Okay, the child on the street was saved, but the passenger inside the self-driving car is now injured. You can ponder whether the action to save the child was worthy in comparison to the result of injuring the passenger. Also, you can contemplate whether the AI failed to take proper action to avoid the injury to the passenger. This kind of ethical dilemma is often depicted via the infamous Trolley Problem, an aspect that I have vehemently argued is very applicable to self-driving cars and deserves much more rapt attention as the advent of self-driving cars continues.

All told, we can seemingly agree that the first rule of Asimov's triad is a helpful aspirational goal for an AI-based true self-driving car, though the fulfillment of that aspiration is going to be pretty tough to achieve and will forever likely remain a conundrum for society to wrestle with.

The second of Asimov's laws is that the robot or in this case the AI driving system is supposed to obey the orders given to it by a human, excluding situations whereby such a human-issued command conflicts with the first rule (i.e., don't harm humans).

This seems straightforward and altogether agreeable.

Yet, even this rule has its problems.

I covered the story of a man that used a car to run over a shooter on a bridge that was randomly shooting and killing people (see my discussion posted June 1, 2020). According to authorities, the driver was heroic by having stopped that shooter.

If the Asimov second law was programmed into the AI driving system of a self-driving car, and suppose a passenger ordered the AI to run over a shooter, presumably the AI would refuse to do so. This is amply obvious because the instruction would harm a human. But, we know that this was a case that seems to override the hard-and-fast always-to-be-obeyed convention that you should not use your car to ram into people.

You might be complaining that this is a rare exception, which I totally concur is absolutely an oddity.

Furthermore, if we were to open the door to allowing passengers in self-driving cars to tell the AI to run over someone, the resulting chaos and mayhem would be untenable. In short, there is certainly a basis for arguing that the second rule ought to be enforced, even if it means that on those rare occasions it would lead to harm due to inaction.

The thing is, you don't have to reach that far beyond the everyday world to find situations that would be nonsensical for an AI driving system to unquestionably obey a passenger. A rider in a self-driving car tells the AI to drive up onto the sidewalk. There are no pedestrians on the sidewalk, thus no one will get hurt.

I ask you, should the AI driving system obey this human uttered command?

No, the AI should not, and we are ultimately going to have to cope with what types of utterances from human passengers the AI driving systems will consider, and which commands will be rejected (see my analysis of the barking of commands problem posted on December 13, 2020).

The third law that Asimov has postulated is that the robot or in this case the AI driving system must protect its own existence, doing so as long as the first and second rules are not countermanded.

Should a self-driving car attempt to preserve its existence?

In a prior column, I mentioned that some believe that self-driving cars will have about a four-year existence, ultimately succumbing to wear-and-tear in just four years of driving (see my posting on September 3, 2019). This seems surprising since we expect cars to last much longer, but the difference with self-driving cars is that they will presumably be operating nearly 24x7 and gain a lot more miles than a conventional car (a conventional car sits unused about 95% to 99% of the time).

Okay, so assume that a self-driving car is nearing its useful end. The vehicle is scheduled to drive itself to the junk heap for recycling.

Is it acceptable that the AI driving system might decide to avoid going to the recycling center and thus try to preserve its existence?

I suppose if a human told it to go there, the second rule wins out and the self-driving car has to obey. The AI might tricky and find some sneaky means to abide by the first and second rule, and nonetheless find a bona fide basis to seek its continued existence (I leave this as a mindful exercise for you to mull over).

Conclusion

Based on the aforementioned logic, it would seem that Asimov's three rules have to be taken with a grain of salt.

The AI driving systems can generally be devised with those rules as part of the overarching architecture, but as might be abundantly evident from this discussion, the rules are aspirations and not ironclad irrefutable and immutable laws.

Perhaps the most important point of this mental workout about Asimov's rules is to shed light on something that few are giving due diligence toward. In the case of AI-based true self-driving cars, there is a lot more to devising and deploying these autonomous vehicles than merely the mechanical facets of driving a car.

Driving a car is a huge ethical dilemma that humans oftentimes take for granted. We need to sort out the reality of how AI driving systems are going to render life-or-death decisions. This must be done before we start flooding our streets and byways with self-driving cars.

Asimov said it best when he lamented a remark that still applies today, some eighty years or so after he implored us with this: "The saddest aspect of life right now is that science gathers knowledge faster than society gathers wisdom."

True words that are greatly worth revisiting.

CHAPTER 21

AI ETHICS AND AI APOLOGIES

A relatively unexplored area of AI Ethics involves the rising use of AI apologies. You see, many AI developers seem to think that their AI should apologize when it has presumably done something wrong. Skeptics would say that this is a dangerous precedent of utilizing AI purposeful anthropomorphic characteristics. Let's take a close look at the matter.

They say that love means never having to say that you are sorry.

When does it make sense though to proffer being sorry and offer someone an apology?

There are AI systems increasingly being designed to emit apologies, doing so when the AI detects that an act of contrition on its part might be suitable or needed.

For example, you apply online for a car loan and the AI system determines that you are not worthy, as it were, and promptly turns you down. The belief is that this would be an ideal moment for the AI to offer you a "heartfelt" apology.

It might go something like this: Dear loan applicant, it is with great sorrow that I must inform you of the unfortunate news that your request to borrow funds to buy a car is hereby denied. Please know that you are not alone in having been spurned and accept this apology for any discomfort that might arise from this outcome. Sincerely, the AI system that reluctantly rebuffed your request.

Do you think this apology will make the person feel any better about the AI-powered decision?

Well, I doubt it would for most people, nonetheless, there is an emerging trend of having AI systems produce these kinds of messages.

We can mull over and debate the tradeoffs involved in having AI that provides these kinds of apologies. There are claimed benefits of having the AI appear to be deferential, while there are criticisms that this is a mockery of humanity and diminishes the potency of apologies all told. Before getting to the overall set of tradeoffs, imagine the myriad of areas that AI is being applied, beyond just adjudicating car loan candidates, and envision how those varied instances might opt to leverage a purposely apologizing AI system.

Here's an intriguing aspect: *Will the advent of AI-based true self-driving cars necessitate the AI being apologetic from time-to-time, and do we really want or expect apologies to be issued by AI driving systems?*

Let's unpack the matter and see.

You might be initially baffled that there would ever be any basis for the AI driving system to issue an apology to the passengers of a self-driving car. We certainly do not expect human drivers to particularly offer apologies, and thus there is no well-established tradition of drivers making such utterances. Sure, on a rare occasion a ride-sharing driver might apologize that their car reeks of tuna salad because they just managed to wolf down their lunch on the way to pick you up, but otherwise the number of apologies we receive while riding in cars has got to be pretty low, nearly zero it so seems.

Well, take a step back and ponder the following scenario.

You are nestled in a self-driving car and enjoying some quiet time on the way to work. The seats can fully recline, due to the facet that there aren't any driving controls inside the vehicle (the steering wheel and pedals for true self-driving cars are expected to be excised from the interior and no longer accessible by humans since the AI is doing all the driving).

The AI is dutifully watching the roadway and attempting to provide you with a safe journey from your home to the office. Thankfully, the AI is coping with the darned traffic on the freeways and the equally exasperating jammed traffic on the busy city streets. You can daydream and meanwhile, the AI is observing the surroundings like an alert hawk.

All of a sudden, the AI detects via its sensors, such as by using cameras, radar, LIDAR, and so on, that a pedestrian is weaving erratically on the sidewalk and appears to be nearing the curb of the street. It is hard to discern whether the person is going to actually come into the street. Maybe they will turn back toward the buildings at the last moment and avoid coming into the roadway. Or, in a worst-case possibility, the person might opt to pop into the street, right in front of where the self-driving car is headed.

What to do?

What would you do?

What should the AI do?

For human drivers, we confront these kinds of driving situations all the time. You have to make split-second judgment choices about whether a pedestrian is going to foolishly wander directly into the path of your moving car, and thus calculate in your mind whether to slow down, speed-up, swerve or take no action. Any of those options might be right. Of course, any of those options might be wrong too.

In the case of AI driving systems, to-date the approach has involved setting up the AI to be extraordinarily cautious, more so than perhaps most human drivers might be. If there is even an inkling of an upcoming car crash or similar incident, the AI is going to try and avert the chances by taking the "safest" course of action (more on this in a moment).

Assume that the AI hits the brakes of the self-driving car, doing so to be at a complete stop before reaching where the pedestrian might end-up being.

By calculating the intersecting points at which the self-driving car and the pedestrian might have arrived, the AI calculated the stopping distance and figured out that an emergency stop could likely ensure that the self-driving car and the meanderer would not come in contact with each other.

Pedestrian is saved.

Suppose though that the person did not come into the street, and at the last moment veered back onto the sidewalk. This means that the self-driving car needlessly came to a halt. You could presumably give the AI some thankful credit for having avoided a potential accident, but the accident never materialized and so you could equally criticize the AI for being an overly reactive scaredy-cat driver.

Meanwhile, remember that there is a passenger inside the self-driving car (we're still pretending it was you). There you were, comfortably reclining and blissfully inattentive to the roadway conditions, rightfully so, reliant upon the AI to tackle the driving and make the proper decisions thereof.

Upon the sharp braking action utilized by the AI driving system, you are tossed around like a sack of potatoes. Maybe a tad bit of whiplash involved.

What the heck happened, you would likely be wondering, having no clue why the AI made the unexpected and utterly unannounced stop.

At this juncture, at least as a minimum, you would be expecting the AI to explain what occurred. If the AI does not indicate why the roughshod driving action was undertaken, you are beset with doubts and would feel uneasy that the AI can adequately drive the self-driving car. Perhaps the AI has gone nuts, or an electronic power surge made its bits go bad.

We are now at the million-dollar question.

Should the AI apologize to you?

Try this: Dear rider, you undoubtedly sensed that the self-driving car came to a sudden halt, which please accept my apologies for having done so. This was done out of an abundance of caution and potentially might have saved the life of an errant pedestrian. As a driving transgression, it is not what I aspire to do while driving, but hopefully, you understand that such moments have merit and your forgiveness on this matter is welcomed. Sincerely, the AI driving the self-driving car.

Notice that this is a twofer, consisting of an explanation and simultaneously an inserted apology.

The explanation would tend to ease your concerns about the AI having gone off the deep end.

Does the apology also make you feel better?

Let's turn our attention to AI that issues apologies and those earlier alluded to tradeoffs involved in having the AI do so.

AI Apologizing and The Merits Or Demerits

Some insist that any apology by an AI system is completely, unabashedly, a fraudulent and hollow act.

The AI is not sentient. For those of you that might be tricked by the barrage of media postings that suggest that AI is sentient or near-to, do not fall for this hogwash. There isn't any AI today that can be construed as sentient and there is nothing on the horizon that implies or purports to show that sentience can be reached in the near future.

Hence, the point is that the AI generating an apology is not the same as a human that proffers an apology. The AI cannot from-the-heart provide you or anyone with a heartfelt apology. This does not compute. In that overall sense, it can be argued that an apology by AI is nothing but fakery.

Worse still is the notion that by providing an apology there is an insidious insinuation that the AI is indeed sentient. In more formal parlance, this is tantamount to anthropomorphizing the AI. When the AI as a computer-based machine is made to seem like it is human, real humans will begin to think that the machine is a human or an equivalent.

That's a dangerous slippery slope.

People that believe the AI can think and act as a human can are going to become reliant upon the AI to do things that the AI cannot achieve. For example, humans have common-sense reasoning (I realize some might chuckle and note that they know humans that are not able to exercise common-sense, but put that cynicism to the side for the moment), but there aren't AI systems yet that have anything of the same. Thus, the AI is not going to apply common-sense to any instructions you might share with it, and nor should you expect the AI to employ common-sense when performing a task for you.

Speaking of cynics, some people are less heated-up about these AI apologies and claim that any human with a modicum of intelligence knows that the apology emitted by AI is merely a made-up artifact by the humans that programmed the AI. In this viewpoint, there is a hardened belief that everyone already should realize that the AI is just a computer and like any computer that spits out a report or displays a message, the whole thing is just a bunch of 1's and 0's being shoveled to-and-fro.

And, it could be argued that getting an apology, albeit from something that does not "know" what an apology is, provides a nice touch of humanity for the circumstances at hand.

The developers of the AI at least realized that sometimes the AI might go afoul. That alone is important and perhaps a shocker since many times an AI system will make a mistake or a misstep and it doesn't realize what has transpired. Thank goodness that there is an apology, acting as a canary in the cage, showing the light that the AI has been embedded with some kind of error detection and response capabilities.

The words too of an apology can be soothing.

Despite the AI not being human or anything akin, the words alone are being spoken and received.

Returning to reclining in a self-driving car that has come to a jolting halt, perhaps the apology can be the icing on the cake, wherein the cake was the explanation and the delightful icing is the supplemental apologetic words.

How far might this go?

There are stratified levels of apologies being cooked into some AI systems. There is a mild apology that is used when the incident or activity was only modestly disturbing for the human. Waiting to be used is the medium level apology that lays out a lengthier indication of what the AI is sorry about. Then there's the heightened apology, profusely seeking to offer a sorrowfulness befitting a Shakespearean play.

The passenger in a self-driving car that got jostled by the sudden halt might get a mild apology if the stopping action was not especially severe. On the other hand, if the stop was the kind that makes your teeth rattle right out of your skull, the heightened version of the apology would likely be issued.

Skeptics have an entirely different viewpoint on these AI-based apologies.

Give me reparations or something tangible to make me whole and soothed, the skeptics exhort, rather than a bunch of gooey words of an apology.

In the case of a self-driving car, the AI ought to inform you that you will be getting a ten percent discount on the driving fare for the ride, or maybe waive the bill entirely. If there is a loyalty program associated with using the self-driving car, perhaps the AI can add some padded miles into your account, doing so to try and appease your dismay at the sudden stopping action. Etc.

In short, there are the where's the beef critics that eschew the apologies if there isn't a bona fide payoff associated with the words themselves. In this view, any apology from either AI or a human is essentially worthless unless it is backed up by money in their pocket or some other form of compensation that deals with the matter underlying the incident that precipitated the apology, to begin with.

Conclusion

Another concern by some about apologies by AI is that it might open a veritable Pandora's box.

Here's how.

The act of the AI apologizing could be construed as an acknowledgment that the AI did something wrong. This admission can be then utilized for any legal action against the company that made or fielded the AI system.

For the self-driving car, potentially the automaker or self-driving tech maker is shooting their own foot, one might say, due to admitting to being at fault.

The next thing you know, there are zillions of lawsuits launched by people that have received AI-based apologies, and they are all going to use as concrete evidence that the AI apologized, which certainly must mean that the AI was in the wrong and that the maker of the AI knew or could have known that the AI was going to bungle things.

Returning to the skeptics, potentially the AI offering an apology is almost like dollars in their pockets, given that the AI is handing them on a silver platter that the AI was at fault and presumably some compensation should be forthcoming accordingly, perhaps by legal court proceedings.

On a final note, there are also the perfectionists that have something to say about AI-based apologies.

In their opinion, there should never be any instance of an apology being necessary, namely, the AI ought to be working perfectly all of the time. If the AI is being built with apologies included, this means that the AI is not being built to achieve perfection. This is obviously then a mistake at the get-go because the AI should not be anywhere in the real world until it is perfected and won't ever need to use an apology.

How do you like those apples?

Realists would laugh at this kind of sentiment and likely say that the perfectionists are idealistic, plus the common line these days is that striving for perfection is allegedly the enemy of the good (ostensibly borrowed from Voltaire, and a variant of the so-called golden mean ascribed by philosophers such as Confucius and Aristotle).

No apologies, no regrets, goes the famous line too.

Now that you know about AI-powered apologies, it might sweeten those human uttered apologies that you get from time-to-time.

Of course, human-generated apologies are not necessarily always genuine and whole, which come to think of it, even once AI does become sentient, perhaps we won't know if the AI is just trying to offer hollow platitudes to appease us versus sincerely expressing a deepfelt sorrow.

That seems like a good juncture to wrap things up on this topic and offer this sage quote by the Bard: Parting is such sweet sorrow that I shall say goodnight till it be morrow.

CHAPTER 22
AI ETHICS FAST TRACKING

Some assert that we are witnessing a type of "fast tracking" of AI Ethics that tends to undercut and undervalue the full importance of sincerely giving attention to devising Ethical AI. Many AI systems of today are criticized that had there been concentrated attention toward incorporating AI Ethics precepts, perhaps those scurrying to push out an AI beneficial application would have been more likely to consider the downsides of their creation too.

For clarification, AI Ethics is a set of ethics-oriented guidelines or principles that offer guidance when designing, building, testing, fielding, and maintaining an AI system (for examples, see my analysis of the set by the Vatican, and another similar one by the U.S. DoD. There is currently a multitude of such proposed AI Ethics indications and no single set has become the one-and-only globally accepted standard, though nonetheless they all pretty much adhere to a similar theme and core values.

In that sense, those that try to use as an excuse that there isn't an anointed all-hands standard are disingenuous at best, and by readily embracing nearly any of the bona fide ones they would be doing well and able to proceed unabated.

Okay, so let's hope that entities developing AI will see the light and opt to adopt a viable AI Ethics code set. Doing so is intended to make them aware of the qualms about AI such as the potential for privacy intrusions, the potential for inherent hidden biases in AI-based decision making, and so on. One assumes that with that awareness will spark AI development efforts that foundationally detect those kinds of problematic and endangering issues, beforehand, rather than after shipping the AI into the hands of the public.

Letting the horse out of the barn prematurely is a bad idea and the goal ought to be making sure first and foremost that the horse is ready to be let loose.

But what happens to AI Ethics when it is crunch time and a kind of panic occurs to rollout AI?

While in the throes of a crisis, it can seem daunting to keep AI Ethics at the forefront, since the usual perception is that worrying about those AI Ethics codifications are bound to stymy the pace of development and undercut the urgent tempo to get AI into the hands of end-users.

That is a decidedly short-minded viewpoint and though it might seem like the value of being quick to market is a worthwhile tradeoff, the result can reverberate for a long time to come. The public will not especially remember that there was a presumed urgency and instead will only tend to know that the AI fostered into the world was insidious and ultimately nefarious.

If enough of those kinds of haphazard make-and-bake AI apps are tossed into the market, we will inevitably witness a colossal backlash that will make the so-far optional AI Ethics principles and guidelines into becoming mandatory and potentially overly onerous as a reaction to those that scrimped at the beginning.

Maybe AI will get banned entirely.

Somehow, there needs to be a balance found that can appropriately make use of the AI Ethics precepts and yet allow for flexibility when there is a real and fully tangible basis to partially cut corners, as it were.

Of course, some would likely abuse the possibility of a slimmer version and always go that route, regardless of any truly needed urgency of timing. Thus, there is a chance of opening a Pandora's box whereby a less-than fully AI Ethics protocol becomes the default norm, rather than serving as a break-glass exception when rarely so needed.

It can be hard to put the Genie back into the bottle. In any case, there are already some attempts at trying to craft a fast-track variant of AI Ethics principles. We can perhaps temper those that leverage the urgent version with both a stick and a carrot.

The carrot is obvious that they are seemingly able to get their AI completed sooner, while the stick is that they will be held wholly accountable for not having taken the full nine yards on the use of the AI Ethics. This is a crucial point that might be used against those taking such a route and be a means to extract penalties via a court of law, along with penalties in the court of public opinion.

Let's next take a look at a well-known set of AI Ethics, promulgated by the OECD, and see if we can shape those into offering a fast-track variant.

The OECD has proffered these five foundational precepts as part of undertaking AI efforts:

1) AI should benefit people and the planet by driving inclusive growth, sustainable development, and well-being.
2) AI systems should be designed in a way that respects the rule of law, human rights, democratic values, and diversity, and they should include appropriate safeguards – for example, enabling human intervention where necessary – to ensure a fair and just society.
3) There should be transparency and responsible disclosure around AI systems to ensure that people understand AI-based outcomes and can challenge them.
4) AI systems must function in a robust, secure, and safe way throughout their life cycles and potential risks should be continually assessed and managed.
5) Organizations and individuals developing, deploying, or operating AI systems should be held accountable for their proper functioning in line with the above principles.

For ease of reference, this is the official shorthand list of the five AI Ethics principles:

1. Inclusive growth, sustainable development, and well-being
2. Human-centered values and fairness
3. Transparency and explainability
4. Robustness, security, and safety
5. Accountability

What can be done to fast-track this set of AI Ethics?

Some might leap to the easy way out by simply lopping one or more from the list.

In other words, just cut the stack down to four, or maybe three, or heaven forbid even just one or two of the precepts.

It isn't apparent as to which of the five would be "best" to ditch.

You could liken this to having to cut off a limb and be arguing about which appendage is the less vital one.

No, I don't think this will do.

Each of the five has a distinct purpose. None of the other five will make up for having omitted one of the other precepts. Knocking out any of them is akin to taking out the leg of a stool, wherein the stool no longer properly stands.

For those that have suggested to chop out one or more of the five, it seems to defy any reasonable logic and you are essentially arbitrarily willing to wholly weaken and undermine the concrete flooring upon which any AI has to be properly constructed.

Case rejected.

That might seem stubborn and unyielding, lest there are some other means to try and turn these precepts into a slimmer variant.

Consider these possibilities:

- **Prioritize the five and weight your effort accordingly** – they are all essential but you could argue that in a pinch they are not all equal, thus, for a given AI, assign weights to each of the five, and then structure your AI development effort according to those with the greater importance or weighting.

- **Take the shortened version of one or more of the precepts** – for each of the five there are lots of subordinated items to normally be considered, but for a bona fide crunch you could shorten some of those underlying elements and knowingly skip a few underlings, keep track as you do so and realize what you are missing accordingly.

- **Double-up on the precepts** – the principles do not need to necessarily be considered one-at-a-time, and there are synergies to be had by considering simultaneously more than one while undertaking your AI effort, thus a double-up is bound to reduce the time and effort, though be careful that it does not become a morass and a gigantic blur.

- **Borrow from a similar AI app** – many that are embarking upon developing AI are doing so for the first time and as such they have little or no prior base to build upon, yet for those that are actively in AI and have other AI systems under their belt they can readily reuse prior aspects that already passed the AI Ethics precepts (just be mindful and do not blindly and falsely borrow something unlike what you are doing now).

- **Parcel out wisely the precepts** – in some instances an AI effort places the rigors of the AI Ethics precepts onto the shoulder of one person that becomes the AI Ethics guru, this might be handy, unfortunately, this can also become a bottleneck and slows down the entire effort, reconsider if there is a single link in the chain and how to better parcel out the workload.

- **Cautiously crowdsource the precepts** – in an open-source manner some are doing AI that relishes using crowdsourcing to either perform the AI development or serve to scrutinize and test it, in which case you could have the AI Ethics become likewise crowdsourced, just as long as the crowd knows what it is doing and this is not an unbridled castoff that undermines the precepts.

- **Combine these fast-tracks** – the aforementioned fast-tracks can be combined in various sensible ways and produce even larger short-cuts accordingly, but do not cut to the bone and end-up losing the core by taking too many slimdowns at once.

As mentioned, you can use one or more of the fast-track facets at the same time.

How will you know that you have gone too far?

Here are the key supplementals for taking on a fast-track approach with the AI Ethics principles:

- **Establish internal checks-and-balances** – make sure to set up the responsibilities for the AI Ethics precepts and include numerous checks-and-balances for gauging how they are proceeding.

- **Potentially use an external third-party auditor** – in addition to internal checks-and-balances, it can be helpful to use an external auditor that does not presumably feel attached to what has been done and therefore will independently and forthrightly conduct their review.

- **Explicitly plan to include the AI Ethics considerations** – sometimes the AI Ethics considerations are belatedly shoved into an AI effort as though a second class citizen and not worthy of resources and nor priority, rate them instead as primary for all AI implementations and include them dutifully in all of your AI planning accordingly.

- **Boost the fail-safe catchall of the AI** – properly devised AI should already have fail-safe catchalls so that if it goes awry in the field the AI will presumably realize troubles are afoot and will do something prudent as a contingency, this is even more so a crucial component when taking the fast-track.

All told, I've provided a workable semblance of how to fast-track an AI effort as it pertains to using AI Ethics guidelines during the project.

Again, do not interpret this as a license to wildly proceed and merely try to skate through the AI Ethics precepts.

Your AI is going to be better if it undergoes a robust and complete AI Ethics effort, and likewise, those using your AI will benefit, and the totality of AI adoption will be kept enlivened.

You might be wondering how the AI Ethics principles come to play in real-world AI applications. A handy exemplar would be the development of AI-based true self-driving cars.

Many of the automakers and self-driving tech firms have been adopting the AI Ethics precepts (this varies from firm-to-firm).

One can argue that all of them ought to be doing so, which is worthwhile to mention herein as an impetus to get some of them off-the-dime and get in gear with including AI Ethics facets.

Please do so.

Let's next consider an example of how AI Ethics applies to self-driving cars.

Besides the bevy of sensors facing outward to detect the roadway, self-driving cars are likely to have a camera or two that are facing inward too.

Why so?

It is assumed that self-driving cars will be mainly used in fleets for purposes of ridesharing. The fleet owners will seemingly be large firms like automakers, car rental agencies, ridesharing firms, and the like (though, I am somewhat of a contrarian and argue that individuals will also own self-driving cars).

With those self-driving cars roaming around and taking on passengers, there is quite obviously the chance that a rowdy rider will decide to mark graffiti on the interior or maybe rip up the seats. By having a camera that points inward, the actions of those unruly people can be tracked. The AI might be trained to look for such behavior and immediately warn or scold the person, potentially stopping the miscreant from doing any further damage.

The inward-facing cameras are readily recording whatever happens inside the vehicle.

Seems innocent and sensible.

Consider another perspective.

Suppose you went to the bar after work and opted to take a self-driving car home, doing so rightfully rather than driving yourself in your conventional car while drunk. During the journey home, you blabber about your work, your personal life, and all sorts of confidential commentary that is spilling out of you while intoxicated.

It is all captured on video.

Who owns that video?

What will they do with it?

Currently, this is an open question and each self-driving car owner is presumably going to decide whatever they believe is appropriate to do about those videos.

Meanwhile, you personally have inadvertently created a personal privacy exposure for yourself and are potentially left in the lurch.

How does this relate to AI Ethics precepts?

Take a look again at the OECD five.

You might hopefully realize that at least one of the AI Ethics principles applies, and indeed it could readily be argued that all five apply to this scenario.

Some of the automakers and self-driving tech firms would currently say that the inward-facing camera is merely a piece of technology and they would absolve themselves of any duty related to how it might be used.

Likewise, if they have an AI monitoring system that can examine the video in real-time or after-the-fact to catch those that are doing something untoward, the makers of that AI would almost surely claim that however it might be used is not their concern.

If those organizations were fully embracing the AI Ethics guidelines, they would instead be having serious and contemplative discussions about the societal implications of that feature. Also, they would aim to figure out how to best put the feature into use and including for those that buy their self-driving cars and opt to use them as ridesharing vehicles.

Without the nudge of the AI Ethics precepts, it can be quite easy to overlook important and societally impactful facets such as this and meanwhile naively profess a type of head-in-the-sand rationale for not dealing with thorny issues.

Conclusion

AI Ethics are only now becoming prominent and we will need to wait and see how those involved in making and fielding AI opt to adopt such guidelines.

The excuse that incorporating AI Ethics is too much effort or will needlessly delay getting AI onto the streets is false and frankly, hogwash.

You can potentially fast-track the AI Ethics facets when (and only when) there is an AI that might be instrumental for the benefit of humanity and for which the timing presupposes an urgency, but this is not the norm and those doing a wink-wink to undercut the AI Ethics elements are doing a disservice to themselves and the rest of us.

Maybe there ought to be an inward-facing camera watching those making AI and we could catch those kinds of scoundrels in the act.

APPENDIX

APPENDIX A
TEACHING WITH THIS MATERIAL

The material in this book can be readily used either as a supplemental to other content for a class, or it can also be used as a core set of textbook material for a specialized class. Classes where this material is most likely used include any classes at the college or university level that want to augment the class by offering thought provoking and educational essays about AI.

In particular, here are some aspects for class use:

- Computer Science. Studying AI, ethics, etc.
- Business. Exploring technology and ethical adoption for business.
- Sociology. Ethical views on the adoption and advancement of technology.

Specialized classes at the undergraduate and graduate level can also make use of this material.

For each chapter, consider whether you think the chapter provides material relevant to your course topic. There is plenty of opportunity to get the students thinking about the topic and force them to decide whether they agree or disagree with the points offered and positions taken. I would also encourage you to have the students do additional research beyond the chapter material presented (I provide next some suggested assignments they can do).

RESEARCH ASSIGNMENTS ON THESE TOPICS

Your students can find background material on these topics, doing so in various business and technical publications. I list below the top ranked AI related journals. For business publications, I would suggest the usual culprits such as the Harvard Business Review, Forbes, Fortune, WSJ, and the like.

Here are some suggestions of homework or projects that you could assign to students:

a) Assignment for foundational AI research topic: Research and prepare a paper and a presentation on a specific aspect of Deep AI, Machine Learning, ANN, etc. The paper should cite at least 3 reputable sources. Compare and contrast to what has been stated in this book.

b) Assignment for the Ethics topic: Research and prepare a paper and ethics. Cite at least 3 reputable sources and analyze the characterizations. Compare and contrast to what has been stated in this book.

c) Assignment for a Business topic: Research and prepare a paper and a presentation on businesses and advanced technology. What is hot, and what is not? Cite at least 3 reputable sources. Compare and contrast to the depictions in this book.

d) Assignment to do a Startup: Have the students prepare a paper about how they might startup a business in this realm. They must submit a sound Business Plan for the startup. They could also be asked to present their Business Plan and so should also have a presentation deck to coincide with it.

You can certainly adjust the aforementioned assignments to fit to your particular needs and the class structure. You'll notice that I ask for 3 reputable cited sources for the paper writing based assignments. I usually steer students toward "reputable" publications, since otherwise they will cite some oddball source that has no credentials other than that they happened to write something and post it onto the Internet. You can define "reputable" in whatever way you prefer, for example some faculty think Wikipedia is not reputable while others believe it is reputable and allow students to cite it.

The reason that I usually ask for at least 3 citations is that if the student only does one or two citations they usually settle on whatever they happened to find the fastest. By requiring three citations, it usually seems to force them to look around, explore, and end-up probably finding five or more, and then whittling it down to 3 that they will actually use.

I have not specified the length of their papers, and leave that to you to tell the students what you prefer. For each of those assignments, you could end-up with a short one to two pager, or you could do a dissertation length paper. Base the length on whatever best fits for your class, and the credit amount of the assignment within the context of the other grading metrics you'll be using for the class.

I mention in the assignments that they are to do a paper and prepare a presentation. I usually try to get students to present their work. This is a good practice for what they will do in the business world. Most of the time, they will be required to prepare an analysis and present it. If you don't have the class time or inclination to have the students present, then you can of course cut out the aspect of them putting together a presentation.

If you want to point students toward highly ranked journals in AI, here's a list of the top journals as reported by *various citation counts sources* (this list changes year to year):

- Communications of the ACM
- Artificial Intelligence
- Cognitive Science
- IEEE Transactions on Pattern Analysis and Machine Intelligence
- Foundations and Trends in Machine Learning
- Journal of Memory and Language
- Cognitive Psychology
- Neural Networks
- IEEE Transactions on Neural Networks and Learning Systems
- IEEE Intelligent Systems
- Knowledge-based Systems

GUIDE TO USING THE CHAPTERS

For each of the chapters, I provide next some various ways to use the chapter material. You can assign the tasks as individual homework assignments, or the tasks can be used with team projects for the class. You can easily layout a series of assignments, such as indicating that the students are to do item "a" below for say Chapter 1, then "b" for the next chapter of the book, and so on.

a) What is the main point of the chapter and describe in your own words the significance of the topic,

b) Identify at least two aspects in the chapter that you agree with, and support your concurrence by providing at least one other outside researched item as support; make sure to explain your basis for disagreeing with the aspects,

c) Identify at least two aspects in the chapter that you disagree with, and support your disagreement by providing at least one other outside researched item as support; make sure to explain your basis for disagreeing with the aspects,

d) Find an aspect that was not covered in the chapter, doing so by conducting outside research, and then explain how that aspect ties into the chapter and what significance it brings to the topic,

e) Interview a specialist in industry about the topic of the chapter, collect from them their thoughts and opinions, and readdress the chapter by citing your source and how they compared and contrasted to the material,

f) Interview a relevant academic professor or researcher in a college or university about the topic of the chapter, collect from them their thoughts and opinions, and readdress the chapter by citing your source and how they compared and contrasted to the material,

g) Try to update a chapter by finding out the latest on the topic, and ascertain whether the issue or topic has now been solved or whether it is still being addressed, explain what you come up with.

The above are all ways in which you can get the students of your class involved in considering the material of a given chapter. You could mix things up by having one of those above assignments per each week, covering the chapters over the course of the semester or quarter. As a reminder, here are the chapters of the book and you can select whichever chapters you find most valued for your particular class:

ABOUT THE AUTHOR

Dr. Lance B. Eliot, Ph.D., MBA is a Stanford Fellow and a globally recognized AI expert and thought leader, an experienced executive and leader, a successful serial entrepreneur, and a noted scholar on AI, including that his Forbes and AI Trends columns have amassed over 5.8+ million views, his books on AI are frequently ranked in the Top 10 of all-time AI books, his articles are widely cited, and he has developed dozens of advanced AI systems.

He currently serves as the CEO of Techbruim, Inc. and has over twenty years of industry experience including serving as a corporate officer in billion-dollar sized firms and was a partner in a major consulting firm. He is also a successful entrepreneur having founded, ran, and sold several high-tech firms.

Dr. Eliot previously hosted the popular radio show *Technotrends* that was also available on American Airlines flights via their in-flight audio program, he has made appearances on CNN, has been a frequent speaker at industry conferences, and his podcasts have been downloaded over 100,000 times.

A former professor at the University of Southern California (USC), he founded and led an innovative research lab on Artificial Intelligence. He also previously served on the faculty of the University of California Los Angeles (UCLA) and was a visiting professor at other major universities. He was elected to the International Board of the Society for Information Management (SIM), a prestigious association of over 3,000 high-tech executives worldwide.

He has performed extensive community service, including serving as Senior Science Adviser to the Congressional Vice-Chair of the Congressional Committee on Science & Technology. He has served on the Board of the OC Science & Engineering Fair (OCSEF), where he is also has been a Grand Sweepstakes judge, and likewise served as a judge for the Intel International SEF (ISEF). He served as the Vice-Chair of the Association for Computing Machinery (ACM) Chapter, a prestigious association of computer scientists. Dr. Eliot has been a shark tank judge for the USC Mark Stevens Center for Innovation on start-up pitch competitions and served as a mentor for several incubators and accelerators in Silicon Valley and in Silicon Beach.

Dr. Eliot holds a Ph.D. from USC, MBA, and Bachelor's in Computer Science, and earned the CDP, CCP, CSP, CDE, and CISA certifications.

ADDENDUM

Advances In AI Ethics

Practical Advances in Artificial Intelligence (AI) and Machine Learning

By
Dr. Lance B. Eliot, MBA, PhD

For special orders of this book, contact:

LBE Press Publishing

Email: LBE.Press.Publishing@gmail.com

Made in the USA
Monee, IL
05 November 2026

67808596R00181